Food Ethics

PAUL POJMAN
Towson University

D1310805

Northwest State Community College

WADSWORTH
CENGAGE Learning

Australia • Brazil • Japan • Korea • Mexico • Singapore • Spain • United Kingdom • United States

WADSWORTH
CENGAGE Learning·

Food Ethics

Paul Pojman

Publisher: Clark Baxter

Sr. Sponsoring Editor: Joann Kozyrev

Assistant Editor: Joshua Duncan

Editorial Assistant: Marri Straton

Media Editor: Kimberly Apfelbaum

Marketing Manager: Mark T. Haynes

Marketing Coordinator: Josh Hendrick

Marketing Communications Manager:
Laura Localio

Content Project Management: PreMediaGlobal

Senior Art Director: Jennifer Wahi

Print Buyer: Mary Beth Hennebury

Senior Rights Acquisitions Specialist, Images:
Jennifer Meyer Dare

Senior Rights Acquisition Specialist, Text:
Katie Huha

Production Service: PreMediaGlobal

Cover Designer: Michelle DiMercurio

Cover Image: © Eric Isselée/Ermin
Gutenberger/Getty Images

Compositor: PreMediaGlobal

For product information and technology assistance, contact us at
Cengage Learning Customer & Sales Support, 1-800-354-9706

For permission to use material from this text or product,
submit all requests online at **www.cengage.com/permissions**.
Further permissions questions can be emailed to
permissionrequest@cengage.com.

Library of Congress Control Number: 2010940887

ISBN-13: 978-1-111-77230-7

ISBN-10: 1-111-77230-4

Wadsworth
20 Channel Center Street
Boston, MA 02210
USA

Cengage Learning is a leading provider of customized learning solutions with office locations around the globe, including Singapore, the United Kingdom, Australia, Mexico, Brazil and Japan. Locate your local office at **international.cengage.com/region**.

Cengage Learning products are represented in Canada by Nelson Education, Ltd.

For your course and learning solutions, visit **www.cengage.com**.

Purchase any of our products at your local college store or at our preferred online store **www.cengagebrain.com**.

Instructors: Please visit **login.cengage.com** and log in to access instructor-specific resources.

Printed in the United States of America
1 2 3 4 5 6 7 14 13 12 11 10

To Louis and Theo Pojman: From Ancestors to Descendants

Contents

Preface

This text provides an introduction to the complex issues arising from the question, "How should we eat?" Food Ethics has become one of the central fields within Environmental Ethics, developing to the point where it can be considered its own field. Three of the early issues at the core of 1960's and 70's environmentalism, animal rights, population and consumption dynamics, and toxic pollutants, form the center of modern food ethics debates, but new questions have also arisen, responding to developments in both food technologies and the globalization of land use.

The essays in this anthology are, with the exception of the introductory essay, derived from a larger anthology, *Environmental Ethics*, 6th edition (Wadsworth, 2011), the first four editions of which were edited by Louis Pojman. He is thus responsible for the selection and editing of the majority of the following essays. His influence is indeed greater than this; the moral standard that he attempted to live by has been the single greatest influence in my own life and thinking on environmental matters. This book is dedicated to him and to his grandson, from ancestors to descendents.

Acknowledgments

I wish to acknowledge to the Cengage, Wadsworth Editorial team including Joann Kozyrev, Sr. Sponsoring Editor; Mark T. Haynes, Marketing Manager; Nathan Gamache, Assistant Editor; and Katie Huha and Karyn Morrison for help with the permissions process as well as the production editor at PreMedia Global, Rathi Thirumalai.

Paul Pojman
Towson University, 2010
Food Ethics

Live simply so others can simply live.
—Gandhi

CHAPTER 1

Introduction

DAVID KAPLAN

FOOD

Food poses a variety of philosophical issues such as the ethical treatments of animals, the moral and political dimensions of genetically modified food, hunger and obligations to poor, and the role of food in gender and personal identity. Yet food has received scant attention in the philosophical literature compared to subjects like science, technology, and the environment, perhaps because food is perceived to be too physical and transient to deserve serious philosophical reflection or because food production and preparation have traditionally been regarded as women's work and, therefore, unworthy topics for male philosophers. As contemporary philosophy continues to challenge conventional notions of what constitutes "real" and "serious" topics of analysis, and as a feminist "hermeneutic of suspicion" yields important insights previously ignored in mainstream scholarship, philosophers have shown an increasing interest in the moral, political, metaphysical, and aesthetic dimensions of food.

Since World War II, changes in the technological and cultural landscape have affected views of food and eating. In the mid-twentieth century, the methods and machinery of industrialization were applied to food production, culminating in the so-called Green Revolution, which brought forth great increases in agricultural productivity in both the industrialized and developing nations. In addition to yielding more food, the Green Revolution also spawned social and environmental changes and raised questions about the appropriate use of land, environmental harms, effects on women, hunger and trade policy, and the ethical treatment of animals.

Further changes in the technological and cultural landscape in the industrialized global north have spurred an increasing awareness of the effects of industrial agriculture, the dubious nutritional value of highly processed foods, the potential health and environmental risks of genetically modified organisms (GMO) and foods, the globalization of food trade and production, and food scarcity and steep price increases in staples brought about by the increasing affluence in China and India and the deepening impact of the biofuels industry on the market for maize.

1

Natural and Artificial Food

Almost everything humans eat has been processed in some way; technologies and techniques transform raw, whole plants or animals into food. Food-processing techniques include cooking, drying, fermenting, slicing, peeling, and butchering. More technologically complex forms of processing include pasteurizing, canning, freezing, irradiating, and artificially sweetening. Some processed food contains additives, substances designed to help prevent spoilage and contamination or to make food look and taste better. Some processed foods include dietary supplements with nutritional properties, such as vitamins, minerals, proteins, herbs, or enzymes. Among the benefits of food processing are improved preservation, increased distribution potential, fortification, consumer choice, and convenience. Among the harms and risks often associated with processed food are reduced nutritional value, adverse health effects, pollution, and the amount of energy expended in processing.

By contrast, the so-called natural foods are purported to be free of artificial ingredients and are often less processed than conventional food. Natural foods—if they are really natural—do not contain artificial food additives, coloring, flavoring, or sweeteners. Nor do they contain refined flour, refined sugar, or hydrogenated oils. "Whole foods" are even less processed or refined. Proponents of a "whole-food diet" claim it is more healthful than a processed-food diet and results in less harm to the environment.

"Raw foods" are "whole foods" that have undergone little or no processing at all. A "raw-food diet" is one composed of entirely uncooked whole food. Advocates of such a regimen believe that increasing the intake of raw foods produces significant health benefits. They claim that it promotes weight loss, prevents disease, and helps mitigate the effects of chronic illness.

"Organic foods" are supposed to be grown without the use of pesticides, synthetic fertilizers, sewage sludge, genetically modified organisms, or ionizing radiation. Animals that produce organic meat, poultry, eggs, and dairy products are not supposed to be given antibiotics or growth hormones. Organic foods are not necessarily whole foods, nor are whole food necessarily organic. The term *organic* refers to the method of growing food or raising livestock, not to the amount of processing it undergoes.

According to the 1995 U.S. Department of Agriculture National Organic Standards Board, organic agriculture is an ecological production-management system that promotes and enhances biodiversity, biological cycles, and soil biological activity. Organic agriculture is based, in theory, on minimal use of off-farm inputs and on practices and materials that restore, maintain, and enhance ecological harmony and health within the farm and beyond.

Organic agriculture aims to optimize the health and productivity of interdependent communities of soil life, plants, animals, and people. Champions of organic food claim that reducing or eliminating the use of agricultural and industrial chemicals leads to cleaner air, water, and soil, and yields more nutritious, more healthful, and better-tasting food. Critics claim that the health and environmental benefits of organic food are questionable, that it is costly to consumers, and that the slippage in standards for organic production and lack of regulatory oversight leave consumers unsure whether their food is as "organic" as advertised.

Industrial Agriculture and Environmental Degradation

Intensive farming, or the industrialization of agriculture, became the norm in twentieth-century North America, Western Europe, and other developed regions of the world. During the latter half of the twentieth century, this model was exported —some would say imposed on—much of the rest of the world. Industrial agriculture involves highly productive systems based on the use of systematic plant breeding (since the 1990s augmented by genetic engineering); monoculture crops; fossil-fuel energy; farm machinery; artificial chemical fertilizers, pesticides, and herbicides; and mechanized irrigation, processing, and long-distance transportation of both bulk raw foods and packaged processed foods. Intensive agriculture has resulted in higher yields, increased productivity, greater availability, and lower prices, but it has also raised significant health and environmental concerns stemming from the use of chemical fertilizers, pesticides, and herbicides, all of which can pollute the air and soil and contaminate water supplies. These contaminants often enter into the food supply, posing health risks to humans and animals and threatening aquatic habitats and ecosystems. One of most intensive aspects of "intensive farming" is its liberal use of energy, especially the fossil fuels that contribute to increased atmospheric and oceanic carbon dioxide, which in turn cause global climate change, and marine acidification, all with unknown consequences.

Industrial agriculture also exposes the soil to the erosive effects of wind and rain, often leading to a severe loss of topsoil. Erosion has other harmful effects: It washes vast amounts of silt into bodies of water, damaging plant and animal life, and it increases the amount of dust, which is an air pollutant and a carrier of infectious diseases that can cost nations financial and productivity losses. If production is to be sustained, nutrients lost to erosion must be replaced, usually by chemical fertilizers, which compromise water quality and biodiversity and diminish the quality of the soil.

Industrialized agriculture involves the planting of monoculture crops, which are single crops grown over thousands of kilometers of land. Such vast monoculture planting threatens the loss of the genetic diversity represented by "land races," the local varieties of crops once grown on smaller scales on those lands. Monoculture crops create an ecological vacuum that insects and diseases exploit, further reducing the quality of the soil while increasing the possibility of crop failure. These declines in agricultural genetic biodiversity, which in turn reduce natural species biodiversity, have consequences throughout the food chain. Farmers must increasingly rely on chemical fertilizers and pesticides to compensate for the resilience formerly afforded by genetic diversity.

The industrialized production of livestock, poultry, and fish, also known as "factory farming," has many of the same benefits and harms associated with intensive farming. The benefits include efficiency, high yields, widespread availability, low prices, and contributions to local and national economies. Among the harms are the abuse of animals, environmental hazards, health risks to farmworkers, and food-safety problems. Industrial livestock production uses vast amounts of water, fossil fuels, inorganic fertilizers, and field machinery; it involves elaborate technologies such as food manufacturing, packaging, refrigeration, and transportation. The environment surrounding factory farms is often heavily polluted by animal wastes and offal, which foul the air and seep into groundwater and surface waters.

By contrast, "sustainable agriculture" aims to produce food indefinitely without causing environmental degradation. Sustainable agriculture may or may not be the same as "traditional farming," which often has a claim to be sustainable because forms of it have, in fact, been sustained for many hundreds of years; it attempts to combine responsible environmental management, high levels of farm productivity, respect for animals and workers, and support for rural farming communities. Sustainable agriculture might augment or replace traditional methods with postindustrial technologies such as drip irrigation or highly bred perennial polycultures.

In the 1990 "Farm Bill," the U.S. Department of Agriculture defined "sustainable agriculture" as an integrated system of plant and animal production practices having a site-specific applications that will, over the long term, satisfy human food and fiber needs, enhance environmental quality and the natural-resource base upon which the agricultural economy depends, make the most efficient use of nonrenewable resources and on-farm resources and integrate natural biological cycles and controls, sustain the economic viability of farm operations, and enhance the quality of life for farmers and society as a whole.

Farmers who take a sustainable approach substitute knowledge for pesticides and fertilizers. They use crop rotations and other adjustments of the agricultural system to solve problems. Among the benefits of sustainable agriculture are soil enrichment, which produces healthy plants that resist disease; the growth of cover crops (ancillary crops that cover the soil during otherwise fallow seasons), which retard erosion and control weeds; and the use of natural predators to help control pests. Sustainable farming minimizes the use of inputs of pesticides and fertilizers, thereby saving money and protecting the environment.

Global and Local Food

Trade and the globalization of agriculture are increasingly "delocalizing" the origin of food and the political authority over food policy. Transnational agribusiness and the global political and financial institutions that support them exercise great influence over food production, with growing consequences for food security and safety and the social fabric of communities. One social consequence of intensive agriculture is the consolidation of small farms into large, monocrop operations. As industrialized farming replaces human labor with machinery, each year millions of people are displaced, disrupting societies based on rural farming and swelling the population of urban areas.

The globalized food trade tends not to improve the lot of poor countries; to the contrary, it often aggravates poverty in those nations as subsidized foodstuffs from industrialized nations artificially drive crop prices down. Local farmers cannot compete with the factory-farm imports, so poor countries are forced into dependency on wealthier nations for food. A further consequence is that traditional, local diets are being replaced by a globalized, homogenized, animal-sourced diet of supermarket foods infused with high-calorie sweeteners and vegetable oils. These dietary changes and lifestyle changes have led to the globalization of the unhealthy European and North American diet, with attendant rises in rates of obesity, diabetes, and heart disease.

Two food movements have emerged in response to the increasing globalization of food production and commerce. One is the local-food movement. Its proponents maintain that locally and sustainably produced food enhances the economic, environmental, health, and well-being of communities. A locavore is someone who aims to eat only food grown or produced within a short distance from his or her home—preferably within a radius of 100 miles. Local food networks of small farms, community gardens, seed banks, community-supported agriculture, coops, and farmers markets enhance local relationships among farmers and communities while providing alternatives to global food production.

The slow-food movement was started in Italy by Carlos Petrini in the late 1980s as counterforce to the global corporate fast-food juggernaut. This movement champions the consumption of locally grown food that uses land-race seed stocks and traditional methods of production in the particular ecoregions in which they evolved. Its proponents claim that this regional form of agriculture protects the environment; promotes local traditional culinary practices and lifestyles; enhances relationships among farmers, communities, and environments; and yields superior-tasting food.

Critics of the local-food and slow-food movements argue that newly industrialized export-oriented farmers in developing countries are harmed when consumers refuse to support international food production and trade. The moral obligation to alleviate suffering abroad, they argue, takes priority over the obligation to mitigate environmental degradation and to support local "hobby" farmers, who have many economic alternatives that are unavailable in less affluent parts of the world and who are producing expensive fad foods for fashion-conscious, high-end bourgeois consumers in the developed world.

Critics also note that transportation is only part of the total environmental impact of food production and consumption. Thorough environmental assessments of food include analyses of methods of production and amounts of energy used. Often the total energy used in food produced and transported great distances is less than that expended in local production. Proponents and critics alike agree that food and agricultural practices should be subject to more stringent moral and political scrutiny in order to promote food safety, nutrition, and taste while protecting farmworkers, food producers, animals, and regional biodiversity.

Biofuels vs. Food

At the turn of the twenty-first century, one of the most hotly contested issues in the ethics of food is the advisability of using foodstuffs such as maize to produce biofuels. Partly as a consequence of this shift in the commodities market, food prices doubled between 2007 and 2008, threatening many poor people throughout the world with chronic hunger, malnutrition, and even starvation. Unlike the controversy over slow and local foods, this debate does not involve individual consumer choice because ethanol, made mostly from maize, is added indiscriminately to gasoline, and ethanol-free gasoline is not offered to consumers as an ethical alternative, even at a higher price. Rather, this is a collective moral issue, to be dealt with at the level of public policy enacted in response to popular outrage over farmers converting food to energy rather than making it available for people to eat.

Critics of the biofuels industry point out that ethanol produced from maize may require more energy to produce—in the form of tractor fuel, petroleum-based fertilizers, the energy involved in distilling it, and other energy-intensive inputs and processes—than is contained in the ethanol derivative. At best, the net energy gain is marginal. Second, other nonfood, less energy-intensive crops such as switchgrass can be used as the raw material for ethanol and other biofuels. The current U.S. policy of encouraging rather than discouraging the growing of maize for ethanol production has been criticized as pork-barrel legislation favoring the economic interests of farm states while masquerading virtuously as a means of achieving U.S. "energy independence."

Another cause of the steep worldwide rise in food prices from 2007 to 2008 is the growing prosperity of the Chinese and Indian populations, which has led to an increased global demand for meat. Producing meat, except on lands incapable of producing crops, involves feeding animals food that might otherwise be available to hungry humans. Only about 10 percent of the "feed" consumed by cows, pigs, chickens, and other animals in factory farming is converted to meat; or, put the other way around, 90 percent of the food value of feed crops consumed by animals for meat production is lost. This indeed can be construed as an individual moral choice. Animal ethicists argue that if the slaughter of sentient beasts cannot penetrate the conscience of the mass of meat eaters, perhaps the prospect of massive human hunger, malnutrition, and starvation will.

A problem remains, however, what economists call the "free-rider" issue. Morally motivated consumers may choose to be vegetarians, but their choice may register such a weak signal in the global marketplace that if many others do not make the same choice, food prices will remain unaffected. In that case government-enforced remedies are the only workable alternative. A luxury tax, for example, might be put on meat to discourage consumption and thus ease price pressure on agricultural commodities, diverting them from animal feedlots and onto the plates of hungry poor people.

SEE ALSO *Agricultural Ethics; Agriculture; Factory Farms; Farms; Genetically Modified Organisms and Biotechnology; Pollen Flow; Seed Banks; Soils; Sustainable Agriculture; U.S. Food and Drug Administration; Vegetarianism.*

Bibliography

Berry, Wendell. 1977. *The Unsettling of America.* San Francisco: Sierra Club Books.

Comstock, Gary. 2002. *Vexing Nature? On the Ethical Case Against Agricultural Biotechnology.* New York: Springer.

Food, Agriculture, Conservation, and Trade Act of 1990 (FACTA), P.L. 101-624, Title XVI, Subtitle A, Section 1603.

Government Printing Office, Washington, DC, 1990. NAL Call # KF1692.A31.

Holland, Alan. 1997. *Animal Biotechnology and Ethics.* New York: Springer.

Jackson, Wes. 1985. *New Roots for Agriculture*, new edition. Lincoln: University of Nebraska Press. First edition, 1980.

Kaplan, David M., ed. 2009. *The Philosophy of Food*. Berkeley: University of California Press.

Korthals, Michiel. 2004. *Before Dinner: Philosophy and Ethics of Food*. New York: Springer.

Shiva, Vandana. 1992. *The Violence of the Green Revolution: Ecological Degradation and Political Conflict in Punjab*. London: Zed Press.

Shiva, Vandana. 2000. *Stolen Harvest: The Hijacking of the Global Food Supply*. Cambridge, MA: South End Press.

Singer, Peter. 2006. *The Way We Eat: Why Our Food Choices Matter*. New York: Rodale.

Thompson, Paul. 1994. *The Spirit of the Soil: Agriculture and Environmental Ethics*. New York: Routledge.

Chapter 2

Animal Rights

WHAT SORT OF BEINGS are deserving of moral regard? Only human beings? Or nonhuman animals as well? How ought we to treat animals? Do they have moral rights? Is their suffering to be equated with human suffering? Should experimentation on animals cease? Should large-scale commercial ("factory") farms be abolished because they tend to cause animals great suffering? Do we have a moral duty to become vegetarians? What exactly is the moral status of animals?

In 1975, a book that opened with the following words appeared: "This book is about the tyranny of human over nonhuman animals. This tyranny has caused and today is still causing an amount of pain and suffering that can only be compared with that which resulted from the centuries of tyranny by white humans over black humans." Thus, Peter Singer began his epoch-making *Animal Liberation*, which launched the modern animal rights movement.

Before the 1970s, vegetarianism was restricted to Hindus, Buddhists, and small numbers of other people with relevant moral or spiritual convictions. Today, hundreds of millions more are vegetarians. Exact numbers are, of course, hard to locate, but various polls indicate that 20% to 30% of the people in the United States lean toward vegetarianism (that is, they look for vegetarian food on restaurant menus or at least generally prefer it). The number of strict vegetarians is probably around 5%. There are of course other reasons to be vegetarian other than concern for animals. For some, the belief that a vegetarian diet is healthier suffices, and increasingly, the environmental impact of meat eating is being raised as a reason in itself. For instance, meat eating contributes more to global climate change than transportation. These issues will be discussed in Chapter 8 on Food Ethics; in this chapter, we focus on the question of the moral status of nonhuman animals.

There are two separate defenses of the moral status (or rights) of animals: the utilitarian and the deontological[1] arguments. Peter Singer is the main representative of the utilitarian argument. Utilitarians follow Jeremy Bentham in asserting that what makes beings morally considerable is not reason but *sentience*. All sentient creatures have the ability to suffer and, as such, have interests. The frustration of those interests leads to suffering. Utilitarianism seeks to maximize the satisfaction of interests whether they be those of humans or animals. In some cases, human interests will make special claims on us; for example, humans but not mice or pigs will need schools and books. But if a pig and a child are in pain and you only have one pain reliever, you may have a moral dilemma as to who should receive the pain reliever. Utilitarians will generally allow some animal experimentation; for example, if experimenting on chimpanzees promises to help us find a cure for AIDS, it's probably justified, but a utilitarian animal liberationist like Singer would also be willing to experiment on retarded children if it maximized utility.

The second type of defense of animal rights is the deontological *rights* position, of which Tom Regan is the foremost proponent. The equal-rights position on animal rights contends that the same essential psychological properties—desires, memory, intelligence, and so on—link all animals and the human animal and thereby give us equal intrinsic value upon which equal rights are founded. These rights are inalienable and cannot be forfeited. Contrary to Singer's position, we have no right to experiment on chimpanzees in order to maximize the satisfaction of interests—that's exploitation. Animals like people are "ends in themselves," so utility is not sufficient to override these rights. Regan is thus more radical than Singer. He calls not for reform but for the total dissolution of commercial animal farming, the total elimination of hunting and trapping, and the total abolition of animal experiments. Just as we would condemn a scientist who took children and performed dangerous experiments on them for the good of others, so we must condemn the institutions that use coercion on animals.

Both utilitarian and deontological animal rights proponents have been attacked on their own grounds. R. G. Frey, for example, has argued that utilitarianism does not justify the sweeping indictments or proposals that Singer advocates. He says that because of the greater complexity of the human psyche and its social system, utility will be maximized by exploiting animals. What is needed is an amelioration of existing large-scale farms and safeguards in animal experimentation to ensure against unnecessary suffering.

In our readings, Mary Anne Warren attacks Regan's deontological position for failing to see important differences between human beings and animals (even other primates), especially our ability to reason. Warren—who agrees that we do have duties to be kind to animals, not to kill them without good reason, and to do what we can to make their lives enjoyable—points out that Regan's notion of inherent value is obscure.

We begin our readings with Kant's view that because animals are not self-conscious rational agents capable of forming the moral law, they are not directly morally considerable, followed by Holly Wilson. She examines Kant's argument over animal egalitarianism (whether all animals are equal).

NOTE

1. *Utilitarianism* is the view that the morally right act is the one that maximizes utility. It aims at producing the best overall consequences. *Deontological* ethics holds that certain features in the moral act itself have intrinsic value regardless of the consequences. It is wrong to kill innocent people even to procure good consequences. Some utilitarians deny animals have rights but argue that we should seek to procure their welfare.

1

Rational Beings Alone Have Moral Worth

IMMANUEL KANT

Immanuel Kant (1724–1804) was born into a deeply pietistic Lutheran family in Königsberg, Germany, and was a professor of philosophy at the University of Königsberg. He is a premier philosopher in the Western tradition, setting forth major works in metaphysics, philosophy of religion, ethics, epistemology, political theory, and philosophy of science.

Here, Kant first argues that rational beings are ends in themselves and must never be used as mere means. Only they have intrinsic moral worth. Animals are not persons because they are not rational, self-conscious beings capable of grasping the moral law. Since they are not part of the kingdom of moral legislators, we who are members of that "kingdom" do not owe them anything. But we should be kind to them since that will help develop good character in us and help us treat our fellow human beings with greater consideration. That is, our duties to animals are simply indirect duties to other human beings. See the next reading for further interpretation.

I. SECOND FORMULATION OF THE CATEGORICAL IMPERATIVE: HUMANITY AS AN END IN ITSELF

The will is conceived as a faculty of determining oneself to action in *accordance with the conception of certain laws*. And such a faculty can be found only in rational beings. Now that which serves the will as the objective ground of its self-determination is the *end*, and if this is assigned by reason alone, it must hold for all rational beings. On the other hand, that which merely contains the ground of possibility of the action of which the effect is the end, this is called the *means*. The subjective ground of the desire is the *spring*, the objective ground of the volition is the *motive*; hence the distinction between subjective ends which rest on springs, and objective ends which depend on motives valid for every rational being. Practical principles are *formal* when they abstract from all subjective ends; they are *material* when they assume these, and therefore particular springs of action. The ends which a rational being proposes to himself at pleasure as *effects* of his actions (material ends) are all only relative, for it is only their relation to the particular desires of the subject that gives them their worth, which therefore cannot furnish principles universal and necessary for all rational beings and for every volition, that is to say practical laws. Hence all these relative ends can give rise only to hypothetical imperatives.

Supposing, however, that there were something *whose existence* has *in itself* an absolute worth, something which, being *an end in itself,* could be a source of definite laws, then in this and this alone would lie the source of a possible categorical imperative, *i.e.* a practical law.

The first section is from Kant's *Foundations of the Metaphysics of Morals* (1873), trans. by T. K. Abbott. The second section is from Kant's *Lectures on Ethics*, trans. by Louis Infield (New York: Harper & Row, 1963).

Now I say: man and generally any rational being *exists* as an end in himself, *not merely as a means* to be arbitrarily used by this or that will, but in all his actions, whether they concern himself or other rational beings, must be always regarded at the same time as an end. All objects of the inclinations have only a conditional worth; for if the inclinations and the wants founded on them did not exist, then their object would be without value. But the inclinations themselves being sources of want are so far from having an absolute worth for which they should be desired, that, on the contrary, it must be the universal wish of every rational being to be wholly free from them. Thus the worth of any object which is *to be acquired* by our action is always conditional. Beings whose existence depends not on our will but on nature's, have nevertheless, if they are nonrational beings, only a relative value as means, and are therefore called *things*; rational beings, on the contrary, are called *persons*, because their very nature points them out as ends in themselves, that is as something which must not be used merely as means, and so far therefore restricts freedom of action (and is an object of respect). These, therefore, are not merely subjective ends whose existence has a worth *for us* as an effect of our action, but *objective ends*, that is things whose existence is an end in itself: an end moreover for which no other can be substituted, which they should subserve *merely* as means, for otherwise nothing whatever would possess *absolute worth*; but if all worth were conditioned and therefore contingent, then there would be no supreme practical principle of reason whatever.

If then there is a supreme practical principle or, in respect of the human will, a categorical imperative, it must be one which, being drawn from the conception of that which is necessarily an end for everyone because it is an *end in itself*, constitutes an *objective* principle of will, and can therefore serve as a universal practical law. The foundation of this principle is: *rational nature exists as an end in itself*. Man necessarily conceives his own existence as being so: so far then this is a *subjective* principle of human actions. But every other rational being regards its existence similarly, just on the same rational principle that holds for me: so that it is at the same time an objective principle, from which as a supreme

practical law all laws of the will must be capable of being deduced. Accordingly the practical imperative will be as follows: *So act as to treat humanity, whether in thine own person or in that of any other, in every case as an end-withal, never as means only.* We will now inquire whether this can be practically carried out.

II.

Baumgarten speaks of duties towards beings which are beneath us and beings which are above us. But so far as animals are concerned, we have no direct duties. Animals are not self-conscious and are there merely as a means to an end. That end is man. We can ask, "Why do animals exist?" But to ask, "Why does man exist?" is a meaningless question. *Our duties towards animals are merely indirect duties towards humanity.* Animal nature has analogies to human nature, and by doing our duties to animals in respect of manifestations of human nature, we indirectly do our duty towards humanity. Thus, if a dog has served his master long and faithfully, his service, on the analogy of human service, deserves reward, and when the dog has grown too old to serve, his master ought to keep him until he dies. Such action helps to support us in our duties towards human beings, where they are bounden duties. If then any acts of animals are analogous to human acts and spring from the same principles, we have duties towards the animals because thus we cultivate the corresponding duties towards human beings. If a man shoots his dog because the animal is no longer capable of service, he does not fail in his duty to the dog, for the dog cannot judge, but his *act is inhuman and damages in himself that humanity which it is his duty to show towards mankind.* If he is not to stifle his human feelings, he must practise kindness towards animals, for he who is cruel to animals becomes hard also in his dealing with men. We can judge the heart of a man by his treatment of animals. Hogarth depicts this in his engravings. He shows how cruelty grows and develops. He shows the child's cruelty to animals, pinch the tail of a dog or a cat; he then depicts the grown man in his cart running over a child; and lastly, the culmination of cruelty in murder. He thus brings home to us in a terrible fashion the rewards of cruelty, and this should be an impressive lesson to children. The more we come in contact with animals and observe their behaviour, the more we love them, for we see how great is their care for their young. It is then difficult for us to be cruel in thought even to a wolf. Leibnitz used a tiny worm for purposes of observation, and then carefully replaced it with its leaf on the tree so that it should not come to harm through any act of his. He would have been sorry—a natural feeling for a humane man—to destroy such a creature for no reason. Tender feelings towards dumb animals develop humane feelings towards mankind. In England butchers and doctors do not sit on a jury because they are accustomed to the sight of death and hardened. Vivisectionists, who use living animals for their experiments, certainly act cruelly, although their aim is praiseworthy, and they can justify their cruelty, since animals must be regarded as man's instruments; but any such cruelty for sport cannot be justified. A master who turns out his ass or his dog because the animal can no longer earn its keep manifests a small mind. The Greeks' ideas in this respect were highminded, as can be seen from the fable of the ass and the bell of ingratitude. Our duties towards animals, then, are indirect duties towards mankind.

STUDY QUESTIONS

1. According to Kant, do animals have rights? What capacity do they lack that deprives them of rights?

2. Why should we be kind to animals? Do you agree with Kant? How would an opponent respond to Kant's arguments?

2

The Green Kant: Kant's Treatment of Animals

HOLLY L. WILSON

Holly Wilson is the author of Kant's Pragmatic Anthropology. *Here she argues that the central reason Kant gave animals lower moral status is that raising the status of animals would diminish the status of humans. She further points out that Kant is thus naturally able to address the problem of animal egalitarianism and that Kant should no longer be seen as in opposition to environmental thinking.*

Some environmental theorists want to give animals rights and in so doing raise their moral status. None of these theorists seem at all concerned that this move may lower the moral status of human beings. It is simply assumed that human status will remain unaffected when the status of some or all animals is

The Green Kant: Kant's Treatment of Animals by Holly L. Wilson. Printed by permission of the author.

raised. Kant, on the other hand, was very concerned about maintaining the moral status and dignity of human beings, and for him that meant that animals cannot have rights and must be conceived of as being "mere means" to the end of humanity. It is important to note that he did not mean that they have the same status as things when he says "mere means"; but they also do not have the same status as human beings because they are not ends-in-themselves. Kant spent a lot of time distinguishing between humans and animals ontologically, and in doing so it appears that he did not want human status to decline to that of animals. For him, human dignity depended on human beings distancing themselves from their animality.

Although Kant is criticized for holding that animals are "mere means," none of the interpreters understand correctly what he meant by "mere means" or why he thought that characterization is important. I will show that Kant, by using teleological judgment, does not mean that animals have no moral status and are no more than things. I will also show that his use of teleological judgment has a lot to offer environmental philosophy. I will hold that his position on humans is able to deal with some of the problems environmental philosophers are struggling with, while sidestepping the problems these philosophers ascribe to Kant. Kant's views on animals are consistent with green concerns and are more positive than is usually assumed.

KANT'S VIEWS ON ANIMALS

Kant holds that animals have souls because they move. This is already an ontological distinction between things and animals. In a *Metaphysics* lecture note Kant writes,

> Animals are not mere machines or just matter, for they do have souls, and they do so because everything in nature is either inanimate or animate. When, e.g., we see a mote on a paper, we look to see whether it moves. If it doesn't we'll take it as inanimate matter but as soon as it moves, we'll look to see whether it does so

voluntarily. If we see *that* in the mote, we'll see that it is *animate*, an animal. So an animal is animated matter, for life is the power to determine oneself from an inner principle. Matter as such lacks an inner principle of spontaneity of motion while all matter that is animate has it, as an object of inner sense. Thus: all matter that lives is alive because of a principle of life…. And to the extent it is animated, to that extent it is besouled.[1]

Animals, in contrast to matter, have an inner principle that gives rise to spontaneous movement. Here is a clear and significant difference between things and animals. Such a distinction gives rise to the presumption that animals should be treated differently from things. Yet, at the same time, having a soul does not mean that an animal is an end-in-itself. To further determine the nature of animals, we turn to the *Critique of Teleological Judgment* where Kant makes the distinction between organized beings and things.

Our teleological judgment recognizes that there is a distinction between organized beings and artifacts and other natural realities. Kant holds that organized beings (living beings) have intrinsic purposiveness.[2] By this he means that we judge the inner organization of an organized being to be constituted by parts (organs), which are means to the ends of the organism and also means to each other's ends. There is a kind of organization that one does not find in a watch, for example. The inner organs of the organized being are mutually means and ends for each other, whereas this is not the case in a watch.[3] In a body the blood is the means of distributing oxygen to the brain; the brain is the means for keeping the blood supplied with nutrients (through eating, for instance). In a watch, one part may make the other part move, but that part is not the productive cause of the other part. The watch does not produce other watches, nor does it produce new parts when old ones malfunction. Even a tree is an organized being for Kant, and hence differs from things. The tree produces itself (maintains itself), reproduces, and its parts are teleological wholes in their own right insofar as a branch can be taken from a tree and grafted onto another tree.[4] Organized beings have formative forces [*Bildungstrieb*]; things do not.[5] Organized beings have intrinsic purposiveness; things do not. Again we find an important distinction between animals and plants, and things.

The distinction extends even further. Kant contrasts natural things like rivers and mountains with organized beings. Here too we find a significant difference between natural objects. Organized beings do not have only intrinsic purposiveness; they are also things for which other things can be extrinsically purposive.[6] Kant writes that the sandy soil "enabled extensive spruce forests to establish themselves, for which unreasonable destruction we often blame our ancestors."[7] The sandy soil was extrinsically purposive for the forests, but the forests were not extrinsically purposive for the soil. When we make such purposive judgments it is with regard to beings that are themselves intrinsically purposive. Hence, animals and plants are intrinsically purposive and things for which other things are extrinsically purposive.[8] We make such judgments whenever we characterize an ecosystem as something in which organized beings find a "habitat." That habitat is purposive for the organized being, and that organized being may well be purposive for other organized beings, but the spotted owl is not purposive for the natural objects like dirt or stones or any other objects in the ecosystem.

Hence, organized beings (animals and plants) have another distinction from things. They can be beings for which other things are purposive, which means that they are ends for the sake of which means exist. That they are intrinsically purposive already means that they are ends for which the means of their parts exist, but we can go even further and now say they are ends for which other things and beings exist. Things don't have this kind of distinction.

There is a qualified sense in which one can say that animals have inherent worth, according to Kant, because they are intrinsically and extrinsically purposive. With respect to human beings as natural beings, we are no different from other organized beings in terms of intrinsic and extrinsic purposiveness. We too are intrinsically purposive, we too may be beings for which other beings and things are purposive, and we too may well be means to another organized being's ends (especially for the ends of bacteria and viruses). Several times Kant exclaims that there is no reason why a human being needs to exist as far as ecosystems are concerned.[9] As natural beings we too have the qualified sense of inherent worth, but as natural animals we certainly are not ends-in-ourselves according to Kant. In this limited sense we are no better than animals. However, he makes an argument that it is only as "beings under moral laws" that we have a status of being ends-in-ourselves.[10] Because animals are not capable of 'being under moral laws,' they do not have this same status. In this human beings distinguish themselves from animals.

There is an additional way in which animals distinguish themselves from things and also may be compared to human beings. Namely, animals have a will [*Willkür*]. A will, Kant writes in the *Critique of Pure Reason,* "is purely *animal* (*arbitrium brutum*), which cannot be determined save through sensuous impulses, that is, pathologically."[11] These wills are not determined by the concept of a law but rather by forces that are impelled from outside.[12] For instance, a lion may well choose between this zebra and that antelope in the hunt, and hence it exhibits freedom of choice (*arbitrium brutum*). Yet, the lion does not have the freedom not to hunt. It is heteronomously impelled by the presentation of the prey and reacts compelled by its instincts. The prey triggers the impulse to pursue and kill and hence the motive of the pursuit is heteronomous. The lion does not have the autonomy to choose not to be a predator, and hence it does not have a free will (*Wille*), only the freedom of choice (*Willkür*). Animals, as distinct from human beings, do not have the capacity to resist their inclinations (instincts or impulses) based on the concept of a law (for instance, a maxim that would say "refrain from killing animals"). In contrast, a human being may well choose to be a vegetarian based on the concept that killing animals is wrong. Human beings then have the possibility of autonomous action based on the free will (*Wille*).[13] As a result, human beings can act contrary to sensuously determined carnivorous inclinations. Kant assumes animals are driven by instincts rather than by concepts of laws and in this way, animals, though like human beings, are different from human beings.

KANT'S VIEWS ON HUMAN BEINGS

There is another way in which animals differ from human beings. Human beings are capable of the idea of "I." The fact, Kant claims,

> that man can have the idea "I" raises him infinitely above all other beings living on earth. By this he is a person; and by virtue of his unity of consciousness through all the changes he may undergo, he is one and the same person.[14]

Animals are indeed conscious, have presentations,[15] and also reflect,[16] but they are not self-conscious and do not have an "I." As a student from Kant's anthropology class notes, "If a horse could grasp the idea of I, then I would dismount and regard it as my society."[17] If animals don't have an "I," then they are not our equals.

Kant does a curious thing at this point in the *Anthropology*. Right after the preceding quote he goes on to say that a human being is "altogether different in rank and dignity from things, such as irrational animals, which we can dispose of as we please." First of all, he makes it a point to say that animals are things [*Sachen*], and from this he concludes that they do not have the same rank and dignity that human beings have. He emphasizes that we may dispose of animals as we please, just like we may dispose of things as we please. But why is it so important for him now (1798) to equate animals and things after he has made it so clear that animals are not things in his earlier writings? Systematically and ontologically, Kant has established a distinction between things and animals, but now he equates them and claims we may treat them the same way. Is this a considered position, or is there another reason why Kant is taking pains to distance animals from human beings?

I think we can find a clue to unravel this mystery within Kant's essay *The Speculative Beginning of Human History* (1786). Kant acknowledges he is writing a speculative flight of fancy about the beginnings of human freedom and the departure from animality. It is about the first appearance of reason in the human species. In the experience of reason, human beings are raised "beyond any community with animals."[18] A human being (Adam) views himself for the first time as the "true end of nature" because "nothing living on earth can compete with him." He says to the sheep,

> 'the pelt you bear was given to you by nature not for yourself, but for me'; the first time he took that pelt off the sheep and put it on himself (Gen. 3:21); at that same time he saw within himself a privilege by virtue of which his nature surpassed that of all animals, which he now no longer regarded as his fellows in creation, but as subject to his will as means and tools for achieving his own chosen objectives.[19]

This story of using a sheepskin is not about how we ought to relate to animals but rather about how we can indeed use animals as mere means, because we are superior in our ability to compete with animals. It is an account of how human beings, through skills, are able to use animals as means toward human's arbitrarily chosen ends. Kant is right: In the struggle for survival, human beings have clearly outperformed other animals. Our success means that nonhuman animals are no longer our equals, our fellows, or our society.

Yet this experience entails even more. Human beings draw the conclusion that they are not only the last end of nature (*letzter Zweck*), but that they, unlike animals, are ends-in-themselves (*Endzweck*) and that no fellow human being ought to be used "merely as a means to any other end." In other words, human beings are "the equal of all rational beings." Kant ties the moment of recognition of our human dignity to the moment we are able to recognize our ability to use animals as mere means.[20] This association of the two insights is exactly what he is doing in the *Anthropology*. Our dignity as humans is in part determined by our ability to distance ourselves from animals, by using them as means to our ends. This distancing is not just from animals, but also from our own animality because we no longer identify with animal society. The very capacity to turn animals into mere means is one way in which we distance ourselves from our own animality. Is it possible to come to this recognition without having to see animals are mere means? Could we have come to this recognition of our dignity with the use of tools?

Kant seems to think that before we used reason we were animals and that our society was with other animals. Thus, the earliest use of reason required our distancing ourselves not only from other animals but also from our own animality. That distancing doesn't seem to be something we could accomplish just by becoming aware of the possibility of using tools because we are not like tools. We are like animals. For Kant we are animals that have the capacity for reason (*animal rationabilis*).[21] One use of reason is found in our technical predisposition, that is, our capacity for skills that are capable of manipulating things "in any way whatsoever."[22] It is because of this predisposition that we are capable of turning animals into "mere means." We have the capacity to develop skills for survival nonspecific ends, or, as Kant puts it in the *Critique of Teleological Judgment*, for arbitrary ends.[23] Kant goes on to say that the culture of skill is "not adequate to assist the will in the determination and selection of its purposes...."[24] Nothing about our technical predisposition and technical skills specifies only worthy ends, and hence there is nothing about these skills that would keep us from turning animals into mere means.

But our technical predisposition is only one of reason's expressions. We also have a pragmatic predisposition and a moral predisposition. These two present necessary ends for reason. The pragmatic predisposition is expressed in the skill of prudence, which aims at our happiness, a necessary end. Prudence is the capacity we have for using other human beings as means to our own ends. The moral predisposition is expressed in our capacity for limiting and refusing specific technical and pragmatic ends for moral reasons.[25] Treating animals as mere

means may well have a detrimental effect on our happiness, and we may hence put a limit on how we relate to animals. Many people love animals, become friends with them, and as a result treat them very well, sometimes even like children, because it brings them happiness to do so. This treatment is the result of our pragmatic predisposition, because we are limiting our use of animals in order to allow them to bring us happiness. Some people refuse to eat animals because they are saddened by the way animals are farm-raised and slaughtered. This refusal too is a result of our pragmatic predisposition. Others want to protect animals from cruelty because they believe that animals are like us (feel pain and pleasure) and that it is ethically wrong to cause them suffering. This protection is possible using moral reasoning. Still others want to limit our ability to treat animals as mere means by even stronger measures. They want to accord animals rights to ensure their safety and well-being. They do not want our limits to be based on internal measures, mere subjective feelings for animals (as in the pragmatic predisposition), or even benevolence and good will (as in the moral predisposition). They want external coercive juridical forces to come to the aid of animals. They believe that granting animal rights would ensure to a greater extent the well-being of animals and that it would raise the status of animals to that of humans because we would no longer be able to treat animals as mere means.

CAN ANIMALS HAVE RIGHTS?

For Kant, a lot would be at stake if we did move toward according animals rights. First of all, it would entail that we could never use animals, even as we use human beings, because we could never gain their informed consent. According to the third formulation of the categorical imperative we may never treat the humanity in ourselves or in others as means only. This formulation means we may never use human beings as means only. Yet we use people all the time, and our pragmatic predisposition is precisely for that purpose. Kant says in the *Lectures on Ethics*, "A person can, indeed, serve as a means for others, by his work, for example, but in such a way that he does not cease to exist as a person and an end."[26] The reason we can use others without turning them into mere means is because we have the other's consent or free choice.[27] I use students as students, and they use me as a professor. What makes it morally permissible to use another human being is the informed consent she gives ahead of time, which is why students register for their classes themselves and I give out a syllabus at the start of every semester. They are consenting to take the class, and I am giving them the information they need to make an informed decision about whether to permit me to evaluate them. It is impossible to gain the informed consent from animals, however, because we would need to convey information regarding the means used and the possible consequences, and we would need to procure a sure sign of their consent. Such a rigorous requirement would make it impossible for me to take my cat to the vet. She doesn't consent to being in the cat carrier, in the car, at the vet's, and she certainly doesn't consent to the vaccine shots. Having to gain animals' informed consent can be a hindrance to helping them as well as making it impossible to treat them as means. Clearly, by treating animals as "mere means" Kant means *inter alia* that we do not have to gain their consent to use them or take care of them, although, for the most part, it is preferable to treat a pet in a way it wants to be treated whenever possible.

This position, however, raises the marginal case of humans for whom we also cannot gain informed consent (children, the mentally handicapped, and those who are comatose). If we include these marginal cases as persons, why can we not also include animals, or at least animals that exhibit some rationality? Why should animals who exhibit some form of rationality be denied moral personhood while human beings not exhibiting rationality are accorded moral personhood? Kant's answer would be that it is not important for each member of the human species to exhibit all features of rationality; it is enough that the species exhibits all forms. That view is implicit in his formulation of the human species as the *animal rationabilis*, rather than the rational animal.[28]

Human beings are the animals who have the capacity for reason. Each human being, as a member of the species, has the potential for rationality even if she never exhibits it. This potential entails that we must still treat humans who do not exhibit rationality as ends-in-themselves. When it is impossible to gain their consent, it does not inhibit our ability to help them.

What is crucial here is that Kant does not want to isolate an individual human being and evaluate whether that particular individual has the capacity for reason. His position is that human nature is intrinsically communal, and hence the capacity for reason is something we share as a species rather than as individuals. Human beings are defined as the animals capable of developing reason (*animal rationabilis*), so that whether any one individual human being does or does not exhibit reason will not affect one's status and nature. Our natural predispositions, which define human nature for Kant, relate us to all other members of the human species.[29] Hence, to treat any one human being as less than an end-in-herself is already to call into question the status of all other human beings. Nonetheless, Kant's definition of human nature as *animal rationabilis* does not exclude other animals as being "like human beings" in that they exhibit "reason-like" capacities.

So, what about those cases in which animals exhibit primitive forms of rationality? Shouldn't they be granted moral personhood? How would Kant deal with animals who are very much like us? That animals are like us is relevant to moral consideration of them. In the very same section, "Of Duties to Animals and Spirits" in the *Lectures on Ethics*, where Kant grants us permission to use animals as mere means, he also claims we have indirect duties with regard to dogs that serve us and wolves that, like us, care for their young.[30] First, he makes it clear that they are like us (analogues of us), and then he claims that our mistreatment of them (animals like us) would result in diminishing our humanity. The duty is then only indirect because it is contingent upon whether our humanity is furthered or diminished. We have a direct duty to our own humanity, but Kant is equally convinced that our treatment of animals matters because they are like us. By implication one could draw the conclusion that the more like us they are, the more consideration they deserve. This conclusion makes Kantian sense of the problem of marginal cases. Animals who exhibit rudimentary rationality certainly deserve more consideration than flies, because they are more like us. Kant's position also solves the obvious problem with animal egalitarianism, which outrageously implies that all animate beings deserve equal consideration. The less like human beings an animate being is, the less it deserves consideration. The more like us they are, the more consideration they deserve. And Kant does not have to be taken as implying that animals are like us only insofar as they exhibit reasonlike capacities. Dogs are like us in that they exhibit loyalty. Wolves are like us in that they care for their young. Thus animals can be like us in many different ways, not only in that they can suffer pain and pleasure or have capacities for reason.

Kant is also right to give human beings only indirect duties to nonhuman animals because they do not have moral rationality. They are not capable of acting on the conception of a law. They do exhibit cooperation and social behaviors, but these traits appear to be a result of survival mechanisms and conditioned inclinations and not a result of acting on the concept of treating animality as an end and never as a means only. Their behaviors do exhibit order and uniformity, but this display is due to the natural organization in their instincts and to socialized learned behavior, not due to considered reflection on whether every chimp could act on that maxim. Human beings exhibit order and character only when they submit their maxims to the moral law. Humans are held to higher standards morally because there are ontological differences between human beings and animals. We have the capacity for technical and pragmatic reason, and we need morality to limit these ends to morally permissible and worthy ends.

What about the position that would say, 'granted, animals cannot give informed consent, develop character, and act on the conception of the law, but that is just the case with children'? We have the authority to make children do what is in their own best interest, while according them rights not to be mistreated. Why not treat animals

the same way? But are there no ontological differences between animals and children? Children have the potential to develop reason. Should this not inform their treatment? Children should be raised rather than trained. They need to be taught in a way that develops their free will. They need to be given alternatives and to be encouraged to evaluate consequences for their actions. Eventually, they also need to be encouraged to deliberate and reflect on possible actions and on the reasons and motives for those actions. Animals, on the other hand, should be trained. They can be trained to associate reward and punishment with certain behaviors. We cannot reason with them and encourage them to choose between alternative behaviors. Would we be blurring the distinction between children and animals if we were to treat animals like children?

The blurring of the distinction between human beings and nonhuman animals is already occurring in evolutionary psychology, evolutionary ethics, and behaviorism. Human behavior is being understood on the animal model of behaviors. Focus is being put on behavior rather than action. More concern is attached to explaining and controlling behavior than developing ways to teach and instill the importance of making choices and taking responsibility for those choices. A Kantian ought to be concerned about this, and I think Kant would be were he here today.

Clearly humans need to be treated differently from animals because they are different, and animals need to be treated differently from humans. Animals should not be treated as things, but they should also not be treated as humans. The locus of our treatment of animals should be ethical rather than juridical. Cruelty to animals should be against the law, not only because it harms animals but also because it harms our humanity and makes us more likely to be cruel to humans. We can and are able to treat animals humanely without giving animals rights. We ought not to treat animal nature as an end-in-itself, as Christine Korsgaard proposes, however, because animal nature is pursued by animals heteronomously, pathologically, and reactively. To treat animal nature as an end-in-itself would mean having to cooperate in the ends that animal nature pursues, and that would make our actions hetero-nomously motivated.

IN CONCLUSION

Human beings, for Kant, are under moral laws and animals are not. We find ourselves obligated not by the needs of animals but by the moral law. Animals do not find themselves obligated by the moral law nor by us and hence they cannot directly obligate us. Nevertheless, animals, in their vulnerabilities and needs, present reasons for taking them into consideration and reasons for refraining from harming them. Insofar as I have a maxim of benevolence toward human beings who have needs, and I can see those same needs in animals, then out of care for the humanity in myself, I can feel obligated to care about animals, but always by virtue of my concern for the state of my own humanity. Kant is asking us to value the best in ourselves, our humanity, and out of that to find motivation for caring for animals. When we do so it solves the problem of the apparent conflict between doing what is good for us and doing what is good for animals. Taking care of animals and not being cruel to them is good for us. Finding our care for animals in our care for our humanity does not preclude legislating against cruel or arbitrary treatment of animals, but rather gives us reason to legislate against such treatment. We can do this without considering animals to be ends-in-themselves, and thereby lowering the worth of human beings and blurring the ontological and moral lines between human life and animal life.

For Kant, animals, like human beings, are organic beings and do have a sense of inherent worth insofar as they are intrinsically and extrinsically purposive. Animals can be ends for which our actions are means, and we treat them as ends when we treat animals kindly, with benevolence, and when we refrain from harming them and their habitats. What is at stake for Kant is the motive for not treating animals cruelly. Animal rights theorists want people to be coercively motivated to keep them from treating animals cruelly by giving animals rights. If animals have a right not to be treated cruelly, then human beings can be punished if they do treat them cruelly. Kant wants us to be motivated out of respect for our own humanity to keep us from treating animals cruelly, because he knows that our dignity as human beings is always at stake in our treatment of animals. Kant holds that we preserve our moral and inherent dignity by treating animals kindly because in so doing we take our humanity as an end-in-itself since animals are like us. It would be like treating our own humanity as a mere means if we were to be arbitrarily cruel to animals like us. Kant wants us not only to treat animals well but also to learn to respect our own humanity and dignity. And for that we have to distinguish between animals and humans.

NOTES

1. Immanuel Kant, *Metaphysik L1,* in KGS 28:275 (1776), translation by Martin Schönfeld.

2. Immanuel Kant, KU, KGS V:372–76; pp. 251–56.

3. Immanuel Kant, KU, KGS V:373; p. 252.

4. Immanuel Kant, KU, KGS V:371; pp. 249–250.

5. Immanuel Kant, KU, KGS V:374; p. 253.

6. Immanuel Kant, KU, KGS V:367–68; p. 245.

7. Immanuel Kant, Ibid.

8. Immanuel Kant, KU, KGS V:369; p. 246.

9. Immanuel Kant, KU, KGS V:369; p. 247; KU, KGS V:378; p. 258.

10. Immanuel Kant, KU, KGS 435; p. 323.

11. Immanuel Kant, *Critique of Pure Reason* [A802/B830].

12. Immanuel Kant, LoE, KGS 27:344; p. 125. Friedländer, KGS 25 (2,1):577.

13. Immanuel Kant, GR, KGS IV:412; p. 23.

14. Immanuel Kant, Anth, KGS VII:127; p. 9.

15. Immanuel Kant, KU, KGS V:464n; p. 356n.

16. Immanuel Kant, First Intro, KGS, XX:211; p. 400.

17. Immanuel Kant, Menschenkunde, KGS 25(2): 859.

18. Immanuel Kant, Mut, KGS VIII:114; p. 52.

19. Immanuel Kant, Mut, KGS VIII:114; p. 52–3.

20. Immanuel Kant, Ibid.

21. Immanuel Kant, Anth, KGS VII:321; p. 183.

22. Immanuel Kant, Anth, KGS VII:323; p. 184.

23. Immanuel Kant, KU, KGS V:430; p. 317.

24. Immanuel Kant, KU, KGS V:432; p. 319.

25. Immanuel Kant, Anth, KGS VII:323–4; p. 185.

26. Immanuel Kant, LoE, KGS 27:343; p. 124.

27. Immanuel Kant, LoE, KGS 27:384; p. 155.

28. Immanuel Kant, Anth, KGS VI:321; p. 183.

29. Holly L. Wilson, *Kant's Pragmatic Anthropology*, Chapter 3.

30. Immanuel Kant, LoE, KGS 27:459; p. 212.

STUDY QUESTIONS

1. According to Kant, what are the differences among humans, nonhuman animals, and plants?

2. What does it mean to treat an entity as an 'end-in-itself '? Why is it problematic to treat animals this way?

3. Animal egalitarianism claims that all animals deserve equal moral consideration. Discuss this view and Kant's account of why this is wrong.

BIBLIOGRAPHY

Citations from Immanuel Kant are from, *Kant's Gesammelte Schriften*, edited by the Königlich Preußische [now Deutsche] Akademie der Wissenschaft, vols. 1–29 (Berlin: G. Reimer [now de Gruyter], 1902–) [KGS].

Immanuel Kant, *Kritik der Urteilskraft*, in KGS V; *Critique of Judgment*, trans. by Werner S. Pluhar (Indianapolis: Hackett Publishing Co., 1987) [KU].

Immanuel Kant, "Erste Einleitung in die Kritik der Urteilskraft" in KGS XX; "First Introduction to the Critique of Judgment" in *Critique of Judgment*, trans. by Werner S. Pluhar (Indianapolis: Hackett Publishing Co., 1987) [First Intro].

Immanuel Kant, *Critique of Pure Reason*, trans. by Normen Kemp Smith (New York: St. Martin's Press, 1965) [A/B].

Immanuel Kant, *Lectures on Ethics*, in KGS, 27, trans. by Peter Heath (Cambridge: Cambridge University Press, 1997) [LoE].

Immanuel Kant, *Grundlegung zur Metaphysik der Sitten*, in KGS IV; Grounding for the Metaphysics of Morals, trans. by James W. Ellington (Indianapolis: Hackett Publishing Co., Inc., 1981) [GR].

Immanuel Kant, *Anthropologie im pragmatischer Hinsicht*, in KGS, VII; *Anthropology from a Pragmatic Point of View*, trans. by Mary Gregor (The Hague: Maritinus Nijhoff, 1974).

Immanuel Kant, *Menschenkunde*, in KGS, XXV(2) [Menschenkunde].

Immanuel Kant, "Muthmaßlicher Anfang der Menschengeschichte" in KGS VIII; "Speculative Beginning of Human History" in *Perpetual Peace and other Essays on Politics, History, and Morals*, trans. by Ted Humphrey (Indianapolis: Hackett Publishing Co., 1983) [Mut].

Christine M. Korsgaard, "Fellow Creatures: Kantian Ethics and Our Duties to Animals" in *The Tanner Lectures on Human Values*, Volume 25/26, ed. by Grethe B. Peterson. Salt Lake City: Utah University Press, 2004.

Holly L. Wilson, *Kant's Pragmatic Anthropology: Its Origin, Meaning, and Critical Significance* (New York: State University of New York Press, 2006).

3

A Utilitarian Defense of Animal Liberation

PETER SINGER

Peter Singer, professor of philosophy at Princeton University, was included in Time *magazine's 2005 list of the world's most influential people. His book* Animal Liberation *(1975), from which the following selection is taken, is the most influential book written on the subject, having in a sense started the animal rights movement. Singer argues that animal liberation today is analogous to racial and gender injustice in the past. Just as people once thought it incredible that women or blacks should be treated as equal to white men, so now speciesists mock the idea that all animals should be given equal consideration. Singer defines* speciesism *(a term devised by Richard Ryder) as the prejudice (unjustified bias) that favors one's own species over every other. What equalizes all sentient beings is our ability to suffer. In that, we and animals are equal and deserving equal consideration of interests. Singer's argument is a utilitarian one, having as its goal the maximization of interest satisfaction.*

In recent years a number of oppressed groups have campaigned vigorously for equality. The classic instance is the Black Liberation movement, which demands an end to the prejudice and discrimination that has made blacks second-class citizens. The immediate appeal of the black liberation movement and its initial, if limited, success made it a model for other oppressed groups to follow. We became familiar with liberation movements for Spanish-Americans, gay people, and a variety of other minorities. When a majority group—women—began their campaign, some thought we had come to the end of the road. Discrimination on the basis of sex, it has been said, is the last universally accepted form of discrimination, practiced without secrecy or pretense even in those liberal circles that have long prided themselves on their freedom from prejudice against racial minorities.

One should always be wary of talking of "the last remaining form of discrimination." If we have

learnt anything from the liberation movements, we should have learnt how difficult it is to be aware of latent prejudice in our attitudes to particular groups until this prejudice is forcefully pointed out.

A liberation movement demands an expansion of our moral horizons and an extension or reinterpretation of the basic moral principle of equality. Practices that were previously regarded as natural and inevitable come to be seen as the result of an unjustifiable prejudice. Who can say with confidence that all his or her attitudes and practices are beyond criticism? If we wish to avoid being numbered amongst the oppressors, we must be prepared to re-think even our most fundamental attitudes. We need to consider them from the point of view of those most disadvantaged by our attitudes, and the practices that follow from these attitudes. If we can make this unaccustomed mental switch we may discover a pattern in our attitudes and practices that consistently operates so as to benefit one

Reprinted from *Animal Rights and Human Obligations* (Englewood Cliffs, N.J.: Prentice Hall, 1976) by permission of Peter Singer.

group—usually the one to which we ourselves belong—at the expense of another. In this way we may come to see that there is a case for a new liberation movement. My aim is to advocate that we make this mental switch in respect of our attitudes and practices towards a very large group of beings: members of species other than our own—or, as we popularly though misleadingly call them, animals. In other words, I am urging that we extend to other species the basic principle of equality that most of us recognize should be extended to all members of our own species.

All this may sound a little far-fetched, more like a parody of other liberation movements than a serious objective. In fact, in the past the idea of "The Rights of Animals" really has been used to parody the case for women's rights. When Mary Wollstonecroft, a forerunner of later feminists, published her *Vindication of the Rights of Women* in 1792, her ideas were widely regarded as absurd, and they were satirized in an anonymous publication entitled *A Vindication of the Rights of Brutes*. The author of this satire (actually Thomas Taylor, a distinguished Cambridge philosopher) tried to refute Wollstonecroft's reasonings by showing that they could be carried one stage further. If sound when applied to women, why should the arguments not be applied to dogs, cats, and horses? They seemed to hold equally well for these "brutes"; yet to hold that brutes had rights was manifestly absurd; therefore the reasoning by which this conclusion had been reached must be unsound, and if unsound when applied to brutes, it must also be unsound when applied to women, since the very same arguments had been used in each case.

One way in which we might reply to this argument is by saying that the case for equality between men and women cannot validly be extended to nonhuman animals. Women have a right to vote, for instance, because they are just as capable of making rational decisions as men are; dogs, on the other hand, are incapable of understanding the significance of voting, so they cannot have the right to vote. There are many other obvious ways in which men and women resemble each other closely, while humans and other animals differ

greatly. So, it might be said, men and women are similar beings, and should have equal rights, while humans and nonhumans are different and should not have equal rights.

The thought behind this reply to Taylor's analogy is correct up to a point, but it does not go far enough. There *are* important differences between humans and other animals, and these differences must give rise to *some* differences in the rights that each have. Recognizing this obvious fact, however, is no barrier to the case for extending the basic principle of equality to nonhuman animals. The differences that exist between men and women are equally undeniable, and the supporters of Women's Liberation are aware that these differences may give rise to different rights. Many feminists hold that women have the right to an abortion on request. It does not follow that since these same people are campaigning for equality between men and women they must support the right of men to have abortions too. Since a man cannot have an abortion, it is meaningless to talk of his right to have one. Since a pig can't vote, it is meaningless to talk of its right to vote. There is no reason why either Women's Liberation or Animal Liberation should get involved in such nonsense. The extension of the basic principle of equality from one group to another does not imply that we must treat both groups in exactly the same way, or grant exactly the same rights to both groups. Whether we should do so will depend on the nature of the members of the two groups. The basic principle of equality, I shall argue, is equality of consideration; and equal consideration for different beings may lead to different treatment and different rights.

So there is a different way of replying to Taylor's attempt to parody Wollstonecroft's arguments, a way which does not deny the differences between humans and nonhumans, but goes more deeply into the question of equality, and concludes by finding nothing absurd in the idea that the basic principle of equality applies to so called "brutes." I believe that we reach this conclusion if we examine the basis on which our opposition to discrimination on grounds of race or sex ultimately rests. We will then see that we would be on shaky ground if we were to demand equality for blacks, women, and other groups of oppressed humans while denying equal consideration to nonhumans.

When we say that all human beings, whatever their race, creed or sex, are equal, what is it that we are asserting? Those who wish to defend a hierarchical, inegalitarian society have often pointed out that by whatever test we choose, it simply is not true that all humans are equal. Like it or not, we must face the fact that humans come in different shapes and sizes; they come with differing moral capacities, differing intellectual abilities, differing amounts of benevolent feeling and sensitivity to the needs of others, differing abilities to communicate effectively, and differing capacities to experience pleasure and pain. In short, if the demand for equality were based on the actual equality of all human beings, we would have to stop demanding equality. It would be an unjustifiable demand.

Still, one might cling to the view that the demand for equality among human beings is based on the actual equality of the different races and sexes. Although humans differ as individuals in various ways, there are no differences between the races and sexes *as such*. From the mere fact that a person is black, or a woman, we cannot infer anything else about that person. This, it may be said, is what is wrong with racism and sexism. The white racist claims that whites are superior to blacks, but this is false—although there are differences between individuals, some blacks are superior to some whites in all of the capacities and abilities that could conceivably be relevant. The opponent of sexism would say the same: a person's sex is no guide to his or her abilities, and this is why it is unjustifiable to discriminate on the basis of sex.

This is a possible line of objection to racial and sexual discrimination. It is not, however, the way that someone really concerned about equality would choose, because taking this line could, in some circumstances, force one to accept a most inegalitarian society. The fact that humans differ as individuals, rather than as races or sexes, is a valid reply to someone who defends a hierarchical society like, say, South Africa, in which all whites are superior in status to all blacks. The existence of individual variations that cut across the lines of

race or sex, however, provides us with no defence at all against a more sophisticated opponent of equality, one who proposes that, say, the interests of those with I.Q. ratings above 100 be preferred to the interests of those with I.Q.s below 100. Would a hierarchical society of this sort really be so much better than one based on race or sex? I think not. But if we tie the moral principle of equality to the factual equality of the different races or sexes, taken as a whole, our opposition to racism and sexism does not provide us with any basis for objecting to this kind of inegalitarianism.

There is a second important reason why we ought not to base our opposition to racism and sexism on any kind of factual equality, even the limited kind which asserts that variations in capacities and abilities are spread evenly between the different races and sexes: we can have no absolute guarantee that these abilities and capacities really are distributed evenly, without regard to race or sex, among human beings. So far as actual abilities are concerned, there do seem to be certain measurable differences between both races and sexes. These differences do not, of course, appear in each case, but only when averages are taken. More important still, we do not yet know how much of these differences is really due to the different genetic endowments of the various races and sexes, and how much is due to environmental differences that are the result of past and continuing discrimination. Perhaps all of the important differences will eventually prove to be environmental rather than genetic. Anyone opposed to racism and sexism will certainly hope that this will be so, for it will make the task of ending discrimination a lot easier; nevertheless it would be dangerous to rest the case against racism and sexism on the belief that all significant differences are environmental in origin. The opponent of, say, racism who takes this line will be unable to avoid conceding that if differences in ability did after all prove to have some generic connection with race, racism would in some way be defensible.

It would be folly for the opponent of racism to stake his whole case on a dogmatic commitment to one particular outcome of a difficult scientific issue which is still a long way from being settled. While attempts to prove that differences in certain selected abilities between races and sexes are primarily genetic in origin have certainly not been conclusive, the same must be said of attempts to prove that these differences are largely the result of environment. At this stage of the investigation we cannot be certain which view is correct, however much we may hope it is the latter.

Fortunately, there is no need to pin the case for equality to one particular outcome of this scientific investigation. The appropriate response to those who claim to have found evidence of genetically based differences in ability between the races or sexes is not to stick to the belief that the genetic explanation must be wrong, whatever evidence to the contrary may turn up: instead we should make it quite clear that the claim to equality does not depend on intelligence, moral capacity, physical strength, or similar matters of fact. Equality is a moral ideal, not a simple assertion of fact. There is no logically compelling reason for assuming that a factual difference in ability between two people justifies any *difference in the amount of consideration we give to satisfying their needs and interests*. The principle of the equality of human beings is not a description of an alleged actual equality among humans: it is a prescription of how we should treat humans.

Jeremy Bentham incorporated the essential basis of moral equality into his utilitarian system of ethics in the formula: "Each to count for one and none for more than one." In other words, the interests of every being affected by an action are to be taken into account and given the same weight as the like interests of any other being. A later utilitarian, Henry Sidgwick, put the point in this way: "The good of any one individual is of no more importance, from the point of view (if I may say so) of the Universe, than the good of any other."[1] More recently, the leading figures in contemporary moral philosophy have shown a great deal of agreement in specifying as a fundamental presupposition of their moral theories some similar requirement which operates so as to give everyone's interests equal consideration—although they cannot agree on how this requirement is best formulated.[2]

It is an implication of this principle of equality that our concern for others ought not to depend on what they are like, or what abilities they possess—although precisely what this concern requires us to do may vary according to the characteristics of those affected by what we do. It is on this basis that the case against racism and the case against sexism must both ultimately rest; and it is in accordance with this principle that speciesism is also to be condemned. If possessing a higher degree of intelligence does not entitle one human to use another for his own ends, how can it entitle humans to exploit nonhumans?

Many philosophers have proposed the principle of equal consideration of interests, in some form or other, as a basic moral principle; but, as we shall see in more detail shortly, not many of them have recognized that this principle applies to members of other species as well as to our own. Bentham was one of the few who did realize this. In a forward-looking passage, written at a time when black slaves in British dominions were still being treated much as we now treat nonhuman animals, Bentham wrote:

> The day **may** come when the rest of the
> animal creation may acquire those rights
> which never could have been witholden
> from them but by the hand of tyranny.
> The French have already discovered that
> the blackness of the skin is no reason why a
> human being should be abandoned
> without redress to the caprice of a
> tormentor. It may one day come to be
> recognized that the number of the legs, the
> villoscity of the skin, or the termination of
> the **os sacrum**, are reasons equally
> insufficient for abandoning a sensitive
> being to the same fate. What else is it that
> should trace the insuperable line? Is it the
> faculty of reason, or perhaps the faculty of
> discourse? But a full grown horse or dog is
> beyond comparison a more rational, as
> well as a more conversable animal, than
> an infant of a day, or a week, or even
> a month, old. But suppose they
> were otherwise, what would it avail?

The question is not, Can they reason? nor
Can they **talk**? but, **Can they suffer?**[3]

In this passage Bentham points to the capacity
for suffering as the vital characteristic that gives a
being the *right* to equal consideration. The capacity
for suffering—or more strictly, for suffering and/or
enjoyment or happiness—is not just another characteristic like the capacity for language, or for
higher mathematics. Bentham is not saying that
those who try to mark the "insuperable line" that
determines whether the interests of a being should
be considered happen to have selected the wrong
characteristic. The capacity for suffering and enjoying things is a prerequisite for having interests at all,
a condition that must be satisfied before we can
speak of interests in any meaningful way. It would
be nonsense to say that it was not in the interests of
a stone to be kicked along the road by a schoolboy.
A stone does not have interests because it cannot
suffer. Nothing that we can do to it could possibly
make any difference to its welfare. A mouse, on the
other hand, does have an interest in not being tor-
mented, because it will suffer if it is.

If a being suffers, there can be no moral justification for refusing to take that suffering into consideration. No matter what the nature of the being,
the principle of equality requires that its suffering be
counted equally with the like suffering—in so far
as rough comparisons can be made—of any other
being. If a being is not capable of suffering, or of
experiencing enjoyment or happiness, there is
nothing to be taken into account. This is why the
limit of sentience (using the term as a convenient, if
not strictly accurate, shorthand for the capacity to
suffer or experience enjoyment or happiness) is the
only defensible boundary of concern for the interests of others. To mark this boundary by some characteristic like intelligence or rationality would be to
mark it in an arbitrary way. Why not choose some
other characteristic, like skin color?

The racist violates the principle of equality by
giving greater weight to the interests of members of
his own race, when there is a clash between their
interests and the interests of those of another race.
Similarly the speciesist allows the interests of his own
species to override the greater interests of members
of other species.[4] The pattern is the same in each
case. Most human beings are speciesists. I shall
now very briefly describe some of the practices
that show this.

For the great majority of human beings, especially in urban, industrialized societies, the most direct form of contact with members of other species
is at mealtimes: we eat them. In doing so we treat
them purely as means to our ends. We regard their
life and well-being as subordinate to our taste for a
particular kind of dish. I say "taste" deliberately—
this is purely a matter of pleasing our palate. There
can be no defence of eating flesh in terms of satisfying nutritional needs, since it has been established
beyond doubt that we could satisfy our need for
protein and other essential nutrients far more efficiently with a diet that replaced animal flesh by soy
beans, or products derived from soy beans, and
other high-protein vegetable products.[5]

It is not merely the act of killing that indicates
what we are ready to do to other species in order to
gratify our tastes. The suffering we inflict on the
animals while they are alive is perhaps an even
clearer indication of our speciesism than the fact
that we are prepared to kill them. In order to have
meat on the table at a price that people can afford,
our society tolerates methods of meat production
that confine sentient animals in cramped, unsuitable
conditions for the entire durations of their lives. Animals are treated like machines that convert fodder
into flesh, and any innovation that results in a higher
"conversion ratio" is liable to be adopted. As one
authority on the subject has said, "cruelty is ac-
knowledged only when profitability ceases."[6] ...

Since, as I have said, none of these practices
cater for anything more than our pleasures of taste,
our practice of rearing and killing other animals
in order to eat them is a clear instance of the sacrifice of the most important interests of other beings
in order to satisfy trivial interests of our own. To
avoid speciesism we must stop this practice, and
each of us has a moral obligation to cease supporting the practice. Our custom is all the support that
the meat-industry needs. The decision to cease giving it that support may be difficult, but it is no more

difficult than it would have been for a white South-
erner to go against the traditions of his society and
free his slaves: if we do not change our dietary habits, how can we censure those slaveholders who
would not change their own way of living?

The same form of discrimination may be observed in the widespread practice of experimenting
on other species in order to see if certain substances
are safe for human beings, or to test some psychological theory about the effect of severe punishment
on learning, or to try out various new compounds
just in case something turns up....

In the past, argument about vivisection has often missed this point, because it has been put in
absolutist terms: Would the abolitionist be prepared
to let thousands die if they could be saved by experimenting on a single animal? The way to reply
to this purely hypothetical question is to pose another: *Would the experimenter be prepared to perform his
experiment on an orphaned human infant, if that were the
only way to save many lives?* (I say "orphan" to avoid
the complication of parental feelings, although in
doing so I am being overfair to the experimenter,
since the nonhuman subjects of experiments are not
orphans.) If the experimenter is not prepared to use
an orphaned human infant, then his readiness to use
nonhumans is simple discrimination, since adult
apes, cats, mice and other mammals are more aware
of what is happening to them, more self-directing
and, so far as we can tell, at least as sensitive to pain,
as any human infant. There seems to be no relevant
characteristic that human infants possess that adult
mammals do not have to the same or a higher degree. (Someone might try to argue that what makes
it wrong to experiment on a human infant is that the
infant will, in time and if left alone, develop into
more than the nonhuman, but one would then, to
be consistent, have to oppose abortion, since the
fetus has the same potential as the infant—indeed,
even contraception and abstinence might be wrong
on this ground, since the egg and sperm, considered
jointly, also have the same potential. In any case,
this argument still gives us no reason for selecting a
nonhuman, rather than a human with severe and
irreversible brain damage, as the subject for our
experiments.)

The experimenter, then, shows a bias in favor
of his own species whenever he carries out an
experiment on a nonhuman for a purpose that he
would not think justified him in using a human
being at an equal or lower level of sentience,
awareness, ability to be self-directing, etc. No one
familiar with the kind of results yielded by most
experiments on animals can have the slightest doubt
that if this bias were eliminated the number of experiments performed would be a minute fraction of
the number performed today.

Experimenting on animals, and eating their
flesh, are perhaps the two major forms of speciesism
in our society. By comparison, the third and last
form of speciesism is so minor as to be insignificant,
but it is perhaps of some special interest to those for
whom this article was written. I am referring to
speciesism in contemporary philosophy.

Philosophy ought to question the basic assumptions of the age. Thinking through, critically
and carefully, what most people take for granted is,
I believe, the chief task of philosophy, and it is this
task that makes philosophy a worthwhile activity.
Regrettably, philosophy does not always live up to
its historic role. Philosophers are human beings and
they are subject to all the preconceptions of the
society to which they belong. Sometimes they succeed in breaking free of the prevailing ideology:
more often they become its most sophisticated defenders. So, in this case, philosophy as practiced in
the universities today does not challenge anyone's
preconceptions about our relations with other species. By their writings, those philosophers who
tackle problems that touch upon the issue reveal
that they make the same unquestioned assumptions
as most other humans, and what they say tends to
confirm the reader in his or her comfortable speciesist habits.

I could illustrate this claim by referring to the
writings of philosophers in various fields—for instance, the attempts that have been made by those
interested in rights to draw the boundary of the
sphere of rights so that it runs parallel to the biological boundaries of the species *homo sapiens,* including infants and even mental defectives, but
excluding those other beings of equal or greater

capacity who are so useful to us at mealtimes and in our laboratories. I think it would be a more appropriate conclusion to this article, however, if I concentrated on the problem with which we have been centrally concerned, the problem of equality.

It is significant that the problem of *equality*, in moral and political philosophy, is invariably formulated in terms of human equality. The effect of this is that the question of the equality of other animals does not confront the philosopher, or student, as an issue itself—and this is already an indication of the failure of philosophy to challenge accepted beliefs. Still, philosophers have found it difficult to discuss the issue of human equality without raising, in a paragraph or two, the question of the status of other animals. The reason for this, which should be apparent from what I have said already, is that if humans are to be regarded as equal to one another, we need some sense of "equal" that does not require any actual, descriptive equality of capacities, talents or other qualities. If equality is to be related to any actual characteristics of humans, these characteristics must be some lowest common denominator, pitched so low that no human lacks them—but then the philosopher comes up against the catch that any such set of characteristics which covers *all* humans will not be possessed *only by humans*. In other words, it turns out that in the only sense in which we can truly say, as an assertion of fact, that all humans are equal, at least some members of other species are also equal—equal, that is, to each other and to humans. If, on the other hand, we regard the statement "All humans are equal" in some non-factual way, perhaps as a prescription, then, as I have already argued, it is even more difficult to exclude nonhumans from the sphere of equality.

This result is not what the egalitarian philosopher originally intended to assert. Instead of accepting the radical outcome to which their own reasonings naturally point, however, most philosophers try to reconcile their beliefs in human equality and animal inequality by arguments that can only be described as devious.

As a first example, I take William Frankena's well-known article "The Concept of Social Justice." Frankena opposes the idea of basing justice on merit, because he sees that this could lead to highly inegalitarian results. Instead he proposes the principle that

> ... all men are to be treated as equals, not because they are equal, in any respect, but *simply because they are human*. They are human because they have **emotions** and **desires**, and are able to **think**, and hence are capable of enjoying a good life in a sense in which other animals are not.[7]

But what is this capacity to enjoy the good life which all humans have, but no other animals? Other animals have emotions and desires, and appear to be capable of enjoying a good life. We may doubt that they can think—although the behavior of some apes, dolphins and even dogs suggests that some of them can—*but what is the relevance of thinking?* Frankena goes on to admit that by "the good life" he means "not so much the morally good life as the happy or satisfactory life," so thought would appear to be unnecessary for enjoying the good life; in fact to emphasize the need for thought would make difficulties for the egalitarian since only some people are capable of leading intellectually satisfying lives, or morally good lives. This makes it difficult to see what Frankena's principle of equality has to do with simply being *human*. Surely every sentient being is capable of leading a life that is happier or less miserable than some alternative life, and hence has a claim to be taken into account. In this respect the distinction between humans and nonhumans is not a sharp division, but rather a continuum along which we move gradually, and with overlaps between the species, from simple capacities for enjoyment and satisfaction, or pain and suffering, to more complex ones.

Faced with a situation in which they see a need for some basis for the moral gulf that is commonly thought to separate humans and animals, but finding no concrete difference that will do the job without undermining the equality of humans, philosophers tend to waffle. They resort to high-sounding phrases like "the intrinsic dignity of the human individual";[8] they talk of the "intrinsic worth of all men" as if men (humans?) had some worth that other beings did not,[9] or they say that humans, and only humans, are "ends in themselves," while "everything other than a person can only have value for a person."[10]

This idea of a distinctive human dignity and worth has a long history; it can be traced back directly to the Renaissance humanists, for instance to Pico della Mirandola's *Oration on the Dignity of Man*. Pico and other humanists based their estimate of human dignity on the idea that man possessed the central, pivotal position in the "Great Chain of Being" that led from the lowliest forms of matter to God himself; this view of the universe, in turn, goes back to both classical and Judeo-Christian doctrines. Contemporary philosophers have cast off these metaphysical and religious shackles and freely invoke the dignity of mankind without needing to justify the idea at all. Why should we not attribute "intrinsic dignity" or "intrinsic worth" to ourselves? Fellow-humans are unlikely to reject the accolades we so generously bestow on them, and those to whom we deny the honor are unable to object. Indeed, when one thinks only of humans, it can be very liberal, very progressive, to talk of the dignity of all human beings. In so doing, we implicitly condemn slavery, racism, and other violations of human rights. We admit that we ourselves are in some fundamental sense on a par with the poorest, most ignorant members of our own species. It is only when we think of humans as no more than a small subgroup of all the beings that inhabit our planet that we may realize that in elevating our own species we are at the same time lowering the relative status of all other species.

The truth is that the appeal to the intrinsic dignity of human beings appears to solve the egalitarian's problems only as long as it goes unchallenged. Once we ask *why* it should be that all humans—including infants, mental defectives, psychopaths, Hitler, Stalin and the rest—have some kind of dignity or worth that no elephant, pig, or chimpanzee can ever achieve, we see that this question is as difficult to answer as our original request for some relevant fact that justifies the inequality of humans and other animals. In fact, these two questions are really one: talk of intrinsic dignity or moral worth only takes the problem back one step, because any satisfactory defence of the claim that all and only humans have intrinsic

dignity would need to refer to some relevant capacities or characteristics that all and only humans possess. Philosophers frequently introduce ideas of dignity, respect and worth at the point at which other reasons appear to be lacking, but this is hardly good enough. Fine phrases are the last resource of those who have run out of arguments.

In case there are those who still think it may be possible to find some relevant characteristic that distinguishes all humans from all members of other species, I shall refer again, before I conclude, to the existence of some humans who quite clearly are below the level of awareness, self-consciousness, intelligence, and sentience, of many nonhumans. I am thinking of humans with severe and irreparable brain damage, and also of infant humans. To avoid the complication of the relevance of a being's potential, however, I shall henceforth concentrate on permanently retarded humans.

Philosophers who set out to find a characteristic that will distinguish humans from other animals rarely take the course of abandoning these groups of humans by lumping them in with the other animals. It is easy to see why they do not. To take this line without re-thinking our attitudes to other animals would entail that we have the right to perform painful experiments on retarded humans for trivial reasons; similarly it would follow that we had the right to rear and kill these humans for food. To most philosophers these consequences are as unacceptable as the view that we should stop treating nonhumans in this way.

Of course, when discussing the problem of equality it is possible to ignore the problem of mental defectives, or brush it aside as if somehow insignificant.[11] This is the easiest way out. What else remains? My final example of speciesism in contemporary philosophy has been selected to show what happens when a writer is prepared to face the question of human equality and animal equality without ignoring the existence of mental defectives, and without resorting to obscurantist mumbo-jumbo. Stanley Benn's clear and honest article "Egalitarianism and Equal Consideration of Interests"[12] fits this description.

Benn, after noting the usual "evident human inequalities" argues, correctly I think, for equality of consideration as the only possible basis for egalitarianism. Yet Benn, like other writers, is thinking only of "equal consideration of human interests." Benn is quite open in his defence of this restriction of equal consideration:

> ... not to possess human shape *is* a disqualifying condition. However faithful or intelligent a dog may be, it would be a monstrous sentimentality to attribute to him interests that could be weighed in an equal balance with those of human beings ... if, for instance, one had to decide between feeding a hungry baby or a hungry dog, anyone who chose the dog would generally be reckoned morally defective, unable to recognize a fundamental inequality of claims.
>
> This is what distinguishes our attitude to animals from our attitude to imbeciles. It would be odd to say that we ought to respect equally the dignity or personality of the imbecile and of the rational man ... but there is nothing odd about saying that we should respect their interests equally, that is, that we should give to the interests of each the same serious consideration as claims to considerations necessary for some standard of well-being that we can recognize and endorse.

Benn's statement of the basis of the consideration we should have for imbeciles seems to me correct, but why should there be any fundamental inequality of claims between a dog and a human imbecile? Benn sees that if equal consideration depended on rationality, no reason could be given against using imbeciles for research purposes, as we now use dogs and guinea pigs. This will not do: "But of course we do distinguish imbeciles from animals in this regard," he says. That the common distinction is justifiable is something Benn does not question; his problem is how it is to be justified. The answer he gives is this:

> ... we respect the interests of men and give them priority over dogs not *insofar* as they

are rational, but because rationality is the human norm. We say it is **unfair** to exploit the deficiencies of the imbecile who falls short of the norm, just as it would be unfair, and not just ordinarily dishonest, to steal from a blind man. If we do not think in this way about dogs, it is because we do not see the irrationality of the dog as a deficiency or a handicap, but as normal for the species. The characteristics, therefore, that distinguish the normal man from the normal dog make it intelligible for us to talk of other men having interests and capacities, and therefore claims, of precisely the same kind as we make on our own behalf. But although these characteristics may provide the point of the distinction between men and other species, they are **not** in fact the qualifying conditions for membership, or the distinguishing criteria of the class of morally considerable persons; **and this is precisely because a man does not become a member of a different species, with its own standards of normality, by reason of not possessing these characteristics**.

The final sentence of this passage gives the argument away. An imbecile, Benn concedes, may have no characteristics superior to those of a dog; nevertheless this does not make the imbecile a member of "a different species" as the dog is. *Therefore* it would be "unfair" to use the imbecile for medical research as we use the dog. But why? That the imbecile is not rational is just the way things have worked out, and the same is true of the dog—neither is any more responsible for their mental level. If it is unfair to take advantage of an isolated defect, why is it fair to take advantage of a more general limitation? I find it hard to see anything in this argument except a defence of preferring the interests of members of our own species because they are members of our own species. To those who think there might be more to it, I suggest the following mental exercise. Assume that it has been proven that there is a difference in the average, or normal, intelligence quotient for two different races, say whites and blacks. Then substitute the term "white" for every occurrence of "men" and "black" for every occurrence of "dog" in the passage quoted; and substitute "high I.Q." for "rationality" and when Benn talks of "imbeciles" replace this term by "dumb whites"—that is, whites who fall well below the normal white I.Q. score. Finally, change "species" to "race." Now re-read the passage. It has become a defence of a rigid, no-exceptions division between whites and blacks, based on I.Q. scores, *not withstanding an admitted overlap* between whites and blacks in this

respect. The revised passage is, of course, outrageous, and this is not only because we have made fictitious assumptions in our substitutions. The point is that in the original passage Benn was defending a rigid division in the amount of consideration due to members of different species, despite admitted cases of overlap. If the original did not, at first reading strike us as being as outrageous as the revised version does, this is largely because although we are not racists ourselves, most of us are speciesists. Like the other articles, Benn's stands as a warning of the ease with which the best minds can fall victim to a prevailing ideology.

NOTES

1. *The Methods of Ethics* (7th Ed.), p. 382.

2. For example, R. M. Hare, *Freedom and Reason* (Oxford, 1963); and J. Rawls, *A Theory of Justice* (Harvard, 1972). For a brief account of the essential agreement on this issue between these and other positions, see R. M. Hare, "Rules of War and Moral Reasoning," *Philosophy and Public Affairs,* vol. 1, no. 2 (1972).

3. *Introduction to the Principles of Morals and Legislation,* ch. XVII.

4. I owe the term "speciesism" to Richard Ryder.

5. In order to produce 1 lb. of protein in the form of beef or veal, we must feed 21 lbs. of protein to the animal. Other forms of livestock are slightly less inefficient, but the average ratio in the U.S. is still 1:8. It has been estimated that the amount of protein lost to humans in this way is equivalent to 90% of the annual world protein deficit. For a brief account, see Frances Moore Lappé, *Diet for a Small Planet* (Friends of The Earth/Ballantine, New York, 1971), pp. 4–11.

6. Ruth Harrison, *Animal Machines* (Stuart, London, 1964). For an account of farming conditions, see my *Animal Liberation* (New York Review Company, 1975).

7. In R. Brandt (ed.), *Social Justice* (Prentice-Hall, Englewood Cliffs, 1962), p. 19.

8. Frankena, *Op. cit.,* p. 23.

9. H. A. Bedau, "Egalitarianism and the Idea of Equality" in *Nomos IX: Equality,* ed. J. R. Pennock and J. W. Chapman (Atherton Press, New York, 1967).

10. G. Vlastos, "Justice and Equality" in Brandt, *Social Justice,* p. 48.

11. For example, Bernard Williams, "The Idea of Equality," in *Philosophy, Politics and Society* (second series), ed. P. Laslett and W. Runciman (Blackwell, Oxford, 1962), p. 118; J. Rawls, *A Theory of Justice,* pp. 509–10.

12. *Nomos IX: Equality;* the passages quoted are on p. 62ff.

STUDY QUESTIONS

1. According to Singer, what is the relationship between civil rights movements and the animal rights movement?

2. What is *speciesism*? Why is it bad, according to Singer? Do you agree?

3. Are all humans equal, according to Singer? In what way are all sentient beings equal?

4. How does Singer apply the notion of equal consideration of interests?

4

The Radical Egalitarian Case for Animal Rights

TOM REGAN

Professor of philosophy at North Carolina State University and a leading animal rights advocate in the United States, Tom Regan is the author of several articles and books on moral philosophy, including The Case for Animal Rights *(1983).*

Regan disagrees with Singer's utilitarian program for animal liberation, for he rejects utilitarianism as lacking a notion of intrinsic worth. Regan's position is that animals and humans all have equal intrinsic value on which their right to life and concern are based. Regan is revolutionary. He calls for not reform but the total abolition of the use of animals in science, the total dissolution of the commercial animal agriculture system, and the total elimination of commercial and sport hunting and trapping. "The fundamental wrong is the system that allows us to view animals as our resources…. Lab animals are not our tasters; we are not their kings."

I regard myself as an advocate of animal rights—as a part of the animal rights movement. That movement, as I conceive it, is committed to a number of goals, including:

1. the total abolition of the use of animals in science
2. the total dissolution of commercial animal agriculture
3. and the total elimination of commercial and sport hunting and trapping.

There are, I know, people who profess to believe in animal rights who do not avow these goals. Factory farming they say, is wrong—violates animals' rights—but traditional animal agriculture is all right. Toxicity tests of cosmetics on animals violate their rights; but not important medical research—cancer research, for example. The clubbing of baby seals is abhorrent; but not the harvesting of adult seals. I used to think I understood this reasoning. Not any more. You don't change unjust institutions by tidying them up.

What's wrong—what's fundamentally wrong—with the way animals are treated isn't the details that vary from case to case. It's the whole system. The forlornness of the veal calf is pathetic—heart wrenching; the pulsing pain of the chimp with electrodes planted deep in her brain is repulsive; the slow, torturous death of the raccoon caught in the leg hold trap, agonizing. But what is fundamentally wrong isn't the pain, isn't the suffering, isn't the deprivation. These compound what's wrong. Sometimes—often—they make it much worse. But they are not the fundamental wrong.

The fundamental wrong is the system that allows us to view animals as our resources, here for us—to be eaten, or surgically manipulated, or put in our cross hairs for sport or money. Once we accept this view of animals—as our resources—the rest is as predictable as it is regrettable. Why worry about their

From *In Defense of Animals*, ed. Peter Singer (Oxford: Basil Blackwell, 1985). Reprinted by permission of Blackwell Publishers.

loneliness, their pain, their death? Since animals exist for us, here to benefit us in one way or another, what harms them really doesn't matter—or matters only if it starts to bother us, makes us feel a trifle uneasy when we eat our veal scampi, for example. So, yes, let us get veal calves out of solitary confinement, give them more space, a little straw, a few companions. But let us keep our veal scampi.

But a little straw, more space, and a few companions don't eliminate—don't even touch—the fundamental wrong, the wrong that attaches to our viewing and treating these animals as our resources. A veal calf killed to be eaten after living in close confinement is viewed and treated in this way: but so, too, is another who is raised (as they say) "more humanely." To right the fundamental wrong of our treatment of farm animals requires more than making rearing methods "more human"—requires something quite different—requires the *total dissolution of commercial animal agriculture.*

How we do this—whether we do this, or as in the case of animals in science, whether and how we abolish their use—these are to a large extent political questions. People must change their beliefs before they change their habits. Enough people, especially those elected to public office, must believe in change—must want it—before we will have laws that protect the rights of animals. This process of change is very complicated, very demanding, very exhausting, calling for the efforts of many hands—in education, publicity, political organization and activity, down to the licking of envelopes and stamps. As a trained and practicing philosopher the sort of contribution I can make is limited, but I like to think, important. The currency of philosophy is ideas—their meaning and rational foundation—not the nuts and bolts of the legislative process say, or the mechanics of community organization. That's what I have been exploring over the past ten years or so in my essays and talks and, more recently, in my book, *The Case for Animal Rights.*[1] I believe the major conclusions I reach in that book are true because they are supported by the weight of the *best arguments.* I believe the idea of animal rights has reason, not just emotion, on its side.

In the space I have at my disposal here I can only sketch, in the barest outlines, some of the main features of the book. Its main themes—and we should not be surprised by this—involve asking and answering deep foundational moral questions, questions about what morality is, how it should be understood, what is the best moral theory all considered. I hope I can convey something of the shape I think this theory is. The attempt to do this will be—to use a word a friendly critic once used to describe my work—cerebral. In fact I was told by this person that my work is "too cerebral." But this is misleading. My feelings about how animals sometimes are treated are just as deep and just as strong as those of my more volatile compatriots. Philosophers do—to use the jargon of the day—have a right side to their brains. If it's the left side we contribute or mainly should—that's because what talents we have reside there.

How to proceed? We begin by asking how the moral status of animals has been understood by thinkers who deny that animals have rights. Then we test the mettle of their ideas by seeing how well they stand up under the heat of fair criticism. If we start our thinking in this way we soon find that some people believe that we have no duties directly to animals—that we owe nothing *to them*—that we can do nothing that *wrongs them.* Rather, we can do wrong acts that involve animals, and so we have duties *regarding* them, though none *to* them. Such views may be called indirect duty views. By way of illustration:

Suppose your neighbor kicks your dog. Then your neighbor has done something wrong. But not to your dog. The wrong that has been done is a wrong to you. After all, it is wrong to upset people, and your neighbor's kicking your dog upsets you. So you are the one who is wronged, not your dog. Or again: by kicking your dog your neighbor damages your property. And since it is wrong to damage another person's property, your neighbor has done something wrong—to you, of course, not to your dog. Your neighbor no more wrongs your dog than your car would be wronged if the windshield were smashed. Your neighbor's duties involving your dog are indirect duties to you. More generally, all of our duties regarding animals are indirect duties to one another—to humanity.

How could someone try to justify such a view? One could say that your dog doesn't feel anything and so isn't hurt by your neighbor's kick, doesn't care about the pain since none is felt, is as unaware of anything as your windshield. Someone could say this but no rational person will since, among other considerations, such a view will commit one who holds it to the position that no human being feels pain either—that human beings also don't care about what happens to them. A second possibility is that though both humans and your dog are hurt when kicked, it is only human pain that matters. But, again, no rational person can believe this. Pain is pain wheresoever it occurs. If your neighbor's causing you pain is wrong because of the pain that is caused, we cannot rationally ignore or dismiss the moral relevance of the pain your dog feels.

Philosophers who hold indirect duty views— and many still do—have come to understand that they must avoid the two defects just noted—avoid, that is, both the view that animals don't feel anything as well as the idea that only human pain can be morally relevant. Among such thinkers the sort of view now favored is one or another form of what is called *contractarianism*.

Here, very crudely, is the root idea: morality consists of a set of rules that individuals voluntarily agree to abide by—as we do when we sign a contract (hence the name: contractarianism). Those who understand and accept the terms of the contract are covered directly—have rights created by, and recognized and protected in, the contract. And these contractors can also have protection spelled out for others who, though they lack the ability to understand morality and so cannot sign the contract themselves, are loved or cherished by those who can. Thus young children, for example, are unable to sign and lack rights. But they are protected by the contract nonetheless because of the sentimental interests of others, most notably their parents. So we have, then, duties involving these children, duties regarding them, but no duties to them. Our duties in their case are indirect duties to other human beings, usually their parents.

As for animals, since they cannot understand the contract, they obviously cannot sign; and since they cannot sign; they have no rights. Like children, however, some animals are the objects of the sentimental interest of others. You, for example, love your dog … or cat. So these animals—those enough people care about: companion animals, whales, baby seals, the American bald eagle—these animals, though they lack rights themselves, will be protected because of the sentimental interests of people. I have, then, according to contractarianism, no duty directly to your dog or any other animal, not even the duty not to cause them pain or suffering; my duty not to hurt them is a duty I have to those people who care about what happens to them. As for other animals, where no or little sentimental interest is present—farm animals, for example, or laboratory rats—what duties we have grow weaker and weaker, perhaps to the vanishing point. The pain and death they endure, though real, are not wrong if no one cares about them.

Contractarianism could be a hard view to refute when it comes to the moral status of animals if it was an adequate theoretical approach to the moral status of human beings. It is not adequate in this latter respect, however, which makes the question of its adequacy in the former—regarding animals— utterly moot. For consider: morality, according to the (crude) contractarian position before us, consists of rules people agree to abide by. What people? Well, enough to make a difference—enough, that is, so that collectively they have the power to enforce the rules that are drawn up in the contract. That is very well and good for the signatories—but not so good for anyone who is not asked to sign. And there is nothing in contractarianism of the sort we are discussing that guarantees or requires that everyone will have a chance to participate equitably in framing the rules of morality. The result is that this approach to ethics could sanction the most blatant forms of social, economic, moral, and political injustice, ranging from a repressive caste system to systematic racial or sexual discrimination. Might, on this theory, does make right. Let those who are the victims of injustice suffer as they will. It matters not so long as no one else—no contractor, or too few of them—cares about it. Such a theory takes one's moral breath away ... as if, for example, there is nothing wrong with apartheid in South Africa if too few white South Africans are upset by it. A theory with so little to recommend it at the level of the ethics of our treatment of our fellow humans cannot have anything more to recommend it when it comes to the ethics of how we treat our fellow animals.

The version of contractarianism just examined is, as I have noted, a crude variety, and in fairness to those of a contractarian persuasion it must be noted that much more refined, subtle, and ingenious varieties are possible. For example, John Rawls, in his *A Theory of Justice*, sets forth a version of contractarianism that forces the contractors to ignore the accidental features of being a human being—for example, whether one is white or black, male or female, a genius or of modest intellect. Only by ignoring such features, Rawls believes, can we insure that the principles of justice contractors would agree upon are not based on bias or prejudice. Despite the improvement a view such as Rawls's shows over the cruder forms of contractarianism, it remains deficient: it systematically denies that we have direct duties to those human beings who do not have a sense of justice—young children, for instance, and many mentally retarded humans. And yet it seems reasonably certain that, were we to torture a young child or a retarded elder, we would be doing something that wrongs them, not something that is wrong if (and only if) other humans with a sense of justice are upset. And since this is true in the case of these humans, we cannot rationally deny the same in the case of animals.

Indirect duty views, then, including the best among them, fail to command our rational assent. Whatever ethical theory we rationally should accept, therefore, it must at least recognize that we have some duties directly to animals, just as we have some duties directly to each other. The next two theories I'll sketch attempt to meet this requirement.

The first I call the *cruelty-kindness* view. Simply stated, this view says that we have a direct duty to be kind to animals and a direct duty not to be cruel to them. Despite the familiar, reassuring ring of these ideas, I do not believe this view offers an adequate theory. To make this clearer, consider kindness. A kind person acts from a certain kind of motive—compassion or concern, for example. And that is a virtue. But there is no guarantee that a kind act is a right act. If I am a generous racist, for example, I will be inclined to act kindly toward members of my own race, favoring their interests above others. My kindness would be real and, so far as it goes, good. But I trust it is too obvious to require comment that my kind acts may not be above moral reproach—may, in fact, be positively wrong because rooted in injustice. So kindness, not withstanding its status as a virtue to be encouraged, simply will not cancel the weight of a theory of right action.

Cruelty fares no better. People or their acts are cruel if they display either a lack of sympathy for or, worse, the presence of enjoyment in, seeing another suffer. Cruelty in all its guises *is* a bad thing—is a tragic human failing. But just as a person's being motivated by kindness does not guarantee that they do what is right, so the absence of cruelty does not assure that they avoid doing what is wrong. Many people who perform abortions, for example, are not cruel, sadistic people. But that fact about their character and motivation does not settle the terribly difficult question about the morality of abortion. The case is no different when we examine the ethics of our treatment of animals. So, yes, let us be for kindness and against cruelty. But let us not suppose that being for the one and against the other answers questions about moral right and wrong.

Some people think the theory we are looking for is *utilitarianism*. A utilitarian accepts two moral principles. The first is a principle of *equality: everyone's interests count, and similar interests must be counted as having similar weight or importance*. White or black, male or female, American or Iranian, human or animal: everyone's pain or frustration matter and matter equally with the like pain or frustration of anyone else. The second principle a utilitarian accepts is the principle of *utility: do that act that will bring about the best balance of satisfaction over frustration for everyone affected by the outcome.*

As a utilitarian, then, here is how I am to approach the task of deciding what I morally ought to do: I must ask who will be affected if I choose to do one thing rather than another, how much each individual will be affected, and where the best results are most likely to lie—which option, in other words, is most likely to bring about the best results, the best balance of satisfaction over frustration. That option, whatever it may be, is the one I ought to choose. That is where my moral duty lies.

The great appeal of utilitarianism rests with its uncompromising *egalitarianism:* everyone's interests count and count equally with the like interests of everyone else. The kind of odious discrimination some forms of contractarianism can justify—discrimination based on race or sex, for example—seems disallowed in principle by utilitarianism, as is speciesism—systematic discrimination based on species membership.

The sort of equality we find in utilitarianism, however, is not the sort an advocate of animal or human rights should have in mind. Utilitarianism has no room for the *equal moral rights of different individuals because it has no room for their equal inherent value or worth.* What has value for the utilitarian is the satisfaction of an individual's interests, not the individual whose interests they are. A universe in which you satisfy your desire for water, food, and warmth, is, other things being equal, better than a universe in which these desires are frustrated. And the same is true in the case of an animal with similar desires. But neither you nor the animal have any value in your own right. *Only your feelings do.*

Here is an analogy to help make the philosophical point clearer: a cup contains different liquids—sometimes sweet, sometimes bitter, sometimes a mix of the two. What has value are the liquids: the sweeter the better, the bitter the worse. The cup—the container—has no value. It's what goes into it, not what they go into, that has value. For the utilitarian, you and I are like the cup; we have no value as individuals and thus no equal value. What has value is what goes into us, what we serve as receptacles for; our feelings of satisfaction have positive value, our feelings of frustration have negative value.

Serious problems arise for utilitarianism when we remind ourselves that it enjoins us to bring about the best consequences. What does this mean? It doesn't mean the best consequences for me alone, or for my family or friends, or any other person taken individually. No, what we must do is, roughly, as follows: we must add up—somehow!—the separate satisfactions and frustrations of everyone likely to be affected by our choice, the satisfactions in one column, the frustrations in the other. We must total each column for each of the opinions before us. That is what it means to say the theory is aggregative. And then we must choose that option which is most likely to bring about the best balance of totaled satisfactions over totaled frustrations. Whatever act would lead to this outcome is the one we morally ought to perform—is where our moral duty lies. And that act quite clearly might not be the same one that would bring about the best results for me personally, or my family or friends, or a lab animal. The best aggregated consequences for everyone concerned are not necessarily the best for each individual.

That utilitarianism is an aggregative theory—that different individuals' satisfactions or frustrations are added, or summed, or totaled—is the key objection to this theory. My Aunt Bea is old, inactive, a cranky, sour person, though not physically ill. She prefers to go on living. She is also rather rich. I could make a fortune if I could get my hands on her money, money she intends to give me in any event, after she dies, but which she refuses to give me now. In order to avoid a huge tax bite, I plan to donate a handsome sum of my profits to a local children's hospital. Many, many children will benefit from my generosity, and much joy will be brought to their parents, relatives, and friends. If I don't get the money rather soon, all these ambitions will come to naught. The once-in-a-lifetime-opportunity to make a real killing will be gone. Why, then, not really kill my Aunt Bea? Oh, of course I *might* get caught. But I'm no fool and, besides, her doctor can be counted on to cooperate (he has an eye for the same investment and I happen to know a good deal about his shady past). The deed can be done ... professionally, shall we say. There is *very* little chance of getting caught. And as for my conscience being guilt ridden, I am a resourceful sort of fellow and will take more than sufficient comfort—as I lie on the beach at Acapulco—in contemplating the joy and health I have brought to so many others.

Suppose Aunt Bea is killed and the rest of the story comes out as told. Would I have done anything wrong? Anything immoral? One would have thought that I had. But not according to utilitarianism. Since what I did brought about the best balance of totaled satisfaction over frustration for all those affected by the outcome, what I did was not wrong. Indeed, in killing Aunt Bea the physician and I did what duty required.

This same kind of argument can be repeated in all sorts of cases, illustrating time after time, how the utilitarian's position leads to results that impartial people find morally callous. It is wrong to kill my Aunt Bea in the name of bringing about the best results for others. A good end does not justify an evil means. Any adequate moral theory will have to explain why this is so. Utilitarianism fails in this respect and so cannot be the theory we seek.

What to do? Where to begin anew? The place to begin, I think, is with the utilitarian's view of the value of the individual—or, rather, lack of value. In its place suppose we consider that you and I, for example, do have value as individuals—what we'll call *inherent value*. To say we have such value is to say that we are something more than, something different from, mere receptacles. Moreover, to insure that we do not pave the way for such injustices as slavery or sexual discrimination, we must believe that all who have inherent value have it equally, regardless of their sex, race, religion, birthplace, and so on. Similarly to be discarded as irrelevant are one's talents or skills, intelligence and wealth, personality or pathology, whether one is loved and admired—or despised and loathed. The genius and the retarded child, the prince and the pauper, the brain surgeon and the fruit vendor, Mother Theresa and the most unscrupulous used car salesman—all have inherent value, all possess it *equally*, and *all have an equal right to be treated with respect*, to be treated in ways that do not reduce them to the status of

things, as if they exist as resources for others. My value as an individual is independent of my usefulness to you. Yours is not dependent on your usefulness to me. For either of us to treat the other in ways that fail to show respect for the other's independent value is to act immorally—is to violate the individual's rights.

Some of the rational virtues of this view—what I call the rights view—should be evident. Unlike (crude) contractarianism, for example, the rights view *in principle* denies the moral tolerability of any and all forms of racial, sexual, or social discrimination; and unlike utilitarianism, this view *in principle* denies that we can justify good results by using evil means that violate an individual's rights—denies, for example, that it could be moral to kill my Aunt Bea to harvest beneficial consequences for others. That would be to sanction the disrespectful treatment of the individual in the name of the social good, something the rights view will not—categorically will not—ever allow.

The rights view—or so I believe—is rationally the most satisfactory moral theory. It surpasses all other theories in the degree to which it illuminates and explains the foundation of our duties to one another—the domain of human morality. On this score, it has the best reasons, the best arguments, on its side. Of course, if it were possible to show that only human beings are included within its scope, then a person like myself, who believes in animal rights, would be obliged to look elsewhere than to the rights view.

But attempts to limit its scope to humans only can be shown to be rationally defective. Animals, it is true, lack many of the abilities humans possess. They can't read, do higher mathematics, build a bookcase, or make *baba ghanoush*. Neither can many human beings, however, and yet we don't say—and shouldn't say—that they (these humans) therefore have less inherent value, less of a right to be treated with respect, than do others. It is the similarities between those human beings who most clearly, most noncontroversially have such value—the people reading this, for example—it is our similarities, not our differences, that matter most. And the really crucial, the basic similarity is simply this; *we are each of us the experiencing subject of a life, each of us a conscious creature having an individual welfare that has importance to us whatever our usefulness to others.* We want and prefer things; believe and feel things; recall and expect things. And all these dimensions of our life, including our pleasure and pain, our enjoyment and suffering, our satisfaction and frustration, our continued existence or our untimely death—all make a difference to the quality of our life as lived, as experienced by us as individuals. As the same is true of those animals who concern us (those who are eaten and trapped, for example), they, too, must be viewed as the experiencing subjects of a life with inherent value of their own.

There are some who resist the idea that animals have inherent value. "Only humans have such value," they profess. How might this narrow view be defended? Shall we say that only humans have the requisite intelligence, or autonomy, or reason? But there are many, many humans who will fail to meet these standards and yet who are reasonably viewed as having value above and beyond their usefulness to others. Shall we claim that only humans belong to the right species—the species *Homo sapiens*? But this is blatant speciesism. Will it be said, then, that all—and only—humans have immortal souls? Then our opponents more than have their work cut out for them. I am myself not ill-disposed to there being immortal souls. Personally, I profoundly hope I have one. But I would not want to rest my position on a controversial, ethical issue on the even more controversial question about who or what has an immortal soul. That is to dig one's hole deeper, not climb out. Rationally, it is better to resolve moral issues without making more controversial assumptions than are needed. The question of who has inherent value is such a question, one that is more rationally resolved without the introduction of the idea of immortal souls than by its use.

Well, perhaps some will say that animals have some inherent value, only *less* than we do. Once again, however, attempts to defend this view can be shown to lack rational justification. What could be the basis of our having more inherent value than animals? Will it be their lack of reason, or autonomy, or intellect? Only if we are willing to make

the same judgment in the case of humans who are similarly deficient. But it is not true that such humans—the retarded child, for example, or the mentally deranged—have less inherent value than you or I. Neither, then, can we rationally sustain the view that animals like them in being the experiencing subjects of a life have less inherent value. *All who have inherent value have it equally, whether they be human animals or not.*

Inherent value, then, belongs equally to those who are the experiencing subjects of a life. Whether it belongs to others—to rocks and rivers, trees and glaciers, for example—we do not know. And may never know. But neither do we need to know, if we are to make the case for animal rights. We do not need to know how many people, for example, are eligible to vote in the next presidential election before we can know whether I am. Similarly, we do not need to know *how many* individuals have inherent value before we can know that some do. When it comes to the case for animal rights, then what we need to know is whether the animals who, in our culture are routinely eaten, hunted, and used in our laboratories, for example, are like us in being subjects of a life. And we *do* know this. We do *know* that many—literally, billions and billions—of these animals are subjects of a life in the sense explained and so have inherent value if we do. And since, in order to have the best theory of our duties to one another, we must recognize our equal inherent value, as individuals, *reason*—not sentiment, not emotion—*reason compels us to recognize the equal inherent value of these animals.* And, with this, their equal right to be treated with respect.

That, *very* roughly, is the shape and feel of the case for animal rights. Most of the details of the supporting argument are missing. They are to be found in the book I alluded to earlier. Here, the details go begging and I must in closing, limit myself to four final points.

The first is how the theory that underlies the case for animal rights shows that the animal rights movement is a part of, not antagonistic to, the human rights movement. The theory that rationally grounds the rights of animals also grounds the rights of humans. Thus are those involved in the animal rights movement partners in the struggle to secure respect for human rights—the rights of women, for example, or minorities and workers. The animal rights movement is cut from the same moral cloth as these.

Second, having set out the broad outlines of the rights view, I can now say why its *implications for farming and science*, for example, are both clear and uncompromising. In the case of using animals in science, the rights view is categorically abolitionist. *Lab animals are not our tasters; we are not their kings.* Because these animals are treated—routinely, systematically— as if their value is reducible to their usefulness to others, they are routinely systematically treated with a lack of respect, and thus their rights routinely, systematically violated. This is just as true when they are used in trivial, duplicative, unnecessary or unwise research as it is when they are used in studies that hold out real promise of human benefits. We can't justify harming or killing a human being (my Aunt Bea, for example) just for these sorts of reasons. Neither can we do so even in the case of so lowly a creature as a laboratory rat. It is not just refinement or reduction that are called for, not just larger, cleaner cages, not just more generous use of anesthetic or the elimination of multiple surgery, not just tidying up the system. It is replacement— completely. The best we can do when it comes to using animals in science is—not to use them. That is where our duty lies, according to the rights view.

As for commercial animal agriculture, the rights view takes a similar abolitionist position. The fundamental moral wrong here is not that animals are kept in stressful close confinement, or in isolation, or that they have their pain and suffering, their needs and preferences ignored or discounted. *All* these *are* wrong, of course, but they are not the fundamental wrong. They are symptoms and effects of the deeper, systematic wrong that allows these animals to be viewed and treated as lacking independent value, as resources for us—as, indeed, a renewable resource. Giving farm animals more space, more natural environments, more companions does not right the fundamental wrong, any more than giving lab animals more anesthesia or bigger, cleaner cages would right the fundamental wrong in their case. Nothing less than the total dissolution of commercial animal agriculture will do this, just as, for

similar reasons I won't develop at length here, morality requires nothing less than the total elimination of commercial and sport hunting and trapping. The rights view's implications, then, as I have said, are clear—and are uncompromising.

My last two points are about philosophy—my profession. It is most obviously, no substitute for political action. The words I have written here and in other places by themselves don't change a thing. It is what we do with the thoughts the words express—our acts, our deeds—that change things. All that philosophy can do, and all I have attempted, is to offer a vision of what our deeds could aim at. And the why. But not the how.

Finally, I am reminded of my thoughtful critic, the one I mentioned earlier, who chastised me for being "too cerebral." Well, cerebral I have been: indirect duty views, utilitarianism, contractarianism—hardly the stuff deep passions are made of. I am also reminded, however, of the image another friend once set before me—the image of the ballerina as expressive of disciplined passion. Long hours of sweat and toil, of loneliness and practice, of doubt and fatigue; that is the discipline of her craft. But the passion is there, too: the fierce drive to excel, to speak through her body, to do it right, to pierce our minds. That is the image of philosophy I would leave with you; not "too cerebral," but *disciplined passion*. Of the discipline, enough has been seen. As for the passion:

There are times, and these are not infrequent, when tears come to my eyes when I see, or read, or hear of the wretched plight of animals in the hands of humans. Their pain, their suffering, their loneliness, their innocence, their death. Anger. Rage. Pity. Sorrow. Disgust. The whole creation groans under the weight of the evil we humans visit upon these mute, powerless creatures. It *is* our heart, not just our head, that calls for an end, that demands of us that we overcome, for them, the habits and forces behind their systematic oppression. All great movements, it is written, go through three stages: ridicule, discussion, adoption. It is the realization of this third stage—adoption—that demands both our passion and our discipline, our heart and our head. *The fate of animals is in our hands. God grant we are equal to the task.*

NOTE

1. Tom Regan, *The Case for Animal Rights* (Berkeley: University of California Press, 1983).

STUDY QUESTIONS

1. How is Regan's position on animal rights different from Singer's? Explain.

2. What are Regan's reasons for granting animals equal moral rights?

3. Does Regan allow for experimentation on animals? If we have to test a dangerous AIDS vaccine, on whom should we test it?

5

A Critique of Regan's Animal Rights Theory

MARY ANNE WARREN

The author of many articles in moral philosophy, Mary Anne Warren teaches philosophy at San Francisco State University.

Warren reconstructs Regan's argument for animal rights and criticizes it for depending on the obscure notion of inherent value. She then argues that all rational human beings are equally part of the moral community since we can reason with each other about our behavior, whereas we cannot so reason with an animal. She puts forth a "weak animal rights theory," which asserts that we ought not to be cruel to animals or kill them without good reason.

Tom Regan has produced what is perhaps the definitive defense of the view that the basic moral rights of at least some non-human animals are in no way inferior to our own. In *The Case for Animal Rights*, he argues that all normal mammals over a year of age have the same basic moral rights.[1] Non-human mammals have essentially the same right not to be harmed or killed as we do. I shall call this "the strong animal rights position," although it is weaker than the claims made by some animal liberationists in that it ascribes rights to only some sentient animals.[2]

I will argue that Regan's case for the strong animal rights position is unpersuasive and that this

Reprinted from *Between the Species*, Vol. 2, No. 4 (Fall 1987) by permission of Mary Anne Warren.

position entails consequences which a reasonable person cannot accept. I do not deny that some non-human animals have moral rights; indeed, I would extend the scope of the rights claim to include all sentient animals, that is, all those capable of having experiences, including experiences of pleasure or satisfaction and pain, suffering, or frustration.[3] However, I do not think that the moral rights of most non-human animals are identical in strength to those of persons.[4] The rights of most non-human animals may be overridden in circumstances which would not justify overriding the rights of persons. There are, for instance, compelling realities which sometimes require that we kill animals for reasons which could not justify the killing of persons. I will call this view "the weak animal rights" position, even though it ascribes rights to a wider range of animals than does the strong animal rights position.

I will begin by summarizing Regan's case for the strong animal rights position and noting two problems with it. Next, I will explore some consequences of the strong animal rights position which I think are unacceptable. Finally, I will outline the case for the weak animal rights position.

REGAN'S CASE

Regan's argument moves through three stages. First, he argues that normal, mature mammals are not only sentient but have other mental capacities as well. These include the capacities for emotion, memory, belief, desire, the use of general concepts, intentional action, a sense of the future, and some degree of self-awareness. Creatures with such capacities are said to be subjects-of-a-life. They are not only alive in the biological sense but have a psychological identity over time and an existence which can go better or worse for them. Thus, they can be harmed or benefited. These are plausible claims, and well defended. One of the strongest parts of the book is the rebuttal of philosophers, such as R. G. Frey, who object to the application of such mentalistic terms to creatures that do not use a human-style

language.[5] The second and third stages of the argument are more problematic.

In the second stage, Regan argues that subjects-of-a-life have inherent value. His concept of inherent value grows out of his opposition to utilitarianism. Utilitarian moral theory, he says, treats individuals as "mere receptacles" for morally significant value, in that harm to one individual may be justified by the production of a greater net benefit to other individuals. In opposition to this, he holds that subjects-of-a-life have a value independent of both the value they may place upon their lives or experiences and the value others may place upon them.

Inherent value, Regan argues, does not come in degrees. To hold that some individuals have more inherent value than others is to adopt a "perfectionist" theory, i.e., one which assigns different moral worth to individuals according to how well they are thought to exemplify some virtue(s), such as intelligence or moral autonomy. Perfectionist theories have been used, at least since the time of Aristotle, to rationalize such injustices as slavery and male domination, as well as the unrestrained exploitation of animals. Regan argues that if we reject these injustices, then we must also reject perfectionism and conclude that all subjects-of-a-life have equal inherent value. Moral agents have no more inherent value than moral patients, i.e., subjects-of-a-life who are not morally responsible for their actions.

In the third phase of the argument, Regan uses the thesis of equal inherent value to derive strong moral rights for all subjects-of-a-life. This thesis underlies the Respect Principle, which forbids us to treat beings who have inherent value as mere receptacles, i.e., mere means to the production of the greatest overall good. This principle, in turn, underlies the Harm Principle, which says that we have a direct *prima facie* duty not to harm beings who have inherent value. Together, these principles give rise to moral rights. Rights are defined as valid claims, claims to certain goods and against certain beings, i.e., moral agents. Moral rights generate duties not only to refrain from inflicting harm upon beings with inherent value but also to come to their aid when they are threatened by other moral agents. Rights are not absolute but may be overridden in certain circumstances. Just what these circumstances are we will consider later. But first, let's look at some difficulties in the theory as thus far presented.

THE MYSTERY OF INHERENT VALUE

Inherent value is a key concept in Regan's theory. It is the bridge between the plausible claim that all normal, mature mammals—human or otherwise—are subjects-of-a-life and the more debatable claim that they all have basic moral rights of the same strength. But it is a highly obscure concept, and its obscurity makes it ill-suited to play this crucial role.

Inherent value is defined almost entirely in negative terms. It is not dependent upon the value which either the inherently valuable individual or anyone else may place upon that individual's life or experiences. It is not (necessarily) a function of sentience or any other mental capacity, because, Regan says, some entities which are not sentient (e.g., trees, rivers, or rocks) may, nevertheless, have inherent value (p. 246). It cannot attach to anything other than an individual; species, ecosystems, and the like cannot have inherent value.

These are some of the things which inherent value is not. But what is it? Unfortunately, we are not told. Inherent value appears as a mysterious non-natural property which we must take on faith. Regan says that it is a *postulate* that subjects-of-a-life have inherent value, a postulate justified by the fact that it avoids certain absurdities which he thinks follow from a purely utilitarian theory (p. 247). But why is it a postulate that *subjects-of-a-life* have inherent value? If the inherent value of a being is completely independent of the value that it or anyone else places upon its experiences, then why does the fact that it has certain sorts of experiences constitute evidence that it has inherent value? If the reason is that subjects-of-a-life have an existence which can go better or worse for them, then why isn't the appropriate conclusion that all sentient beings have inherent value, since they would all seem to meet that condition? Sentient but mentally unsophisticated beings may have a less extensive range of possible satisfactions and frustrations, but

why should it follow that they have—or may have—no inherent value at all?

In the absence of a positive account of inherent value, it is also difficult to grasp the connection between being inherently valuable and having moral rights. Intuitively, it seems that value is one thing, and rights are another. It does not seem incoherent to say that some things (e.g., mountains, rivers, redwood trees) are inherently valuable and yet are not the sorts of things which can have moral rights. Nor does it seem incoherent to ascribe inherent value to some things which are not individuals, e.g., plant or animal species, though it may well be incoherent to ascribe moral rights to such things.

In short, the concept of inherent value seems to create at least as many problems as it solves. If inherent value is based on some natural property, then why not try to identify that property and explain its moral significance, without appealing to inherent value? And if it is not based on any natural property, then why should we believe in it? That it may enable us to avoid some of the problems faced by the utilitarian is not a sufficient reason, if it creates other problems which are just as serious.

IS THERE A SHARP LINE?

Perhaps the most serious problems are those that arise when we try to apply the strong animal rights position to animals other than normal, mature mammals. Regan's theory requires us to divide all living things into two categories: those which have the same inherent value and the same basic moral rights that we do, and those which have no inherent value and presumably no moral rights. But wherever we try to draw the line, such a sharp division is implausible.

It would surely be arbitrary to draw such a sharp line between normal, mature mammals and all other living things. Some birds (e.g., crows, magpies, parrots, mynahs) appear to be just as mentally sophisticated as most mammals and thus are equally strong candidates for inclusion under the subject-of-a-life criterion. Regan is not in fact advocating that we draw the line here. His claim is only that normal mature mammals are clear cases, while other cases are less clear. Yet, on his theory, there must be such a sharp line *somewhere,* since there are no degrees of inherent value. But why should we believe that there is a sharp line between creatures that are subjects-of-a-life and creatures that are not? Isn't it more likely that "subjecthood" comes in degrees, that some creatures have only a little self-awareness, and only a little capacity to anticipate the future, while some have a little more, and some a good deal more?

Should we, for instance, regard fish, amphibians, and reptiles as subjects-of-a-life? A simple yes-or-no answer seems inadequate. On the one hand, some of their behavior is difficult to explain without the assumption that they have sensations, beliefs, desires, emotions, and memories; on the other hand, they do not seem to exhibit very much self-awareness or very much conscious anticipation of future events. Do they have enough mental sophistication to count as subjects-of-a-life? Exactly how much is enough?

It is still more unclear what we should say about insects, spiders, octopi, and other invertebrate animals which have brains and sensory organs but whose minds (if they have minds) are even more alien to us than those of fish or reptiles. Such creatures are probably sentient. Some people doubt that they can feel pain, since they lack certain neurological structures which are crucial to the processing of pain impulses in vertebrate animals. But this argument is inconclusive, since their nervous systems might process pain in ways different from ours. When injured, they sometimes act as if they are in pain. On evolutionary grounds, it seems unlikely that highly mobile creatures with complex sensory systems would not have developed a capacity for pain (and pleasure), since such a capacity has obvious survival value. It must, however, be admitted that we do not *know* whether spiders can feel pain (or something very like it), let alone whether they have emotions, memories, beliefs, desires, self-awareness, or a sense of the future.

Even more mysterious are the mental capacities (if any) of mobile microfauna. The brisk and efficient way that paramecia move about in their incessant search for food *might* indicate some kind of sentience, in spite of their lack of eyes, ears, brains, and other organs associated with sentience in more complex organisms. It is conceivable—though not very probable—that they, too, are subjects-of-a-life.

The existence of a few unclear cases need not pose a serious problem for a moral theory, but in this case, the unclear cases constitute most of those with which an adequate theory of animal rights would need to deal. The subject-of-a-life criterion can provide us with little or no moral guidance in our interactions with the vast majority of animals. That might be acceptable if it could be supplemented with additional principles which would provide such guidance. However, the radical dualism of the theory precludes supplementing it in this way. We are forced to say that either a spider has the same right to life as you and I do, or it has no right to life whatever—and that only the gods know which of these alternatives is true.

Regan's suggestion for dealing with such unclear cases is to apply the "benefit of the doubt" principle. That is, when dealing with beings that may or may not be subjects-of-a-life, we should act as if they are.[6] But if we try to apply this principle to the entire range of doubtful cases, we will find ourselves with moral obligations which we cannot possibly fulfill. In many climates, it is virtually impossible to live without swatting mosquitoes and exterminating cockroaches, and not all of us can afford to hire someone to sweep the path before we walk, in order to make sure that we do not step on ants. Thus, we are still faced with the daunting task of drawing a sharp line somewhere on the continuum of life forms—this time, a line demarcating the limits of the benefit of the doubt principle.

The weak animal rights theory provides a more plausible way of dealing with this range of cases, in that it allows the rights of animals of different kinds to vary in strength....

WHY ARE ANIMAL RIGHTS WEAKER THAN HUMAN RIGHTS?

How can we justify regarding the rights of persons as generally stronger than those of sentient beings which are not persons? There are a plethora of bad justifications, based on religious premises or false or unprovable claims about the differences between human and non-human nature. But there is one difference which has a clear moral relevance: people are at least sometimes capable of being moved to action or inaction by the force of reasoned argument. Rationality rests upon other mental capacities, notably those which Regan cites as criteria for being a subject-of-a-life. We share these capacities with many other animals. But it is not just because we are subjects-of-a-life that we are both able and morally compelled to recognize one another as beings with equal basic moral rights. It is also because we are able to "listen to reason" in order to settle our conflicts and cooperate in shared projects. This capacity, unlike the others, may require something like a human language.

Why is rationality morally relevant? It does not make us "better" than other animals or more "perfect." It does not even automatically make us more intelligent. (Bad reasoning reduces our effective intelligence rather than increasing it.) But it is morally relevant insofar as it provides greater possibilities for cooperation and for the nonviolent resolution of problems. It also makes us more dangerous than non-rational beings can ever be. Because we are potentially more dangerous and less predictable than wolves, we need an articulated system of morality to regulate our conduct. Any human morality, to be workable in the long run, must recognize the equal moral status of all persons, whether through the postulate of equal basic moral rights or in some other way. The recognition of the moral equality of other persons is the price we must each pay for their recognition of our moral equality. Without this mutual recognition of moral equality, human society can exist only in a state of chronic and bitter conflict. The war between the sexes will persist so long as there is sexism and male domination; racial conflict will never be eliminated so long as there are racist laws and practices. But, to the extent that we achieve a mutual recognition of equality, we can hope to live together, perhaps as peacefully as wolves, achieving (in part) through explicit moral principles what they do not seem to need explicit moral principles to achieve.

Why not extend this recognition of moral equality to other creatures, even though they cannot do the same for us? The answer is that we cannot. Because we cannot reason with most non-human animals, we cannot always solve the problems which they may cause without harming them—although we are always obligated to try. We cannot negotiate a treaty with the feral cats and foxes, requiring them to stop preying on endangered native species in return for suitable concessions on our part.

> If rats invade our houses … we cannot reason with them, hoping to persuade them of the injustice they do us. We can only attempt to get rid of them.[7]

Aristotle was not wrong in claiming that the capacity to alter one's behavior on the basis of reasoned argument is relevant to the full moral status which he accorded to free men. Of course, he was wrong in his other premise, that women and slaves by nature cannot reason well enough to function as autonomous moral agents. Had that premise been true, so would his conclusion that women and slaves are not quite the moral equals of free men. In the case of most nonhuman animals, the corresponding premise is true. If, on the other hand, there are animals with whom we can learn to reason, then we are obligated to do this and to regard them as our moral equals.

Thus, to distinguish between the rights of persons and those of most other animals on the grounds that only people can alter their behavior on the basis of reasoned argument does not commit us to a perfectionist theory of the sort Aristotle endorsed. There is no excuse for refusing to recognize the moral equality of some people on the grounds that we don't regard them as quite as rational as we are, since it is perfectly clear that most people can reason well enough to determine how to act so as to respect the basic rights of others (if they choose to), and that is enough for moral equality.

But what about people who are clearly not rational? It is often argued that sophisticated mental capacities such as rationality cannot be essential for the possession of equal basic moral rights, since nearly everyone agrees that human infants and mentally incompetent persons have such rights, even though they may lack those sophisticated mental capacities. But this argument is inconclusive, because there are powerful practical and emotional reasons for protecting non-rational human beings, reasons which are absent in the case of most non-human animals. Infancy and mental incompetence are human conditions which all of us either have experienced or are likely to experience at some time. We also protect babies and mentally incompetent people because we care for them. We don't normally care for animals in the same way, and when we do—e.g., in the case of much-loved pets—we may regard them as having special rights by virtue of their relationship to us. We protect them not only for their sake but also for our own, lest we be hurt by harm done to them. Regan holds that such "side-effects" are irrelevant to moral rights, and perhaps they are. But in ordinary usage, there is no sharp line between moral rights and those moral protections which are not rights. The extension of strong moral protections to infants and the mentally impaired in no way proves that non-human animals have the same basic moral rights as people.

WHY SPEAK OF "ANIMAL RIGHTS" AT ALL?

If, as I have argued, reality precludes our treating all animals as our moral equals, then why should we still ascribe rights to them? Everyone agrees that animals are entitled to some protection against human abuse, but why speak of animal *rights* if we are not prepared to accept most animals as our moral equals? The weak animal rights position may seem an unstable compromise between the bold claim that animals have the same basic moral rights that we do and the more common view that animals have no rights at all.

It is probably impossible to either prove or disprove the thesis that animals have moral rights by producing an analysis of the concept of a moral right and checking to see if some or all animals satisfy the conditions for having rights. The concept of a moral right is complex, and it is not clear which of its strands are essential. Paradigm rights holders, i.e., mature and mentally competent persons, are *both* rational and morally autonomous beings and sentient subjects-of-a-life. Opponents of animal rights claim that rationality and moral autonomy are essential for the possession of rights, while defenders of animal rights claim that they are not. The ordinary concept of a moral right is probably not precise enough to enable us to determine who is right on purely definitional grounds.

If logical analysis will not answer the question of whether animals have moral rights, practical considerations may, nevertheless incline us to say that they do. The most plausible alternative to the view that animals have moral rights is that, while they do not have *rights*, we are, nevertheless, obligated not to be cruel to them. Regan argues persuasively that the injunction to avoid being cruel to animals is inadequate to express our obligations towards animals, because it focuses on the mental states of those who cause animal suffering, rather than on the harm done to the animals themselves (p. 158). Cruelty is inflicting pain or suffering and either taking pleasure in that pain or suffering or being more or less indifferent to it. Thus, to express the demand for the decent treatment of animals in terms of the rejection of cruelty is to invite the too easy response that those who subject animals to suffering are not being cruel because they regret the suffering they cause but sincerely believe that what they do is justified. The injunction to avoid cruelty is also inadequate in that it does not preclude the killing of animals—for any reason, however trivial—so long as it is done relatively painlessly.

The inadequacy of the anti-cruelty view provides one practical reason for speaking of animal rights. Another practical reason is that this is an age in which nearly all significant moral claims tend to be expressed in terms of rights. Thus, the denial that animals have rights, however carefully qualified, is likely to be taken to mean that we may do whatever we like to them, provided that we do not violate any human rights. In such a context, speaking of the rights of animals may be the only way to persuade many people to take seriously protests against the abuse of animals.

Why not extend this line of argument and speak of the rights of trees, mountains, oceans, or anything else which we may wish to see protected from destruction? Some environmentalists have not hesitated to speak in this way, and, given the importance of protecting such elements of the natural world, they cannot be blamed for using this rhetorical device. But, I would argue that moral rights can meaningfully be ascribed only to entities which have some capacity for sentience. This is because moral rights are protections designed to protect rights holders from harms or to provide them with benefits which matter *to them*. Only beings capable of sentience can be harmed or benefited in ways which matter to them, for only such beings can like or dislike what happens to them or prefer some conditions to others. Thus, sentient animals, unlike mountains, rivers, or species, are at least logically possible candidates for moral rights. This fact together with the need to end current abuses of animals—e.g., in scientific research ... —provides a plausible case for speaking of animal rights.

CONCLUSION

I have argued that Regan's case for ascribing strong moral rights to all normal, mature mammals is unpersuasive because (1) it rests upon the obscure concept of inherent value, which is defined only in negative terms, and (2) it seems to preclude any plausible answer to questions about the moral status of the vast majority of sentient animals....

The weak animal rights theory asserts that (1) any creature whose natural mode of life includes the pursuit of certain satisfactions has the right not to be forced to exist without the opportunity to pursue those satisfactions; (2) that any creature which is capable of pain, suffering, or frustration has the right that such experiences not be deliberately inflicted upon it without some compelling reason; and (3) that no sentient being should be killed without good reason. However, moral rights are not an all-or-nothing affair. The strength of the reasons required to override the rights of a non-human organism varies, depending upon—among other things—the probability that it is sentient and (if it is clearly sentient) its probable degree of mental sophistication....

NOTES

1. Tom Regan, *The Case for Animal Rights* (Berkeley: University of California Press, 1983). All page references are to this edition.

2. For instance, Peter Singer, although he does not like to speak of rights, includes all sentient beings under the protection of his basic utilitarian principle of equal respect for like interests. (*Animal Liberation* [New York: Avon Books, 1975], p. 3.)

3. The capacity for sentience like all of the mental capacities mentioned in what follows is a disposition. Dispositions do not disappear whenever they are not currently manifested. Thus, sleeping or temporarily unconscious persons or nonhuman animals are still sentient in the relevant sense (i.e., still capable of sentience), so long as they still have the neurological mechanisms necessary for the occurrence of experiences.

4. It is possible, perhaps probable that some nonhuman animals—such as cetaceans and anthropoid apes—should be regarded as persons. If so, then the weak animal rights position holds that these animals have the same basic moral rights as human persons.

5. See R. G. Frey, *Interests and Rights: The Case Against Animals* (Oxford: Oxford University Press, 1980).

6. See, for instance, p. 319, where Regan appeals to the benefit of the doubt principle when dealing with infanticide and late-term abortion.

7. Bonnie Steinbock, "Speciesism and the Idea of Equality," *Philosophy* 53 (1978):253.

STUDY QUESTIONS

1. Examine Warren's critique of Regan's position. What is her main criticism? How strong is her criticism?

2. What is the basis for granting human beings moral rights that we do not grant animals? Do you agree with Warren's arguments?

3. What is the weak animal rights position? What is Warren's argument for it?

Chapter 3

Population and Consumption

THE UNIVERSAL DECLARATION ON HUMAN RIGHTS describes the family as the natural and fundamental unit of society. It follows that any choice and decision with regard to the size of the family must irrevocably rest with the family itself and cannot be made by anyone else.[1]

In evaluating population growth one must keep in mind that such growth increases *exponentially* rather than *linearly*. Linear growth increases by adding 1 unit to the sum: 1, 2, 3, 4, 5, and so forth. Exponential growth increases by a fixed percentage of the whole over a given time. It doubles itself: 1, 2, 4, 8, 16, 32, 64, and so forth.

An ancient Chinese story illustrates this. Once a hero defeated the enemies of his country. The emperor had the hero brought before him and promised the hero anything he wanted. The hero produced a chessboard and asked the Emperor for one grain of rice on the first square, two on the second, four on the third, eight on the fourth, and to continue doubling through all 64 squares. The emperor was astonished. "Is that all you request?" he cried. "You could have had half my kingdom, and all you ask for is a little grain?" But the emperor soon discovered that he could not comply with the hero's request. By the time he had gotten to square 32, he found that on that square alone he owed the hero 8.6 billion grains of rice. By the time he got to square 64, he owed over 10,000,000,000,000,000,000 grains of rice, far more than the entire country produced.

We calculate the doubling time of a given amount by using the *rule of 70*. If a sum increases at 1% per annum, it will double in size in 70 years. If it increases at a 2% rate per annum, it will increase fourfold in 70 years.

About 2,000 years ago, 300 million people existed (about the population of the United States in 2006). It reached a billion in the nineteenth century, and by the end of the twentieth century, it reached 6 billion (about 6.3 billion in 2006). A current estimate is that by 2050, the world's population will be 9.3 billion. How serious is this growth? The more people there are, the more food, water, and energy we need and the more pollution we produce. How many people can Earth reasonably sustain?

As more societies industrialize and achieve middle-class lifestyles, they tend to use more resources and produce more pollution, resulting in more environmental degradation. This use is sometimes referred to as *consumption overpopulation* as opposed to *people overpopulation*. Many countries are rapidly industrializing, including India and China.

For some environmentalists, the picture is quite gloomy; there are simply not enough land resources. Others argue that our problems are moral and political, not demographic. They say we can solve our urban problems if we have the will to live together in equality and harmony. Technology has radically increased our energy and food resources. Enough food exists for all. The real problem is one of just distribution.

Proponents of this view argue that the wealthy nations should moderate their consumptive passions, pointing out that with only 4.5% of the world's population, the United States uses 33% of its resources, 25% of its nonrenewable energy, and produces 33% of its pollution. The average American's negative impact on the environment is about forty or fifty times that of a person in the Third World. In the affluent West, we must reject consumerism and simplify our lives. Those in the poorer developing nations must be allowed to improve their quality of life through education and appropriate technology.

To provide some data, we begin with a reading by Bill McKibben that succinctly sets forth a case for limiting population growth.

Next we turn to Garrett Hardin's classic article, "The Tragedy of the Commons," in which he argues that unless strong social sanctions are enforced, self-interest will lead people to maximize personal utility, which all too often means violating the carrying capacity of the land. With regard to population, he says that unless we have mutually coercive, mutually agreed-on restrictions on procreation, we will not survive, or we will survive with enormous misery.

In our third reading, Jacqueline Kasun takes a diametrically opposite point of view from that of McKibben and Hardin. Citing an impressive array of statistics, Kasun argues that enough food and resources exist to care for a lot more people than presently inhabit Earth and that technology promises to expand our resources efficiently. Population increase, rather than being a liability, is actually a blessing. Such growth stimulates agricultural and economic investment, encourages governments and parents to devote greater resources to education, and inspires both more ideas and the exchange of ideas among people. Contrary to the interests of the ruling elite, we must learn to live creatively with the expanding opportunities that a growing population affords.

Next, Hardin's famous article, "Lifeboat Ethics," argues that affluent societies, like lifeboats, ought to ensure their survival by preserving a safety factor of resources. Giving away its resources to needy nations or admitting needy immigrants is like taking on additional passengers who threaten to capsize the lifeboat. We help neither them nor ourselves. Aiming at perfect distributive justice ends up a perfect catastrophe. Furthermore, we have a duty to our children and grandchildren, which will be compromised if we endeavor to help the poor.

In our final reading, William Murdoch and Allan Oaten take strong issue with Hardin's assessment. They argue that Hardin's arguments rest on misleading metaphors, *lifeboat, commons,* and *ratchet,* and a fuller analysis will reveal that the situation is far more hopeful than Hardin claims. We are responsible for the plight of the poor and must take steps to alleviate their suffering.

NOTE

1. Secretary General of the United Nations U Thant, *International Planned Parenthood News* 168 (February 1968): 3.

6

A Special Moment in History: The Challenge of Overpopulation and Overconsumption

BILL McKIBBEN

Bill McKibben is an environmentalist and writer who lives in the Adirondacks in New York State. In this essay he argues that, because of the environmental crisis we face, we are living in a special time, which could determine the near—and long-term—future of the planet. With the world's population heading for another doubling and with more people consuming more resources and creating more pollutants—and with fewer sinks into which to throw them—the decisions we make in the next few decades may well determine the fate of Earth and prospects for future generations. McKibben's article is valuable for the large amount of data on demographics and global warming (see Chapter 8), which it lucidly sets forth and analyzes.

… We may live in a special time. We may live in the strangest, most thoroughly different moment [of history] since human beings took up farming, 10,000 years ago, and time more or less commenced. Since then time has flowed in one direction—toward *more,* which we have taken to be progress. At first the momentum was gradual, almost imperceptible, checked by wars and the Dark Ages and plagues and taboos; but in recent centuries it has accelerated, the curve of every graph steepening like the Himalayas rising from the Asian steppe. We have climbed quite high. Of course, fifty years ago one could have said the same thing, and fifty years before that, and fifty years before *that.* But in each case it would have been premature. We've increased the population fourfold in that 150 years; the amount of food we grow has gone up faster still; the size of our economy has quite simply exploded.

But now—now may be the special time. So special that in the Western world we might each of us consider, among many other things, having only one child—that is, reproducing at a rate as low as that at which human beings have ever voluntarily reproduced. Is this really necessary? Are we finally running up against some limits?

To try to answer this question, we need to ask another: *How many of us will there be in the near future?* Here is a piece of news that may alter the way we see the planet—an indication that we live at a special moment. At least at first blush the news is hopeful. *New demographic evidence shows that it is at least possible that a child born today will live long enough to see the peak of human population.*

Around the world people are choosing to have fewer and fewer children—not just in China, where the government forces it on them, but in almost every nation outside the poorest parts of Africa. Population growth rates are lower than

Reprinted from *The Atlantic Monthly* (May 1998). Used by permission of the author.

they have been at any time since the Second World War. In the past three decades the average woman in the developing world, excluding China, has gone from bearing six children to bearing four. Even in Bangladesh the average has fallen from six to fewer than four; even in the mullahs' Iran it has dropped by four children. If this keeps up, the population of the world will not quite double again; United Nations analysts offer as their mid-range projection that it will top out at 10 to 11 billion, up from just under six billion at the moment. The world is still growing, at nearly a record pace—we add a New York City every month, almost a Mexico every year, almost an India every decade. But the rate of growth is slowing; it is no longer "exponential," "unstoppable," "inexorable," "unchecked," "cancerous." If current trends hold, the world's population will all but stop growing before the twenty-first century is out.

And that will be none too soon. There is no way we could keep going as we have been. The *increase* in human population in the 1990s has exceeded the *total* population in 1600. The population has grown more since 1950 than it did during the previous four million years. The reasons for our recent rapid growth are pretty clear. Although the Industrial Revolution speeded historical growth rates considerably, it was really the public-health revolution, and its spread to the Third World at the end of the Second World War, that set us galloping. Vaccines and antibiotics came all at once, and right behind came population. In Sri Lanka in the late 1940s life expectancy was rising at least a year every twelve months. How much difference did this make? Consider the United States: If people died throughout this century at the same rate as they did at its beginning, America's population would be 140 million, not 270 million.

If it is relatively easy to explain why populations grew so fast after the Second World War, it is much harder to explain why the growth is now slowing. Experts confidently supply answers, some of them contradictory: "Development is the best contraceptive"—or education, or the empowerment of women, or hard times that force families to postpone having children. For each example

there is a counterexample. Ninety-seven percent of women in the Arab sheikhdom of Oman know about contraception, and yet they average more than six children apiece. Turks have used contraception at about the same rate as the Japanese, but their birth rate is twice as high. And so on. It is not AIDS that will slow population growth, except in a few African countries. It is not horrors like the civil war in Rwanda, which claimed half a million lives—a loss the planet can make up for in two days. All that matters is how often individual men and women decide that they want to reproduce.

Will the drop continue? It had better. UN midrange projections assume that women in the developing world will soon average two children apiece—the rate at which population growth stabilizes. If fertility remained at current levels, the population would reach the absurd figure of 296 billion in just 150 years. Even if it dropped to 2.5 children per woman and then stopped falling, the population would still reach 28 billion.

But let's trust that this time the demographers have got it right. Let's trust that we have rounded the turn and we're in the home stretch. Let's trust that the planet's population really will double only one more time. Even so, this is a case of good news, bad news. The good news is that we won't grow forever. The bad news is that there are six billion of us already, a number the world strains to support. One more near-doubling—four or five billion more people—will nearly double that strain. Will these be the five billion straws that break the camel's back?

BIG QUESTIONS

We've answered the question *How many of us will there be?* But to figure out how near we are to any limits, we need to ask something else: *How big are we?* This is not so simple. Not only do we vary greatly in how much food and energy and water and minerals we consume, but each of us varies over time. William Catton, who was a sociologist at Washington State University before his retirement, once tried to calculate the amount of energy human beings use each day. In hunter-gatherer times it was about 2,500 calories, all of it food. That is the daily energy intake of a common dolphin. A modern human being uses 31,000 calories a day, most of it in the form of fossil fuel. That is the intake of a pilot whale. And the average American uses six times that—as much as a sperm whale. We have become, in other words, different from the people we used to be. Not kinder or unkinder, not deeper or stupider—our natures seem to have changed little since Homer. We've just gotten bigger. We appear to be the same species, with stomachs of the same size, but we aren't. It's as if each of us were trailing a big Macy's-parade balloon around, feeding it constantly.

So it doesn't do much good to stare idly out the window of your 737 as you fly from New York to Los Angeles and see that there's *plenty* of empty space down there. Sure enough, you could crowd lots more people into the nation or onto the planet. The entire world population could fit into Texas, and each person could have an area equal to the floor space of a typical U.S. home. If people were willing to stand, everyone on earth could fit comfortably into half of Rhode Island. Holland is crowded and is doing just fine.

But this ignores the balloons above our heads, our hungry shadow selves, our sperm-whale appetites. As soon as we started farming, we started setting aside extra land to support ourselves. Now each of us needs not only a little plot of cropland and a little pasture for the meat we eat but also a little forest for timber and paper, a little mine, a little oil well. Giants have big feet. Some scientists in Vancouver tried to calculate one such "footprint" and found that although 1.7 million people lived on a million acres surrounding their city, those people required 21.5 million acres of land to support them—wheat fields in Alberta, oil fields in Saudi Arabia, tomato fields in California. People in Manhattan are as dependent on faraway resources as people on the Mir space station.

Those balloons above our heads can shrink or grow, depending on how we choose to live. All over the earth people who were once tiny are suddenly growing like Alice when she ate the cake. In China per capita income has doubled since the early 1980s. People there, though still Lilliputian in comparison with us, are twice their former size. They eat much higher on the food chain, understandably, than they used to: China slaughters more pigs than any other nation, and it takes four pounds of grain to produce one pound of pork. When, a decade ago, the United Nations examined sustainable development, it issued a report saying that the economies of the developing countries needed to be five to ten times as large to move poor people to an acceptable standard of living—with all that this would mean in terms of demands on oil wells and forests.

That sounds almost impossible. For the moment, though, let's not pass judgment. We're still just doing math. There are going to be lots of us. We're going to be big. But lots of us in relation to what? Big in relation to what? It could be that compared with the world we inhabit, we're still scarce and small. Or not. So now we need to consider a third question.

HOW BIG IS THE EARTH?

Any state wildlife biologist can tell you how many deer a given area can support—how much browse there is for the deer to eat before they begin to suppress the reproduction of trees, before they begin to starve in the winter. He can calculate how many wolves a given area can support too, in part by counting the number of deer. And so on, up and down the food chain. It's not an exact science, but it comes pretty close—at least compared with figuring out the carrying capacity of the earth for human beings, which is an art so dark that anyone with any sense stays away from it.

Consider the difficulties. Human beings, unlike deer, can eat almost anything and live at almost any level they choose. Hunter-gatherers used 2,500 calories of energy a day, whereas modern Americans use seventy-five times that. Human beings, unlike deer, can import what they need from thousands of miles away. And human beings, unlike deer, can figure out new ways to do old things. If, like deer, we needed to browse on conifers to survive, we could crossbreed lush new strains, chop down competing trees, irrigate forests, spray a thousand chemicals, freeze or dry the tender buds at the peak of harvest, genetically engineer new strains—and advertise the merits of maple buds until everyone was ready to switch. The variables are so great that professional demographers rarely even bother trying to figure out carrying capacity. The demographer Joel Cohen, in his potent book *How Many People Can the Earth Support?* (1995), reports that at two recent meetings of the Population Association of America, exactly none of the more than 200 symposia dealt with carrying capacity.

But the difficulty hasn't stopped other thinkers. This is, after all, as big a question as the world offers. Plato, Euripides, and Polybius all worried that we would run out of food if the population kept growing; for centuries a steady stream of economists, environmentalists, and zealots and cranks of all sorts have made it their business to issue estimates either dire or benign. The most famous, of course, came from the Reverend Thomas Malthus. Writing in 1798, he proposed that the growth of population, being "geometric," would soon outstrip the supply of food. Though he changed his mind and rewrote his famous essay, it's the original version that people have remembered—and lambasted—ever since. Few other writers have found critics in as many corners. Not only have conservatives made Malthus's name a byword for ludicrous alarmism, but Karl Marx called his essay "a libel on the human race," Friedrich Engels believed that "we are forever secure from the fear of overpopulation," and even Mao Zedong attacked Malthus by name, adding, "Of all things in the world people are the most precious."

Each new generation of Malthusians has made new predictions that the end was near, and has been proved wrong. The late 1960s saw an upsurge of Malthusian panic. In 1967 William and Paul Paddock published a book called *Famine—1975!*, which contained a triage list: "Egypt: Can't-be-saved.... Tunisia: Should Receive Food.... India: Can't-be-saved." Almost simultaneously

Paul Ehrlich wrote, in his best-selling *The Population Bomb* (1968), "The battle to feed all of humanity is over. In the 1970s, the world will undergo famines—hundreds of millions of people will starve to death." It all seemed so certain, so firmly in keeping with a world soon to be darkened by the first oil crisis.

But that's not how it worked out. India fed herself. The United States still ships surplus grain around the world. As the astute Harvard social scientist Amartya Sen points out, "Not only is food generally much cheaper to buy today, in constant dollars, than it was in Malthus's time, but it also has become cheaper during recent decades." So far, in other words, the world has more or less supported us. Too many people starve (60 percent of children in South Asia are stunted by malnutrition), but both the total number and the percentage have dropped in recent decades, thanks mainly to the successes of the Green Revolution. Food production has tripled since the Second World War, outpacing even population growth. We may be giants, but we are clever giants.

So Malthus was wrong. Over and over again he was wrong. No other prophet has ever been proved wrong so many times. At the moment, his stock is especially low. One group of technological optimists now believes that people will continue to improve their standard of living precisely *because* they increase their numbers. This group's intellectual fountainhead is a brilliant Danish economist named Ester Boserup—a sort of anti-Malthus, who in 1965 argued that the gloomy cleric had it backward. The more people, Boserup said, the more progress. Take agriculture as an example: the first farmers, she pointed out, were slash-and-burn cultivators, who might farm a plot for a year or two and then move on, not returning for maybe two decades. As the population grew, however, they had to return more frequently to the same plot. That meant problems: compacted, depleted, weedy soils. But those new problems meant new solutions: hoes, manure, compost, crop rotation, irrigation. Even in this century, Boserup said, necessity-induced invention has meant that "intensive systems of agriculture replaced extensive systems," accelerating the rate of food production.

Boserup's closely argued examples have inspired a less cautious group of popularizers, who point out that standards of living have risen all over the world even as population has grown. The most important benefit, in fact, that population growth bestows on an economy is to increase the stock of useful knowledge, insisted Julian Simon, the best known of the so-called cornucopians, who died earlier this year. We might run out of copper, but who cares? The mere fact of shortage will lead someone to invent a substitute. "The main fuel to speed our progress is our stock of knowledge, and the brake is our lack of imagination," Simon wrote. "The ultimate resource is people—skilled, spirited, and hopeful people who will exert their wills and imaginations for their own benefit, and so, inevitably, for the benefit of us all."

Simon and his ilk owe their success to this: they have been right so far. The world has behaved as they predicted. India hasn't starved. Food is cheap. But Malthus never goes away. The idea that we might grow too big can be disproved only for the moment—never for good. We might always be on the threshold of a special time, when the mechanisms described by Boserup and Simon stop working. It is true that Malthus was wrong when the population doubled from 750 million to 1.5 billion. It is true that Malthus was wrong when the population doubled from 1.5 billion to three billion. It is true that Malthus was wrong when the population doubled from three billion to six billion. Will Malthus still be wrong fifty years from now?

LOOKING AT LIMITS

The case that the next doubling, the one we're now experiencing, might be the difficult one can begin as readily with the Stanford biologist Peter Vitousek as with anyone else. In 1986 Vitousek decided to calculate how much of the earth's "primary productivity" went to support human beings. He added together the grain we ate, the corn we fed our cows, and the forests we cut for timber and paper; he added the losses in food as we overgrazed grassland and turned it into desert. And when he was finished adding, the number he came up with was 38.8 percent. We use 38.8 percent of everything the world's plants don't need to keep themselves alive; directly or indirectly, we consume 38.8 percent of what it is possible to eat. "That's a relatively large number," Vitousek says. "It should give pause to people who think we are far from any limits." Though he never drops the measured tone of an academic, Vitousek speaks with considerable emphasis: "There's a sense among some economists that we're *so* far from any biophysical limits. I think that's not supported by the evidence."

For another antidote to the good cheer of someone like Julian Simon, sit down with the Cornell biologist David Pimentel. He believes that we're in big trouble. Odd facts stud his conversation—for example, a nice head of iceberg lettuce is 95 percent water and contains just fifty calories of energy, but it takes 400 calories of energy to grow that head of lettuce in California's Central Valley, and another 1,800 to ship it east. ("There's practically no nutrition in the damn stuff anyway," Pimentel says. "Cabbage is a lot better, and we can grow it in upstate New York.") Pimentel has devoted the past three decades to tracking the planet's capacity, and he believes that we're already too crowded—that the earth can support only two billion people over the long run at a middle-class standard of living, and that trying to support more is doing great damage. He has spent considerable time studying soil erosion, for instance. Every raindrop that hits exposed ground is like a small explosion, launching soil particles into the air. On a slope, more than half of the soil contained in those splashes is carried downhill. If crop residue—cornstalks, say—is left in the field after harvest, it helps to shield the soil: the raindrop doesn't hit as hard. But in the developing world, where firewood is scarce, peasants burn those corn-stalks for cooking fuel. About 60 percent of crop residues in China and 90 percent in Bangladesh are removed and burned, Pimentel says. When planting season comes, dry soils simply blow away. "Our measuring stations pick up Chinese soil in the Hawaiian air when ploughing time comes," he says. "Every year in Florida we pick up African soils in the wind when they start to plough."

The very things that made the Green Revolution so stunning—that made the last doubling possible—now cause trouble. Irrigation ditches, for instance, water 17 percent of all arable land and help to produce a third of all crops. But when flooded soils are baked by the sun, the water evaporates and the minerals in the irrigation water are deposited on the land. A hectare (2.47 acres) can accumulate two to five tons of salt annually, and eventually plants won't grow there. Maybe 10 percent of all irrigated land is affected.

Or think about fresh water for human use. Plenty of rain falls on the earth's surface, but most of it evaporates or roars down to the ocean in spring floods. According to Sandra Postel, the director of the Global Water Policy Project, we're left with about 12,500 cubic kilometers of accessible runoff, which would be enough for current demand except that it's not very well distributed around the globe. And we're not exactly conservationists—we use nearly seven times as much water as we used in 1900. Already 20 percent of the world's population lacks access to potable water and fights over water divide in many regions. Already the Colorado River usually dries out in the desert before it reaches the Sea of Cortez, making what the mid-century conservationist Aldo Leopold called a "milk and honey wilderness" into some of the nastiest country in North America. Already the Yellow River can run dry for as much as a third of the year. Already only two percent of the Nile's fresh-water flow makes it to the ocean. And we need more water all the time. Producing a ton of grain consumes a thousand tons of water—that's how much the wheat plant breathes out as it grows. "We estimated that biotechnology might cut the amount of water a plant uses by ten percent," Pimentel says. "But plant physiologists tell us that's optimistic—they remind us that water's a pretty important part of photosynthesis. Maybe we can get five percent."...

I said earlier that food production grew even faster than population after the Second World War. Year after year the yield of wheat and corn and rice

rocketed up about three percent annually. It's a favorite statistic of the eternal optimists. In Julian Simon's book *The Ultimate Resource* (1981), charts show just how fast the growth was, and how it continually cut the cost of food. Simon wrote, "The obvious implication of this historical trend toward cheaper food—a trend that probably extends back to the beginning of agriculture—is that real prices for food will continue to drop.... It is a fact that portends more drops in price and even less scarcity in the future."

A few years after Simon's book was published, however, the data curve began to change. That rocketing growth in grain production ceased; now the gains were coming in tiny increments, too small to keep pace with population growth. The world reaped its largest harvest of grain per capita in 1984; since then the amount of corn and wheat and rice per person has fallen by six percent. Grain stockpiles have shrunk to less than two months' supply.

No one knows quite why. The collapse of the Soviet Union contributed to the trend—cooperative farms suddenly found the fertilizer supply shut off and spare parts for the tractor hard to come by. But there were other causes, too, all around the world—the salinization of irrigated fields, the erosion of topsoil, the conversion of prime farmland into residential areas, and all the other things that environmentalists had been warning about for years. It's possible that we'll still turn production around and start it rocketing again. Charles C. Mann, writing in *Science,* quotes experts who believe that in the future a "gigantic, multi-year, multi-billion-dollar scientific effort, a kind of agricultural 'person-on-the-moon project'" might do the trick. The next great hope of the optimists is genetic engineering, and scientists have indeed managed to induce resistance to pests and disease in some plants. To get more yield, though, a corn-stalk must be made to put out another ear, and conventional breeding may have exhausted the possibilities. There's a sense that we're running into walls.

We won't start producing *less* food. Wheat is not like oil, whose flow from the spigot will simply slow to a trickle one day. But we may be getting to the point where gains will be small and hard to come by. The spectacular increases may be behind us. One researcher told Mann, "Producing higher yields will no longer be like unveiling a new model of a car. We won't be pulling off the sheet and there it is, a two-fold yield increase." Instead the process will be "incremental, torturous, and slow." And there are five billion more of us to come.

So far we're still fed; gas is cheap at the pump; the supermarket grows ever larger. We've been warned again and again about approaching limits, and we've never quite reached them. So maybe—how tempting to believe it!—they don't really exist. For every Paul Ehrlich there's a man like Lawrence Summers, the former World Bank chief economist and current deputy secretary of the Treasury, who writes, "There are no … limits to carrying capacity of the Earth that are likely to bind at any time in the foreseeable future." And we are talking about the future—nothing can be *proved*.

But we can calculate risks, figure the odds that each side may be right. Joel Cohen made the most thorough attempt to do so in *How Many People Can the Earth Support?* Cohen collected and examined every estimate of carrying capacity made in recent decades, from that of a Harvard oceanographer who thought in 1976 that we might have food enough for 40 billion people to that of a Brown University researcher who calculated in 1991 that we might be able to sustain 5.9 billion (our present population), but only if we were principally vegetarians. One study proposed that if photosynthesis was the limiting factor, the earth might support a trillion people; an Australian economist proved, in calculations a decade apart, that we could manage populations of 28 billion and 157 billion. None of the studies is wise enough to examine every variable, to reach by itself the "right" number. When Cohen compared the dozens of studies, however, he uncovered something pretty interesting: the median low value for the planet's carrying capacity was 7.7 billion people, and the median high value was 12 billion. That, of course, is just the range that the UN predicts we will inhabit by the middle of the next century. Cohen wrote,

The human population of the Earth now travels in the zone where a substantial fraction of scholars have estimated upper limits on human population size…. The possibility must be considered seriously that the number of people on the Earth has reached, or will reach within half a century, the maximum number the Earth can support in modes of life that we and our children and their children will choose to want.

EARTH2

Throughout the 10,000 years of recorded human history the planet—the physical planet—has been a stable place. In every single year of those 10,000 there have been earthquakes, volcanoes, hurricanes, cyclones, typhoons, floods, forest fires, sandstorms, hailstorms, plagues, crop failures, heat waves, cold spells, blizzards, and droughts. But these have never shaken the basic predictability of the planet as a whole. Some of the earth's land areas—the Mediterranean rim, for instance—have been deforested beyond recovery, but so far these shifts have always been local.

Among other things, this stability has made possible the insurance industry—has underwritten the underwriters. Insurers can analyze the risk in any venture because they know the ground rules. If you want to build a house on the coast of Florida, they can calculate with reasonable accuracy the chance that it will be hit by a hurricane and the speed of the winds circling that hurricane's eye. If they couldn't, they would have no way to set your premium—they'd just be gambling. They're always gambling a little, of course: they don't know if that hurricane is coming next year or next century. But the earth's physical stability is the house edge in this casino. As Julian Simon pointed out, "A prediction based on past data can be sound if it is sensible to assume that the past and the future belong to the same statistical universe."

So what does it mean that alone among the earth's great pools of money and power, insurance companies are beginning to take the idea of global climate change quite seriously? What does it mean that the payout for weather-related damage climbed from $16 billion during the entire 1980s to $48 billion in the years 1990–1994? What does it mean that top European insurance executives have begun consulting with Green-peace about global warming? What does it mean that the insurance giant Swiss Re, which paid out $291.5 million in the wake of Hurricane Andrew, ran an ad in the *Financial Times* showing its corporate logo bent sideways by a storm?

These things mean, I think, that the possibility that we live on a new earth cannot be discounted entirely as a fever dream. Above, I showed attempts to calculate carrying capacity for the world as we have always known it, the world we were born into. But what if, all of a sudden, we live on some other planet? On Earth2?

In 1955 Princeton University held an international symposium on "Man's Role in Changing the Face of the Earth." By this time anthropogenic carbon, sulfur, and nitrogen were pouring into the atmosphere, deforestation was already widespread, and the population was nearing three billion. Still, by comparison with the present, we remained a puny race. Cars were as yet novelties in many places. Tropical forests were still intact, as were much of the ancient woods of the West Coast, Canada, and Siberia. The world's economy was a quarter its present size. By most calculations we have used more natural resources since 1955 than in all of human history to that time.

Another symposium was organized in 1987 by Clark University, in Massachusetts. This time even the title made clear what was happening—not "Man and Nature," not "Man's Role in Changing the Face of the Earth," but "The Earth as Transformed by Human Actions." Attendees were no longer talking about local changes or what would take place in the future. "In our judgment," they said, "the biosphere has accumulated, or is on its way to accumulating, such a magnitude and variety of changes that it may be said to have been transformed."

Many of these changes come from a direction that Malthus didn't consider. He and most of his successors were transfixed by *sources*—by figuring out whether and how we could find enough trees or corn or oil. We're good at finding more stuff; as the price rises, we look harder. The lights never did go out, despite many predictions to the contrary on the first Earth Day. We found more oil, and we still have lots and lots of coal. Meanwhile, we're driving big cars again, and why not? As of this writing, the price of gas has dropped below a dollar a gallon across much of the nation. Who can believe in limits while driving a Suburban? But perhaps, like an audience watching a magician wave his wand, we've been distracted from the real story.

That real story was told in the most recent attempt to calculate our size—a special section in *Science* published last summer. The authors spoke bluntly in the lead article. Forget man "transforming" nature—we live, they concluded, on "a human-dominated planet," where "no ecosystem on Earth's surface is free of pervasive human influence." It's not that we're running out of stuff. What we're running out of is what the scientists call "sinks"—places to put the by-products of our large appetites. Not garbage dumps (we could go on using Pampers till the end of time and still have empty space left to toss them away) but the atmospheric equivalent of garbage dumps.

It wasn't hard to figure out that there were limits on how much coal smoke we could pour into the air of a single city. It took a while longer to figure out that building ever higher smokestacks merely lofted the haze farther afield, raining down acid on whatever mountain range lay to the east. Even that, however, we are slowly fixing, with scrubbers and different mixtures of fuel. We can't so easily repair the new kinds of pollution. These do not come from something going wrong—some engine without a catalytic converter, some waste-water pipe without a filter, some smokestack without a scrubber. New kinds of pollution come instead from things going as they're supposed to go—but at such a high volume that they overwhelm the planet. They come from normal human life—but there are so many of us living those normal lives that something abnormal is happening. And that something is so different from the old forms of pollution that it confuses the issue even to use the word.

Consider nitrogen, for instance. Almost 80 percent of the atmosphere is nitrogen gas. But before plants can absorb it, it must become "fixed"—bonded with carbon, hydrogen, or oxygen. Nature does this trick with certain kinds of algae and soil bacteria, and with lightning. Before human beings began to alter the nitrogen cycle, these mechanisms provided 90–150 million metric tons of nitrogen a year. Now human activity adds 130–150 million more tons. Nitrogen isn't pollution—it's essential. And we are using more of it all the time. Half the industrial nitrogen fertilizer used in human history has been applied since 1984. As a result, coastal waters and estuaries bloom with toxic algae while oxygen concentrations dwindle, killing fish; as a result, nitrous oxide traps solar heat. And once the gas is in the air, it stays there for a century or more.

Or consider methane, which comes out of the back of a cow or the top of a termite mound or the bottom of a rice paddy. As a result of our determination to raise more cattle, cut down more tropical forest (thereby causing termite populations to explode), and grow more rice, methane concentrations in the atmosphere are more than twice as high as they have been for most of the past 160,000 years. And methane traps heat—very efficiently.

Or consider carbon dioxide. In fact, concentrate on carbon dioxide. If we had to pick one problem to obsess about over the next fifty years, we'd do well to make it CO_2—which is not pollution either. Carbon *monoxide* is pollution: it kills you if you breathe enough of it. But carbon *dioxide*, carbon with two oxygen atoms, can't do a blessed thing to you. If you're reading this indoors, you're breathing more CO_2 than you'll ever get outside. For generations, in fact, engineers said that an engine burned clean if it produced only water vapor and carbon dioxide.

Here's the catch: that engine produces a *lot* of CO_2. A gallon of gas weighs about eight pounds.

When it's burned in a car, about five and a half pounds of carbon, in the form of carbon dioxide, come spewing out the back. It doesn't matter if the car is a 1958 Chevy or a 1998 Saab. And no filter can reduce that flow—it's an inevitable by-product of fossil-fuel combustion, which is why CO_2 has been piling up in the atmosphere ever since the Industrial Revolution. Before we started burning oil and coal and gas, the atmosphere contained about 280 parts CO_2 per million. Now the figure is about 360. Unless we do everything we can think of to eliminate fossil fuels from our diet, the air will test out at more than 500 parts per million fifty or sixty years from now, whether it's sampled in the South Bronx or at the South Pole.

This matters because, as we all know by now, the molecular structure of this clean, natural, common element that we are adding to every cubic foot of the atmosphere surrounding us traps heat that would otherwise radiate back out to space. Far more than even methane and nitrous oxide, CO_2 causes global warming—the greenhouse effect—and climate change. Far more than any other single factor, it is turning the earth we were born on into a new planet.

Remember, this is not pollution as we have known it. In the spring of last year the Environmental Protection Agency issued its "Ten-Year Air Quality and Emissions Trends" report. Carbon monoxide was down by 37 percent since 1986, lead was down by 78 percent, and particulate matter had dropped by nearly a quarter. If you lived in the San Fernando Valley, you saw the mountains more often than you had a decade before. The air was *cleaner,* but it was also *different*—richer with CO_2. And its new composition may change almost everything.

Ten years ago I wrote a book called *The End of Nature,* which was the first volume for a general audience about carbon dioxide and climate change, an early attempt to show that human beings now dominate the earth. Even then global warming was only a hypothesis—strong and gaining credibility all the time, but a hypothesis nonetheless. By the late 1990s it has become a fact. For ten years, with heavy funding from governments around the world, scientists launched satellites, monitored weather balloons, and studied clouds. Their work culminated in a long-awaited report from the UN's Intergovernmental Panel on Climate Change, released in the fall of 1995. The panel's 2,000 scientists, from every corner of the globe, summed up their findings in this dry but historic bit of understatement: "The balance of evidence suggests that there is a discernible human influence on global climate." That is to say, we are heating up the planet—substantially. If we don't reduce emissions of carbon dioxide and other gases, the panel warned, temperatures will probably rise 3.6° Fahrenheit by 2100, and perhaps as much as 6.3°.

You may think you've already heard a lot about global warming. But most of our sense of the problem is behind the curve. Here's the current news: the changes are already well under way. When politicians and businessmen talk about "future risks," their rhetoric is outdated. This is not a problem for the distant future, or even for the near future. The planet has already heated up by a degree or more. We are perhaps a quarter of the way into the greenhouse era, and the effects are already being felt. From a new heaven, filled with nitrogen, methane, and carbon, a new earth is being born. If some alien astronomer is watching us, she's doubtless puzzled. This is the most obvious effect of our numbers and our appetites, and the key to understanding why the size of our population suddenly poses such a risk.

STORMY AND WARM

What does this new world feel like? For one thing, it's stormier than the old one. Data analyzed last year by Thomas Karl, of the National Oceanic and Atmospheric Administration, showed that total winter precipitation in the United States had increased by 10 percent since 1900 and that "extreme precipitation events"—rainstorms that dumped more than two inches of water in twenty-four hours and blizzards—had increased by 20 percent. That's because warmer air holds more water vapor than the colder atmosphere of the old earth; more water evaporates from the ocean,

meaning more clouds, more rain, more snow. Engineers designing storm sewers, bridges, and culverts used to plan for what they called the "hundred-year storm." That is, they built to withstand the worst flooding or wind that history led them to expect in the course of a century. Since that history no longer applies, Karl says, "there isn't really a hundred-year event anymore … we seem to be getting these storms of the century every couple of years." When Grand Forks, North Dakota, disappeared beneath the Red River in the spring of last year, some meteorologists referred to it as "a 500-year flood"—meaning, essentially, that all bets are off. Meaning that these aren't acts of God. "If you look out your window, part of what you see in terms of the weather is produced by ourselves," Karl says. "If you look out the window fifty years from now, we're going to be responsible for more of it."

Twenty percent more bad storms, 10 percent more winter precipitation—these are enormous numbers. It's like opening the newspaper to read that the average American is smarter by 30 IQ points. And the same data showed increases in drought, too. With more water in the atmosphere, there's less in the soil, according to Kevin Trenberth, of the National Center for Atmospheric Research. Those parts of the continent that are normally dry—the eastern sides of mountains, the plains and deserts—are even drier, as the higher average temperatures evaporate more of what rain does fall. "You get wilting plants and eventually drought faster than you would otherwise," Trenberth says. And when the rain does come, it's often so intense that much of it runs off before it can soak into the soil.

So—wetter and drier. *Different.*

In 1958 Charles Keeling, of the Scripps Institution of Oceanography, set up the world's single most significant scientific instrument in a small hut on the slope of Hawaii's Mauna Loa volcano. Forty years later it continues without fail to track the amount of carbon dioxide in the atmosphere. The graphs that it produces show that this most important greenhouse gas has steadily increased for forty years. That's the main news.

It has also shown something else of interest in recent years—a sign that this new atmosphere is changing the planet. Every year CO_2 levels dip in the spring, when plants across the Northern Hemisphere begin to grow, soaking up carbon dioxide. And every year in the fall decaying plants and soils release CO_2 back into the atmosphere. So along with the steady upward trend, there's an annual seesaw, an oscillation that is suddenly growing more pronounced. The size of that yearly tooth on the graph is 20 percent greater than it was in the early 1960s, as Keeling reported in the journal *Nature,* in July of 1996. Or, in the words of Rhys Roth, writing in a newsletter of the Atmosphere Alliance, the earth is "breathing deeper." More vegetation must be growing, stimulated by higher temperatures. And the earth is breathing earlier, too. Spring is starting about a week earlier in the 1990s than it was in the 1970s, Keeling said....

[It's] not clear that the grain belt will have the water it needs as the climate warms. In 1988, a summer of record heat across the rain belt, harvests plummeted, because the very heat that produces more storms also causes extra evaporation. What *is* clear is that fundamental shifts are under way in the operation of the planet. And we are very early yet in the greenhouse era.

The changes are basic. The freezing level in the atmosphere—the height at which the air temperature reaches 32°F—has been gaining altitude since 1970 at the rate of nearly fifteen feet a year. Not surprisingly, tropical and subtropical glaciers are melting at what a team of Ohio State researchers termed "striking" rates. Speaking at a press conference last spring, Ellen Mosley-Thompson, a member of the Ohio State team, was asked if she was sure of her results. She replied, "I don't know quite what to say. I've presented the evidence. I gave you the example of the Quelccaya ice cap. It just comes back to the compilation of what's happening at high elevations: the Lewis glacier on Mount Kenya has lost forty percent of its mass; in the Ruwenzori range all the glaciers are in massive retreat. Everything, virtually, in Patagonia, except for just a few glaciers, is retreating.... We've seen ... that plants are moving up the mountains.... I frankly don't know what additional evidence you need."

As the glaciers retreat, a crucial source of fresh water in many tropical countries disappears. These areas are "already water-stressed," Mosley-Thompson told the Association of American Geographers last year. Now they may be really desperate.

As with the tropics, so with the poles. According to every computer model, in fact, the polar effects are even more pronounced, because the Arctic and the Antarctic will warm much faster than the Equator as carbon dioxide builds up. Scientists manning a research station at Toolik Lake, Alaska, 170 miles north of the Arctic Circle, have watched average summer temperatures rise by about seven degrees in the past two decades. "Those who remember wearing down-lined summer parkas in the 1970s—before the term 'global warming' existed—have peeled down to T-shirts in recent summers," according to the reporter Wendy Hower, writing in the *Fairbanks Daily News-Miner.* It rained briefly at the American base in McMurdo Sound, in Antarctica, during the southern summer of 1997—as strange as if it had snowed in Saudi Arabia. None of this necessarily means that the ice caps will soon slide into the sea, turning Tennessee into beachfront. It simply demonstrates a radical instability in places that have been stable for many thousands of years. One researcher watched as emperor penguins tried to cope with the early breakup of ice: their chicks had to jump into the water two weeks ahead of schedule, probably guaranteeing an early death. They (like us) evolved on the old earth....

The effects of that warming can be found in the largest phenomena. The oceans that cover most of the planet's surface are clearly rising, both because of melting glaciers and because water expands as it warms. As a result, low-lying Pacific islands already report surges of water washing across the atolls. "It's nice weather and all of a sudden water is pouring into your living room," one Marshall Islands resident told a newspaper reporter. "It's very clear that something is happening in the Pacific, and these islands are feeling it." Global warming will be like a much more powerful version of El Niño that covers the entire globe and lasts forever, or at least until the next big asteroid strikes.

If you want to scare yourself with guesses about what might happen in the near future, there's no shortage of possibilities. Scientists have already observed large-scale shifts in the duration of the El Niño ocean warming, for instance. The Arctic tundra has warmed so much that in some places it now gives off more carbon dioxide than it absorbs—a switch that could trigger a potent feedback loop, making warming ever worse. And researchers studying glacial cores from the Greenland Ice Sheet recently concluded that local climate shifts have occurred with incredible rapidity in the past—188 in one three-year stretch. Other scientists worry that such a shift might be enough to flood the oceans with fresh water and reroute or shut off currents like the Gulf Stream and the North Atlantic, which keep Europe far warmer than it would otherwise be…. In the words of Wallace Broecker, of Columbia University, a pioneer in the field, "Climate is an angry beast, and we are poking it with sticks." But we don't need worst-case scenarios: best-case scenarios make the point. The population of the earth is going to nearly double one more time. That will bring it to a level that even the reliable old earth we were born on would be hard-pressed to support. Just at the moment when we need everything to be working as smoothly as possible, we find ourselves inhabiting a new planet, whose carrying capacity we cannot conceivably estimate. We have no idea how much wheat this planet can grow. We don't know what its politics will be like: not if there are going to be heat waves like the one that killed more than 700 Chicagoans in 1995; not if rising sea levels and other effects of climate change create tens of millions of environmental refugees; not if a 1.58 jump in India's temperature could reduce the country's wheat crop by 10 percent or divert its monsoons….

We have gotten very large and very powerful, and for the foreseeable future we're stuck with the results. The glaciers won't grow back again anytime soon; the oceans won't drop. We've already done deep and systemic damage. To use a human analogy, we've already said the angry and unforgivable words that will haunt our marriage till its end. And yet we can't simply walk out the door. There's no place to go. We have to salvage what we can of our relationship with the earth, to keep things from getting any worse than they have to be.

If we can bring our various emissions quickly and sharply under control, we *can* limit the damage, reduce dramatically the chance of horrible surprises, preserve more of the biology we were born into. But do not underestimate the task. The UN's Intergovernmental Panel on Climate Change projects that an immediate 60 percent reduction in fossil-fuel use is necessary just to stabilize climate at the current level of disruption. Nature may still meet us halfway, but halfway is a long way from where we are now. What's more, we can't delay. If we wait a few decades to get started, we may as well not even begin. It's not like poverty, a concern that's always there for civilizations to address. This is a timed test, like the SAT: two or three decades, and we lay our pencils down. It's *the* test for our generations, and population is a part of the answer….

STUDY QUESTIONS

1. Explain why McKibben thinks we live in a special moment of history. Do you find his arguments cogent and convincing?

2. Doomsdayers have been wrong before in their prediction that the sky is falling. How does McKibben respond to this charge that he and others, like Paul Ehrlich, are unduly pessimistic?

3. What evidence does McKibben bring to bear on the global warming thesis—that humans are responsible for the greenhouse effect, which is having dramatic effects on Earth's climate? How serious is the greenhouse effect?

7

The Tragedy of the Commons

GARRETT HARDIN

Garrett Hardin argues that some social problems have no technical—that is, scientific or technological—solution, but must be addressed by moral and political means. Exponential population growth is one such problem. Hardin calls our attention to a study by the British mathematician William Forster Lloyd (1794–1852), which demonstrates that in nonregulated areas (the "commons") individual rationality and self-interest leads to disaster. Hardin applies Lloyd's study to human population growth and argues that voluntary restriction of population by families is not adequate to deal with this problem, since many will not respond to voluntary procreation limitations. We must have "mutual coercion, mutually agreed upon by the majority of the people affected."

Garrett Hardin (1915–2003) was emeritus professor at the University of California, Santa Barbara, and the author of several works in biology and ethics, including The Limits of Altruism *and* Exploring New Ethics for Survival.

At the end of a thoughtful article on the future of nuclear war, Wiesner and York[1] concluded that: "Both sides in the arms race are … confronted by the dilemma of steadily increasing military power and steadily decreasing national security. *It is our considered professional judgment that this dilemma has no technical solution.* If the great powers continue to look for solutions in the area of science and technology only, the result will be to worsen the situation."

I would like to focus your attention not on the subject of the article (national security in a nuclear world) but on the kind of conclusion they reached, namely that there is no technical solution to the problem. An implicit and almost universal assumption of discussions published in professional and semi-popular scientific journals is that the problem under discussion has a technical solution. A technical solution may be defined as one that requires a change only in the techniques of the natural sciences, demanding little or nothing in the way of change in human values or ideas of morality.

In our day (though not in earlier times) technical solutions are always welcome. Because of previous failures in prophecy, it takes courage to assert that a desired technical solution is not possible. Wiesner and York exhibited this courage; publishing in a science journal, they insisted that the solution to the problem was not to be found in the natural sciences. They cautiously qualified their statement with the phrase, "It is our considered professional judgment…." Whether they were right or not is not the concern of the present article. Rather, the concern here is with the important concept of a class of human problems which can be called "no technical solution problems," and, more specifically, with the identification and discussion of one of these.

Reprinted with permission from *Science*, Vol. 162: 1243–48 (December 1986). Copyright © 1986 by the American Association for the Advancement of Science.

It is easy to show that the class is not a null class. Recall the game of tick-tack-toe. Consider the problem, "How can I win the game of tick-tack-toe?" It is well known that I cannot, if I assume (in keeping with the conventions of game theory) that my opponent understands the game perfectly. Put another way, there is no "technical solution" to the problem. I can win only by giving a radical meaning to the word "win." I can hit my opponent over the head; or I can drug him; or I can falsify the records. Every way in which I "win" involves, in some sense, an abandonment of the game, as we intuitively understand it. (I can also, of course, openly abandon the game—refuse to play it. This is what most adults do.)

The class of "No technical solution problems" has members. My thesis is that the "population problem," as conventionally conceived, is a member of this class. How it is conventionally conceived needs some comment. It is fair to say that most people who anguish over the population problem are trying to find a way to avoid the evils of overpopulation without relinquishing any of the privileges they now enjoy. They think that farming the seas or developing new strains of wheat will solve the problem—technologically. I try to show here that the solution they seek cannot be found. The population problem cannot be solved in a technical way, any more than can the problem of winning the game of tick-tack-toe.

WHAT SHALL WE MAXIMIZE?

Population, as Malthus said, naturally tends to grow "geometrically," or, as we would now say, exponentially. In a finite world this means that the per capita share of the world's goods must steadily decrease. Is ours a finite world?

A fair defense can be put forward for the view that the world is infinite; or that we do not know that it is not. But, in terms of the practical problems that we must face in the next few generations with the foreseeable technology, it is clear that we will greatly increase human misery if we do not, during the immediate future, assume that the world available to the terrestrial human population is finite. "Space" is no escape.[2]

A finite world can support only a finite population; therefore, population growth must eventually equal zero. (The case of perpetual wide fluctuations above and below zero is a trivial variant that need not be discussed.) When this condition is met, what will be the situation of mankind? Specifically, can Bentham's goal of "the greatest good for the greatest number" be realized?

No—for two reasons, each sufficient by itself. The first is a theoretical one. It is not mathematically possible to maximize for two (or more) variables at the same time. This was clearly stated by von Neumann and Morgenstern,[3] but the principle is implicit in the theory of partial differential equations, dating back at least to D'Alembert (1717–1783).

The second reason springs directly from biological facts. To live, any organism must have a source of energy (for example, food). This energy is utilized for two purposes: mere maintenance and work. For man, maintenance of life requires about 1600 kilocalories a day ("maintenance calories"). Anything that he does over and above merely staying alive will be defined as work, and is supported by "work calories" which he takes in. Work calories are used not only for what we call work in common speech; they are also required for all forms of enjoyment, from swimming and automobile racing to playing music and writing poetry. If our goal is to maximize population it is obvious what we must do: We must make the work calories per person approach as close to zero as possible. No gourmet meals, no vacations, no sports, no music, no literature, no art…. I think that everyone will grant, without argument or proof, that maximizing population does not maximize goods. Bentham's goal is impossible.

In reaching this conclusion I have made the usual assumption that it is the acquisition of energy that is the problem. The appearance of atomic energy has led some to question this assumption. However, given an infinite source of energy, population growth still produces an inescapable problem. The problem of the acquisition of energy is replaced by the problem of its dissipation, as J. H. Fremlin has so wittily shown.[4] The arithmetic signs in the analysis are, as it were, reversed; but Bentham's goal is still unobtainable.

The optimum population is, then, less than the maximum. The difficulty of defining the optimum is enormous; so far as I know, no one has seriously tackled this problem. Reaching an acceptable and stable solution will surely require more than one generation of hard analytical work—and much persuasion.

We want the maximum good per person; but what is good? To one person it is wilderness, to another it is ski lodges for thousands. To one it is estuaries to nourish ducks for hunters to shoot; to another it is factory land. Comparing one good with another is, we usually say, impossible because goods are incommensurable. Incommensurables cannot be compared.

Theoretically this may be true; but in real life incommensurables *are* commensurable. Only a criterion of judgment and a system of weighting are needed. In nature the criterion is survival. Is it better for a species to be small and hideable, or large and powerful? Natural selection commensurates the incommensurables. The compromise achieved depends on a natural weighting of the values of the variables.

Man must imitate this process. There is no doubt that in fact he already does, but unconsciously. It is when the hidden decisions are made explicit that the arguments begin. The problem for the years ahead is to work out an acceptable theory of weighting. Synergistic effects, non-linear variation, and difficulties in discounting the future make the intellectual problem difficult, but not (in principle) insoluble.

Has any cultural group solved this practical problem at the present time, even on an intuitive level? One simple fact proves that none has: there is no prosperous population in the world today that has, and has had for some time, a growth rate of zero. Any people that has intuitively identified its optimum point will soon reach it, after which its growth rate becomes and remains zero.

Of course, a positive growth rate might be taken as evidence that a population is below its optimum. However, by any reasonable standards, the most rapidly growing populations on earth today are (in general) the most miserable. This association (which need not be invariable) casts doubt on the optimistic assumption that the positive growth rate of a population is evidence that it has yet to reach its optimum.

We can make little progress in working toward optimum population size until we explicitly exorcize the spirit of Adam Smith in the field of practical demography. In economic affairs, *The Wealth of Nations* (1776) popularized the "invisible hand," the idea that an individual who "intends only his own gain," is, as it were, "led by an invisible hand to promote ... the public interest."[5] Adam Smith did not assert that this was invariably true, and perhaps neither did any of his followers. But he contributed to a dominant tendency of thought that has ever since interfered with positive action based on rational analysis, namely, the tendency to assume that decisions reached individually will, in fact, be the best decisions for an entire society. If this assumption is correct, it justifies the continuance of our present policy of laissez-faire in reproduction. If it is correct we can assume that men will control their individual fecundity so as to produce the optimum population. If the assumption is not correct, we need to reexamine our individual freedoms to see which ones are defensible.

TRAGEDY OF FREEDOM
IN A COMMONS

The rebuttal to the invisible hand in population control is to be found in a scenario first sketched in a little-known pamphlet[6] in 1833 by a mathematical amateur named William Forster Lloyd (1794–1852). We may well call it "the tragedy of the commons," using the word "tragedy" as the philosopher Whitehead used it[7]: "The essence of dramatic tragedy is not unhappiness. It resides in the solemnity of the remorseless working of things." He then goes on to say, "This inevitableness of destiny can only be illustrated in terms of human life by incidents which in fact involve unhappiness. For it is only by them that the futility of escape can be made evident in the drama."

The tragedy of the commons develops in this way. Picture a pasture open to all. It is to be expected that each herdsman will try to keep as many cattle as possible on the commons. Such an arrangement may work reasonably satisfactorily for centuries because tribal wars, poaching, and disease keep the numbers of both man and beast well below the carrying capacity of the land. Finally, however, comes the day of reckoning, that is, the day when the long-desired goal of social stability becomes a reality. At this point, the inherent logic of the commons remorselessly generates tragedy.

As a rational being, each herdsman seeks to maximize his gain. Explicitly or implicitly, more or less consciously, he asks, "What is the utility *to me* of adding one more animal to my herd?" This utility has one negative and one positive component.

1. The positive component is a function of the increment of one animal. Since the herdsman receives all the proceeds from the sale of the additional animal, the positive utility is nearly +1.

2. The negative component is a function of the additional overgrazing created by one or more animal. Since, however, the effects of overgrazing are shared by all the herdsmen, the negative utility for any particular decision-making herdsman is only a fraction of −1.

Adding together the component partial utilities, the rational herdsman concludes that the only sensible course for him to pursue is to add another animal to his herd. And another; and another.... But this is the conclusion reached by each and every rational herdsman sharing a commons. Therein is the tragedy. Each man is locked into a system that compels him to increase his herd without limit—in a world that is limited. Ruin is the destination toward which all men rush, each pursuing his own best interest in a society that believes in the freedom of the commons. Freedom in a commons brings ruin to all.

Some would say that this is a platitude. Would that it were! In a sense, it was learned thousands of years ago, but natural selection favors the forces of psychological denial.[8] The individual benefits as an individual from his ability to deny the truth even though society as a whole, of which he is a part, suffers. Education can counteract the natural tendency to do the wrong thing, but the inexorable success of generations requires that the basis for this knowledge be constantly refreshed.

A simple incident that occurred a few years ago in Leominster, Massachusetts, shows how perishable the knowledge is. During the Christmas shopping season the parking meters downtown were covered with plastic bags that bore tags reading: "Do not open until after Christmas. Free parking courtesy of the mayor and city council." In other words, facing the prospect of an increased demand for already scarce space, the city fathers reinstituted the system of the commons. (Cynically, we suspect that they gained more votes than they lost by this retrogressive act.)

In an approximate way, the logic of the commons has been understood for a long time, perhaps since the discovery of agriculture or the invention of private property in real estate. But it is understood mostly only in special cases which are not sufficiently generalized. Even at this late date, cattlemen leasing national land on the western ranges demonstrate no more than an ambivalent understanding, in constantly pressuring federal authorities to increase the head count to the point where overgrazing produces erosion and weed-dominance. Likewise, the oceans of the world continue to suffer from the survival of the philosophy of the commons. Maritime nations still respond automatically to the shibboleth of the "freedom of the seas." Professing to believe in the "inexhaustible resources of the oceans," they bring species after species of fish and whales closer to extinction.[9]

The National Parks present another instance of the working out of the tragedy of the commons. At present they are open to all, without limit. The parks themselves are limited in extent—there is only one Yosemite Valley—whereas population seems to grow without limit. The values that visitors seek in the parks are steadily eroded. Plainly, we must soon cease to treat the parks as commons or they will be of no value to anyone.

What shall we do? We have several options. We might sell them off as private property. We might keep them as public property, but allocate the right to enter them. The allocation might be on the basis of wealth, by the use of an auction system. It might be on the basis of merit, as defined by some agreed-upon standards. It might be by lottery. Or it might be on a first-come, first-served basis, administered to long queues. These, I think, are all the reasonable possibilities. They are all objectionable. But we must choose—or acquiesce in the destruction of the commons that we call our National Parks.

POLLUTION

In a reverse way, the tragedy of the commons reappears in problems of pollution. Here it is not a question of taking something out of the commons, but of putting something in—sewage, or chemical, radioactive, and heat wastes into water; noxious and dangerous fumes into the air, and distracting and unpleasant advertising signs into the line of sight. The calculations of utility are much the same as before. The rational man finds that his share of the cost of the wastes he discharges into the commons is less than the cost of purifying his wastes before releasing them. Since this is true for everyone, we are locked into a system of "fouling our own nest," so long as we behave only as independent, rational, free-enterprisers.

The tragedy of the commons as a food basket is averted by private property, or something formally like it. But the air and waters surrounding us cannot readily be fenced, and so the tragedy of the commons as a cesspool must be prevented by different means, by coercive laws or taxing devices that make it cheaper for the polluter to treat his pollutants than to discharge them untreated. We have not progressed as far with the solution of this problem as we have with the first. Indeed, our particular concept of private property, which deters us from exhausting the positive resources of the earth, favors

pollution. The owner of a factory on the bank of a stream—whose property extends to the middle of the stream—often has difficulty seeing why it is not his natural right to muddy the waters flowing past his door. The law, always behind the times, requires elaborate stitching and fitting to adapt it to this newly perceived aspect of the commons.

The pollution problem is a consequence of population. It did not much matter how a lonely American frontiersman disposed of his waste. "Flowing water purifies itself every 10 miles," my grandfather used to say, and the myth was near enough to the truth when he was a boy, for there were not too many people. But as population became denser, the natural chemical and biological recycling processes became overloaded, calling for a redefinition of property rights.

HOW TO LEGISLATE TEMPERANCE?

Analysis of the pollution problem as a function of population density uncovers a not generally recognized principle of morality, namely: *the morality of an act is a function of the state of the system at the time it is performed.*[10] Using the commons as a cesspool does not harm the general public under frontier conditions, because there is no public; the same behavior in a metropolis is unbearable. A hundred and fifty years ago a plainsman could kill an American bison, cut out only the tongue for his dinner, and discard the rest of the animal. He was not in any important sense being wasteful. Today, with only a few thousand bison left, we would be appalled at such behavior.

In passing, it is worth noting that the morality of an act cannot be determined from a photograph. One does not know whether a man killing an elephant or setting fire to the grassland is harming others until one knows the total system in which his act appears. "One picture is worth a thousand words" said an ancient Chinese; but it may take 10,000 words to validate it. It is as tempting to ecologists as it is to reformers in general to try to persuade others by way of the photographic shortcut.

But the essence of an argument cannot be photographed: it must be presented rationally—in words.

That morality is system-sensitive escaped the attention of most codifiers of ethics in the past. "Thou shalt not …" is the form of traditional ethical directives which make no allowance for particular circumstances. The laws of our society follow the pattern of ancient ethics, and therefore are poorly suited to governing a complex, crowded, changeable world. Our epicyclic solution is to augment statutory law with administrative law. Since it is practically impossible to spell out all the conditions under which it is safe to burn trash in the backyard or to run an automobile without smog-control, by law we delegate the details to bureaus. The result is administrative law, which is rightly feared for an ancient reason—*Quis custodiet ipsos custodes?*—"Who shall watch the watchers themselves?" John Adams said that we must have "a government of laws and not men." Bureau administrators, trying to evaluate the morality of acts in the total system, are singularly liable to corruption, producing a government by men, not laws.

Prohibition is easy to legislate (though not necessarily to enforce); but how do we legislate temperance? Experience indicates that it can be accomplished best through the mediation of administrative law. We limit possibilities unnecessarily if we suppose that the sentiment of *Quis custodiet* denies us the use of administrative law. We should rather retain the phrase as a perpetual reminder of fearful dangers we cannot avoid. The great challenge facing us now is to invent the corrective feedbacks that are needed to keep custodians honest. We must find ways to legitimate the needed authority of both the custodians and the corrective feedbacks.

FREEDOM TO BREED
IS INTOLERABLE

The tragedy of the commons is involved in population problems in another way. In a world governed solely by the principle of "dog eat dog"—if indeed there ever was such a world—how many children a family had would not be a matter of public concern. Parents who bred too exuberantly would leave fewer descendants, not more, because they would be unable to care adequately for their children. David Lack and others have found that such a negative feedback demonstrably controls the fecundity of birds.[11] But men are not birds, and have not acted like them for millenniums, at least.

If each human family were dependent only on its own resources; *if* the children of improvident parents starved to death; *if,* thus, overbreeding brought its own "punishment" to the germ line— *then* there would be no public interest in controlling the breeding of families. But our society is deeply committed to the welfare state,[12] and hence is confronted with another aspect of the tragedy of the commons.

In a welfare state, how shall we deal with the family, the religion, the race, or the class (or indeed any distinguishable and cohesive group) that adopts overbreeding as a policy to secure its own aggrandizement?[13] To couple the concept of freedom to breed with the belief that everyone born has an equal right to the commons is to lock the world into a tragic course of action.

Unfortunately this is just the course of action that is being pursued by the United Nations. In late 1967, some 30 nations agreed to the following[14]:

> The Universal Declaration of Human Rights describes the family as the natural and fundamental unit of society. It follows that any choice and decision with regard to the size of the family must irrevocably rest with the family itself, and cannot be made by anyone else.

It is painful to have to deny categorically the validity of this right; denying it, one feels as uncomfortable as a resident of Salem, Massachusetts, who denied the reality of witches in the 17th century. At the present time, in liberal quarters, something like a taboo acts to inhibit criticism of the United Nations. There is a feeling that the United Nations is "our last and best hope," that we shouldn't find fault with it; we shouldn't play into the hands of the archconservatives. However, let us not forget what Robert Louis Stevenson said: "The truth that is suppressed by friends is the readiest weapon of the enemy." If we love the truth we must openly deny the validity of the Universal Declaration of Human Rights, even though it is promoted by the United Nations. We should also join with Kingsley Davis[15] in attempting to get Planned Parenthood–World Population to see the error of its ways in embracing the same tragic ideal.

CONSCIENCE IS SELF-ELIMINATING

It is a mistake to think that we can control the breeding of mankind in the long run by an appeal to conscience. Charles Galton Darwin made this point when he spoke on the centennial of the publication of his grandfather's great book. The argument is straightforward and Darwinian.

People vary. Confronted with appeals to limit breeding, some people will undoubtedly respond to the plea more than others. Those who have more children will produce a larger fraction of the next generation than those with more susceptible consciences. The difference will be accentuated, generation by generation.

In C. G. Darwin's words: "It may well be that it would take hundreds of generations for the progenitive instinct to develop in this way, but if it should do so, nature would have taken her revenge, and the variety *Homo contracipiens* would become extinct and would be replaced by the variety *Homo progenitivus*."[16]

The argument assumes that conscience or the desire for children (no matter which) is hereditary—but hereditary only in the most general formal sense. The result will be the same whether the attitude is transmitted through germ cells, or exosomatically, to use A. J. Lotka's term. (If one denies the latter possibility as well as the former, then what's the point of education?) The argument has here been stated in the context of the population problem, but it applies equally well to any instance in which society appeals to an individual exploiting a commons to restrain himself for the general good—by means of his conscience. To make such an appeal is to set up a selective system that works toward the elimination of conscience from the race.

PATHOGENIC EFFECTS
OF CONSCIENCE

The long-term disadvantage of an appeal to conscience should be enough to condemn it; it has serious short-term disadvantages as well. If we ask a man who is exploiting a commons to desist "in the name of conscience," what are we saying to him? What does he hear?—not only at the moment but also in the wee small hours of the night when, half asleep, he remembers not merely the words we used but also the nonverbal communication cues we gave him unawares? Sooner or later, consciously or subconsciously, he senses that he has received two communications and that they are contradictory: (i) (intended communication) "If you don't do as we ask, we will openly condemn you for not acting like a responsible citizen"; (ii) (the unintended communication) "If you *do* behave as we ask, we will secretly condemn you for a simpleton who can be shamed into standing aside while the rest of us exploit the commons."

Every man then is caught in what Bateson has called a "double bind." Bateson and his coworkers have made a plausible case for viewing the double bind as an important causative factor in the genesis of schizophrenia.[17] The double bind may not always be so damaging, but it always endangers the mental health of anyone to whom it is applied. "A bad conscience," said Nietzsche, "is a kind of illness."

To conjure up a conscience in others is tempting to anyone who wishes to extend his control beyond the legal limits. Leaders at the highest level succumb to this temptation. Has any President during the past generation failed to call on labor unions to moderate voluntarily their demands for higher wages, or to steel companies to honor voluntary guidelines on prices? I can recall none. The rhetoric used on such occasions is designed to produce feelings of guilt in noncooperators.

For centuries it was assumed without proof that guilt was a valuable, perhaps even indispensable, ingredient of the civilized life. Now, in this post-Freudian world, we doubt it.

Paul Goodman speaks from the modern point of view when he says: "No good has ever come from feeling guilty, neither intelligence, policy, nor compassion. The guilty do not pay attention to the object but only to themselves, and not even to their own interests, which might make sense, but to their anxieties."[18]

One does not have to be a professional psychiatrist to see the consequences of anxiety. We in the Western world are just emerging from a dreadful two-centuries-long Dark Ages of Eros that was sustained partly by prohibition laws, but perhaps more effectively by the anxiety-generating mechanisms of education. Alex Comfort has told the story well in *The Anxiety Makers*[19]; it is not a pretty one.

Since proof is difficult, we may even concede that the results of anxiety may sometimes, from certain points of view, be desirable. The larger question we should ask is whether, as a matter of policy, we should ever encourage the use of a technique the tendency (if not the intention) of which is psychologically pathogenic. We hear much talk these days of responsible parenthood; the coupled words are incorporated into the titles of some organizations devoted to birth control. Some people have proposed massive propaganda campaigns to instill responsibility into the nation's (or the world's) breeders. But what is the meaning of the word responsibility in this context? Is it not merely a synonym for the word conscience? When we use the word responsibility in the absence of substantial sanctions are we not trying to browbeat a free man in a commons into acting against his own interest? Responsibility is a verbal counterfeit for a substantial *quid pro quo*. It is an attempt to get something for nothing.

If the word responsibility is to be used at all, I suggest that it be in the sense Charles Frankel uses it.[20] "Responsibility," says this philosopher, "is the product of definite social arrangements." Notice that Frankel calls for social arrangements—not propaganda.

MUTUAL COERCION MUTUALLY AGREED UPON

The social arrangements that produce responsibility are arrangements that create coercion, of some sort. Consider bank-robbing. The man who takes money from a bank acts as if the bank were a commons. How do we prevent such action? Certainly not by trying to control his behavior solely by a verbal appeal to his sense of responsibility. Rather than rely on propaganda we follow Frankel's lead and insist that a bank is not a commons; we seek the definite social arrangements that will keep it from becoming a commons. That we thereby infringe on the freedom of would-be robbers we neither deny nor regret.

The morality of bank-robbing is particularly easy to understand because we accept complete prohibition of this activity. We are willing to say "Thou shalt not rob banks," without providing for exceptions. But temperance also can be created by coercion. Taxing is a good coercive device. To keep downtown shoppers temperate in their use of parking space we introduce parking meters for short periods, and traffic fines for longer ones. We need not actually forbid a citizen to park as long as he wants to; we need merely make it increasingly expensive for him to do so. Not prohibition, but carefully biased options are what we offer him. A Madison Avenue man might call this persuasion; I prefer the greater candor of the word coercion.

Coercion is a dirty word to most liberals now, but it need not forever be so. As with the four-letter words, its dirtiness can be cleansed away by exposure to light, by saying it over and over without apology or embarrassment. To many, the word coercion implies arbitrary decisions of distant and irresponsible bureaucrats; but this is not a necessary part of its meaning. The only kind of coercion I recommend is mutual coercion, mutually agreed upon by the majority of the people affected.

To say that we mutually agree to coercion is not to say that we are required to enjoy it, or even to pretend we enjoy it. Who enjoys taxes? We all grumble about them. But we accept compulsory taxes because we recognize that voluntary taxes would favor the conscienceless. We institute and (grumblingly) support taxes and other coercive devices to escape the horror of the commons.

An alternative to the commons need not be perfectly just to be preferable. With real estate and other material goods, the alternative we have chosen is the institution of private property coupled with legal inheritance. Is this system perfectly just? As a genetically trained biologist I deny that it is. It seems to me that, if there are to be differences in individual inheritance, legal possession should be perfectly correlated with biological inheritance—that those who are biologically more fit to be the custodians of property and power should legally inherit more. But genetic recombination continually makes a mockery of the doctrine of "like father, like son" implicit in our laws of legal inheritance. An idiot can inherit millions, and a trust fund can keep his estate intact. We must admit that our legal system of private property plus inheritance is unjust—but we put up with it because we are not convinced, at the moment, that anyone has invented a better system. The alternative of the commons is too horrifying to contemplate. Injustice is preferable to total ruin.

It is one of the peculiarities of the warfare between reform and the status quo that it is thoughtlessly governed by a double standard. Whenever a reform measure is proposed it is often defeated when its opponents triumphantly discover a flaw in it. As Kingsley Davis has pointed out,[21] worshippers of the status quo sometimes imply that no reform is possible without unanimous agreement, an implication contrary to historical fact. As nearly as I can make out, automatic rejection of proposed reforms is based on one of two unconscious assumptions: (i) that the status quo is perfect; or (ii) that the choice we face is between reform and no action; if the proposed reform is imperfect, we presumably should take no action at all, while we wait for a perfect proposal.

But we can never do nothing. That which we have done for thousands of years is also action. It also produces evils. Once we are aware that the status quo is action, we can then compare its discoverable advantages and disadvantages with the predicted advantages and disadvantages of the proposed reform, discounting as best we can for our lack of experience. On the basis of such a comparison, we can make a rational decision which will not involve the unworkable assumption that only perfect systems are tolerable.

RECOGNITION OF NECESSITY

Perhaps the simplest summary of this analysis of man's population problems is this: the commons, if justifiable at all, is justifiable only under conditions of low-population density. As the human population has increased, the commons has had to be abandoned in one aspect after another.

First we abandoned the commons in food gathering, enclosing farm land and restricting pastures and hunting and fishing areas. These restrictions are still not complete throughout the world.

Somewhat later we saw that the commons as a place for water disposal would also have to be abandoned. Restrictions on the disposal of domestic sewage are widely accepted in the Western world; we are still struggling to close the commons to pollution by automobiles, factories, insecticide sprayers, fertilizing operations, and atomic energy installations.

In a still more embryonic state is our recognition of the evils of the commons in matters of pleasure. There is almost no restriction on the propagation of sound waves in the public medium. The shopping public is assaulted with mindless music, without its consent. Our government is paying out billions of dollars to create supersonic transport which will disturb 50,000 people for every one person who is whisked from coast to coast 3 hours faster. Advertisers muddy the airwaves of radio and television and pollute the view of travelers. We are a long way from outlawing the commons in matters of pleasure. Is this because our Puritan inheritance makes us view pleasure as something of a sin, and pain (that is, the pollution of advertising) as the sign of virtue?

Every new enclosure of the commons involves the infringement of somebody's personal liberty. Infringements made in the distant past are accepted because no contemporary complains of a loss. It is the newly proposed infringements that we vigorously oppose; cries of "rights" and "freedom" fill the air. But what does "freedom" mean? When men mutually agreed to pass laws against robbing, mankind became more free, not less so. Individuals locked into the logic of the commons are free only to bring on universal ruin; once they see the necessity of mutual coercion, they become free to pursue other goals. I believe it was Hegel who said, "Freedom is the recognition of necessity."

The most important aspect of necessity that we must now recognize is the necessity of abandoning the commons in breeding. No technical solution can rescue us from the misery of overpopulation. Freedom to breed will bring ruin to all. At the moment, to avoid hard decisions many of us are tempted to propagandize for conscience and responsible parenthood. The temptation must be resisted, because an appeal to independently acting consciences selects for the disappearance of all conscience in the long run, and an increase in anxiety in the short.

The only way we can preserve and nurture other and more precious freedoms is by relinquishing the freedom to breed, and that very soon. "Freedom is the recognition of necessity"—and it is the role of education to reveal to all the necessity of abandoning the freedom to breed. Only so, can we put an end to this aspect of the tragedy of the commons.

NOTES

1. J. B. Wiesner and H. F. York, *Sci. Amer.* 211 (No. 44), 27 (1964).

2. G. Hardin, *J. Hered.* 50, 68 (1959); S. von Hoernor, *Science* 137, 18 (1962).

3. J. von Neumann and O. Morgenstern, *Theory of Games and Economic Behavior* (Princeton Univ. Press, Princeton, NJ, 1947), p. 11.

4. J. H. Fremlin, *New Sci.,* No. 415 (1964), p. 285.

5. A. Smith, *The Wealth of Nations* (Modern Library, New York, 1937), p. 423.

6. W. F. Lloyd, *Two Lectures on the Checks to Population* (Oxford Univ. Press, Oxford, England, 1833), reprinted (in part) in *Population, Evolution, and Birth Control,* G. Hardin, Ed. (Freeman, San Francisco, 1964), p. 37.

7. A. N. Whitehead, *Science and the Modern World* (Mentor, New York, 1948), p. 17.

8. G. Hardin, Ed., *Population, Evolution and Birth Control* (Freeman, San Francisco, 1964), p. 56.

9. S. McVay, *Sci. Amer.* 216 (No. 8), 13 (1966).

10. J. Fletcher, *Situation Ethics* (Westminster, Philadelphia, 1966).

11. D. Lack, *The Natural Regulation of Animal Numbers* (Clarendon Press, Oxford, 1954).

12. H. Girvetz, *From Wealth to Welfare* (Stanford Univ. Press, Stanford, Calif., 1950).

13. G. Hardin, *Perspec. Biol. Med.* 6, 366 (1963).

14. U Thant, *Int. Planned Parenthood News,* No. 168 (February 1968), p. 3.

15. K. Davis, *Science,* 158, 730 (1967).

16. S. Tax, Ed., *Evolution After Darwin* (Univ. of Chicago Press, Chicago, 1960), vol. 2, p. 469.

17. G. Bateson, D. D. Jackson, J. Haley, and J. Weakland, *Behav. Sci.* 1, 251 (1956).

18. P. Goodman, *New York Rev. Books* 1968, 10 (8), 22 (23 May 1968).

19. A. Comfort, *The Anxiety Makers* (Nelson, London, 1967).

20. C. Frankel, *The Case for Modern Man* (Harper, New York, 1955), p. 203.

21. J. D. Roslansky, *Genetics and the Future of Man* (Appleton-Century-Crofts, New York, 1966), p. 177.

STUDY QUESTIONS

1. What does Hardin mean when he says that the problem of population growth has no technical solution?

2. Explain the idea of the "tragedy of the commons" as first set forth by William Forster Lloyd. How does it work?

3. What does Hardin mean when he says, "Freedom in a commons brings ruin to all"? How does he define true "freedom" at the end of his essay?

4. How does Hardin apply the tragedy of the commons to human population growth? Do you agree with his analysis? Explain.

5. What does Hardin mean by "conscience is self-eliminating"? What is wrong with appealing to conscience to solve environmental problems?

6. How serious is the current population growth? What do you think should be done about it?

8

The Unjust War against Population

JACQUELINE KASUN

Jacqueline Kasun is professor of economics at Humboldt State University in Arcata, California. Her writings have appeared in The Wall Street Journal, The American Spectator, *and* The Christian Science Monitor. *She is the author of* The War against Population *(1988) from which this selection is taken.*

Kasun argues that Doomsdayers like the Smithsonian Institution and Garrett Hardin are carrying out an irrational campaign against our freedom to propagate. The idea that humanity is multiplying at a horrendous rate is one of the unexamined dogmas of our time. Kasun offers evidence to the contrary and charges the Doomsdayers with bad faith and with attempting to take control of our families, churches, and other voluntary institutions around the globe.

It was a traveling exhibit for schoolchildren. Titled "Population: The Problem Is Us," it toured the country at government expense in the mid-1970s. It consisted of a set of illustrated panels with an accompanying script that stated:

… there are too many people in the world. We are running out of space. We are running out of energy. We are running out of food. And, although too few people seem to realize it, we are running out of time.[1]

Reprinted from *The War Against Population* (San Francisco: Ignatius, 1988) by permission. Notes edited.

It told the children that "the birth rate must decrease and/or the death rate must increase" since resources were all but exhausted and mass starvation loomed. It warned that, "driven by starvation, people have been known to eat dogs, cats, bird droppings, and even their own children," and it featured a picture of a dead rat on a dinner plate as an example of future "food sources." Overpopulation, it threatened, would lead not only to starvation and cannibalism but to civil violence and nuclear war.

The exhibit was created at the Smithsonian Institution, the national museum of the U.S. government, using federal funds provided by the National Science Foundation, an agency of the U.S. government.

Concurrently, other American schoolchildren were also being treated to federally funded "population education," instructing them on "the growing pressures on global resources, food, jobs, and political stability." They read Paul Ehrlich's book, *The Population Bomb.* They were taught, falsely, that "world population is increasing at a rate of 2 percent per year whereas the food supply is increasing at a rate of 1 percent per year," and equally falsely, that "population growth and rising affluence have reduced reserves of the world's minerals." They viewed slides of the "biological catastrophes" that would result from overpopulation and held class discussions on "what responsible individuals in a 'crowded world' should or can do about population growth." They learned that the world is like a spaceship or a crowded lifeboat, to deduce the fate of mankind, which faces a "population crisis." And then, closer to home, they learned that families who have children are adding to the problems of overpopulation, and besides, children are a costly burden who "need attention … 24 hours a day" and spoil marriages by making their fathers "jealous" and rendering their mothers "depleted." They were told to "say good-bye" to numerous wildlife species doomed to extinction as a result of the human population explosion.

This propaganda campaign in the public schools, which indoctrinated a generation of children, was federally funded, despite the fact that no law had committed the United States to this policy. Nor, indeed, had agreement been reached among informed groups that the problem of "overpopulation" even existed. To the contrary, during the same period the government drive against population was gaining momentum, contrary evidence was proliferating. One of the world's most prominent economic demographers, Colin Clark of Oxford University, published a book titled *Population Growth: The Advantages;* and economists Peter Bauer and Basil Yamey of the London School of Economics discovered that the population scare "relies on misleading statistics … misunderstands the determinants of economic progress … misinterprets the causalities in changes in fertility and changes in income" and "envisages children exclusively as burdens." Moreover, in his major study of The *Economics of Population Growth,* Julian Simon found that population growth was economically beneficial. Other economists joined in differing from the official antinatalist position.

Commenting on this body of economic findings, Paul Ehrlich, the biologist-author of *The Population Bomb,* charged that economists "continue to whisper in the ears of politicians all kinds of nonsense." If not on the side of the angels, Ehrlich certainly found himself on the side of the U.S. government, which since the mid-1960s has become increasingly committed to a worldwide drive to reduce the growth of population. It has absorbed rapidly increasing amounts of public money, as well as the energies of a growing number of public agencies and publicly subsidized private organizations.

The spirit of the propaganda has permeated American life at all levels, from the highest reaches of the federal bureaucracy to the chronic reporting of overpopulation problems by the media and the population education being pushed in public schools. It has become so much a part of daily American life that its presuppositions and implications are scarcely examined; though volumes are regularly published on the subject, they rarely do more than restate the assumptions as a prelude to proposing even "better" methods of population planning.

But even more alarming are some neglected features inherent in the proposed needs and the probable results of population planning. The factual errors are egregious, true, and the alarmists err when they claim that world food output per person and world mineral reserves are decreasing—that, indeed, the human economic prospect has been growing worse rather than more secure and prosperous by all available objective standards. But these are not the most significant claims made by the advocates of government population planning. The most fundamental, which is often tacit rather than explicit, is that the world faces an unprecedented problem of "crisis" proportions that defies all familiar methods of solution.

Specifically, it is implied that the familiar human response to scarcity—that of economizing—is inadequate under the "new" conditions. Thus the economist's traditional reliance on the individual's ability to choose in impersonal markets is disqualified. Occasionally it is posited that the market mechanism will fail due to "externalities," but it is more often said that mankind is entering by a quantum leap into a new age in which all traditional methods and values are inapplicable. Sometimes it is implied that the uniqueness of this new age inheres in its new technology, and at other times that human nature itself is changing in fundamental respects.

Whatever the cause of this leap into an unmapped future, the widely held conclusion is that since all familiar human institutions are failing and will continue to fail in the "new" circumstances, they must be abandoned and replaced. First among these supposedly failing institutions is the market mechanism, that congeries of institutions and activities by which individuals and groups carry out production and make decisions about the allocation of resources and the distribution of income. Not only the market, but democratic political institutions as well are held to be manifestly unsuitable for the "new" circumstances. Even the traditional family is labeled for extinction because of its inability to adapt to the evolving situation. The new school family life and sex education programs, for example, stress the supposed decline of the traditional

family—heterosexual marriage, blood or adoptive relationships—and its replacement by new, "optional" forms, such as communes and homosexual partnerships. Unsurprisingly, traditional moral and ethical teachings must be abandoned.

The decision to repudiate the market is of interest not only to economists but to both those capitalists and market socialists who have seen how impersonal markets can mediate the innate conflict between consumer desires and resource scarcity. The most elegant models of socialism have incorporated the market mechanism into their fundamental design. Adam Smith's "invisible hand," which leads men to serve one another and to economize in their use of resources as they pursue their own self-interest, is relied upon to a considerable extent in a number of socialist countries. John Maurice Clark called it "our main safeguard against exploitation" because it performs "the simple miracle whereby each one increases his gains by increasing his services rather than by reducing them," and Walter Eucken said it protects individuals by breaking up the great concentrations of economic power. The common element here is, of course, the realization that individual decision-making leads not to chaos but to social harmony.

This view is denied by the population planners and it is here that the debate is, or should be, joined. Why are the advocates of government population planning so sure that the market mechanism cannot handle population growth? Why are they so sure that the market will not respond as it has in the past to resource scarcities—by raising prices so as to induce consumers to economize and producers to provide substitutes? Why can individual families not be trusted to adjust the number of their children to their incomes and thus to the given availability of resources? Why do the advocates of government population control assume that human beings must "overbreed," both to their own detriment and to that of society?

It is occasionally averred that the reason for this hypothetical failure is that individuals do not bear the full costs of their childbearing decisions but transfer a large part to society and therefore tend to have "too many" children. This is a dubious claim, for it overlooks the fact that individual families do not receive all the benefits generated by their childbearing. The lifetime productivity and social contribution of children flows largely to persons other than their parents, which, it might be argued, leads families to have fewer children than would be in the best interests of society. Which of these "externalities" is the more important, or whether they balance one another, is a question that waits not merely for an answer but for a reasoned study.

Another reason commonly given for the alleged failure of personal decisions is that individuals do not know how to control the size of their families. But a deeper look makes it abundantly clear that the underlying reason is that the population planners do not believe that individuals, even if fully informed, can be relied upon to make the proper choice. The emphasis on "outreach" and the incentives that pervade the United States' domestic and foreign population efforts testify to this, as will be shown in more depth shortly.

More important than these arguments, however, is the claim that new advances in technology are not amenable to control by market forces—a traditional argument in favor of socialism. From the time of Saint Simon to that of Veblen and on to our own age, the argument has been advanced that the market forces of supply-and-demand are incapable of controlling the vast powers of modern technology. At the dawn of the nineteenth century Saint Simon called for the redesigning of human society to cope with the new forces being unleashed by science. Only planned organization and control would suffice, he claimed. "Men of business" and the market forces which they represented would have to be replaced by planning "experts." In the middle of the nineteenth century Marx created a theoretic model of the capitalist market that purported to prove that the new technological developments would burst asunder the forms of private property and capitalist markets. Three-quarters of a century later Veblen spoke for the planning mentality when he wrote in 1921:

> The material welfare of the community is unreservedly bound up with the due working of this industrial system, and therefore with its unreserved control by the engineers, who alone are competent to manage it. To do their work as it should be done these men of the industrial general staff must have a free hand, unhampered by commercial considerations....

In our own time, Heilbroner expresses a similar but even more profound distrust of market forces:

> ... the external challenge of the human prospect, with its threats of runaway populations, obliterative war, and potential environmental collapse, can be seen as an extended and growing crisis induced by the advent of a command over natural processes and forces that far exceeds the reach of our present mechanisms of social control.

Heilbroner's position is uniquely modern in its pessimism. Unlike Marx and Veblen, who believed that the profit-seeking aspects of supply-and-demand unduly restricted the new technology from fulfilling its *beneficent* potential, Heilbroner sees the market as incapable of controlling an essentially *destructive* technology. Technology, in Heilbroner's view, brings nuclear arms, industrial pollution, and the reduction in death rates that is responsible for the population "explosion"; all of these stubbornly resist control by the market or by benign technological advance. Heilbroner has little hope that pollution-control technology, for example, will be able to offset the bad effects of industrial pollution.

An additional argument is that mankind is rapidly approaching, or has reached, the "limits to growth" or the "carrying capacity" of an earth with "finite" resources. Far from being a new position, it dates back to Thomas Malthus' *Essay on the Principle of Population* (1798), which held that the growth of population must inevitably outrun the growth of food supply. It must be one of the curiosities of our age that though Malthus' forecast has proved mistaken—that, in fact, the living standards of the average person have reached a level probably unsurpassed in history—doom is still pervasively forecast. The modern literature of "limits" is voluminous, including such works as the much-criticized *Limits to Growth* published by the Club of Rome, and the Carter administration's *Global 2000*. In common, these works predict an impending exhaustion of various world economic resources which are assumed to be absolutely fixed in quantity and for which no substitutes can be found. The world is likened to a "spaceship," as in Boulding's and Asimov's writings; or, even more pessimistically, an overloaded "lifeboat," as in Garrett Hardin's articles.

Now, in the first place, as for the common assumption in this literature that the limits are fixed and known (or, as Garrett Hardin puts it, each country's "lifeboat" carries a sign that indicates its "capacity"), no such knowledge does in fact exist—for the earth, or for any individual country, or with regard to any resource. No one knows how much petroleum exists on earth or how many people can earn their living in Illinois. What is known is that the types and quantities of economic resources are continually changing, as is the ability of given areas to support life. In the same territories in which earlier men struggled and starved, much larger populations today support themselves in comfort. The difference, of course, lies in the *knowledge* that human beings bring to the task of discovering and managing resources.

But then, secondly, the literature of limits rules out all such increasing knowledge. Indeed, in adopting the lifeboat or spaceship metaphor, the apostles of limits not only rule out all new knowledge, but the discovery of new resources, and in fact, virtually all production. Clearly, if the world is really a spaceship or a lifeboat, then both technology and resources are absolutely fixed, and beyond a low limit, population growth would be disastrous. Adherents of the view insist that that limit is either being rapidly approached or has been passed, about which more later. Important here is that even this extreme view of the human situation does not rule out the potential of market forces. Most of mankind throughout history has lived under conditions that would be regarded today as extreme, even

desperate, deprivation. And over the millennia private decisions and private transactions have played an important, often a dominant, role in economic life. The historical record clearly shows that human beings can act and cooperate on their own in the best interests of survival, even under very difficult conditions. But history notwithstanding, the claims that emergencies of one kind or another require the centralized direction of economic life have been recurrent, especially during this century, which, ironically, has been the most economically prosperous. Today's advocates of coercion—the proponents of population control—posit the imminent approach of resource exhaustion, a condition wherein human beings will abandon all semblance of rational and civilized behavior.

To ward off their "emergency," the proponents of population control call for the adoption of measures that they admit would not be normally admissible. This is surely ample reason for a thoughtful and thorough examination of measures already being propagated.

Social and economic planning require an administrative bureaucracy with powers of enforcement. Modern economic analysis clearly shows that there are no impersonal, automatic mechanisms in the public sector that can simply and perfectly compensate for private market "failure." The public alternative is fraught with inequity and inefficiency, which can be substantial and exceedingly important. Although the theory of bureaucratic behavior has received less attention than that of private consumer choice, public administrators have also proved subject to greed, which hardly leads to social harmony. Government employees and contractors have the same incentives to avoid competition and form monopolies as private firms. They can increase their incomes by padding their costs and bloating their projects, and excuse it by exaggerating the need for their services and discrediting alternative solutions.

Managers of government projects have no market test to meet since they give away their products, even force them on an unwilling public, while collecting the necessary funds by force through the tax system. They can use their government grants to lobby for still more grants and to finance legal action to increase their power. They can bribe other bureaucrats and grants recipients to back their projects with the promise of reciprocal services. Through intergovernmental grants and "subventions" they can arrange their financial affairs so that apparently no one is accountable for any given decision or program. In short, the record of bureaucratic behavior confirms the statement of the great socialist scholar Oskar Lange, that "the real danger of socialism is that of a bureaucratization of economic life." The danger may well be more serious than we realize—it could be nothing less than totalitarianism.

Finally, proponents of the "population crisis" believe that not only must the *agencies* and *methods* of control be changed under the "new" circumstances but also the *criteria for choice*. Since, they argue, the technological and demographic developments of the modern age render all traditional standards of value and goodness either obsolete or questionable, these must be revised—under the leadership, of course, of those who understand the implications of the new developments.

Above all, they hold that the traditional concept of the value and dignity of the individual human being must be overhauled. The good of the *species,* as understood fully only by the advocates of the new views, must in all cases supersede the good as perceived and sought after by individuals.

Clearly, in the late twentieth century a worldview has emerged that calls into question not only the presuppositions of much of economics, but some basic political and philosophical thought as well. The history of our age may be determined by the outcome of the confrontation between these views.

It must be emphasized that the essential issue is not birth control or family planning. People have throughout history used various means to determine the size of their families, generating a great deal of discussion and debate. But the critical issue raised by recent history, especially in the United States, is whether government has the right or duty to preside over the reproductive process … for what reasons, to what extent?

Recent official action in the United States has proceeded as if the question had already been answered. The fact is, however, that it has been neither explicitly asked nor discussed, even as we rush toward a future shaped by its affirmative answer. It is this question that must be examined.

SCARCITY OR LIFEBOAT ECONOMICS: WHICH IS RIGHT?

The fact of scarcity is the fundamental concern of economics. As one leading textbook puts it in its opening pages, "wants exceed what is available."[2] It pertains to the rich as well as to the poor, since scarcity is not the same thing as poverty. As another text tells students, "higher production levels seem to bring in their train ever-higher consumption standards. Scarcity remains."[3]

> Yet another explains,
>   we are not able to produce all of
> everything that everyone wants free; thus
> we must "economize" our resources, or
> use them as efficiently as possible …
> human wants, if not infinite, go … far
> beyond the ability of our productive
> resources to satisfy them.…[4]

That scarcity is no less real in affluent societies than in poor ones is explained in more general terms by other economists who stress the need to make *choices* whenever alternatives exist. In the words of McKenzie and Tullock,

> the individual makes **choices** from among
> an array of alternative options … in each
> choice situation, a person must always
> forgo doing one or more things when
> doing something else. Since **cost** is the
> most highly valued alternative forgone, all
> rational behavior involves a cost.[5]

Clearly, the affluent person or society faces a large list of highly valued alternatives, and is likely to have a difficult choice to make—to be more acutely aware of the scarcity and the need to give up one thing in order to have another. It follows that scarcity does not lessen with affluence but is more likely to increase.

Simply put, economists understand scarcity as the inescapable fact that candy bars and ice cream cannot be made out of the same milk and chocolate. A choice must be made, regardless of how much milk and chocolate there is. And the decision to produce milk and chocolate rather than cheese and coffee is another inescapable choice. And so the list continues, endlessly, constituting the core of economics. How to choose what to produce, for whom, and how, is the very stuff of economics.

It is important to notice how different these traditional economic concepts of scarcity and choice are from the notions of "lifeboat economics." In Garrett Hardin's metaphor, the lifeboat's capacity is written on its side. The doomsday literature of limits is shot through with the conceit of absolute capacity, which is alien to economics. Not the least of the differences is that in economics humanity is viewed not only as the *raison d'être* of other forms of wealth but as one of the sources of wealth; human labor and ingenuity are resources, means for creating wealth. In the lifeboat, human beings are pure burdens, straining the capacity of the boat. Which of these views is closer to reality?

Is the earth rapidly approaching or has it surpassed its capacity to support human life? But before delving into the existence and nature of limits, keep in mind that the notion of a limited carrying capacity is not the only argument for population control. The view of people, or at least of more people, as simply a curse or affliction has its adherents. Thus Kingsley Davis writes of the plague, and Paul Ehrlich speaks with obvious repugnance of "people, people, people, people." Other writers, both old and new, attribute, if not a negative, at least a zero value to people. Thus John D. Rockefeller III, submitting the final report of the Commission on Population Growth and the American Future, wrote:

> in the long run, no substantial benefits will result from further growth of the Nation's population, rather ... the gradual stabilization of our population would contribute significantly to the Nation's ability to solve its problems. We have looked for, and have not found, any convincing economic argument for continued population growth. The health of our country does not depend on it, nor does the vitality of business nor the welfare of the average person.[6]

The notion embodied in this statement—that, to validate its claim to existence, a human life should justify itself by contributing to such things as the "vitality of business"—is a perfect example of the utilitarian ethic. Though economics has skirted utilitarianism at times, it was never in this sense, but rather in its belief that human beings could be rational in making choices. Economics has been content to value all things in terms of what they mean to individual human beings; it has never valued human beings in terms of supposedly higher values.

The idea that the earth is incapable of continuing to support human life suffuses United States governmental publications. The House Select Committee on Population reported in 1978 that

> the four major biological systems that humanity depends upon for food and raw materials—ocean fisheries, grasslands, forests, and croplands—are being strained by rapid population growth to the point where, in some cases, they are actually losing productive capacity.[7]

The Carter administration's *Global 2000* report, which was much criticized by research experts, predicted:

> With the persistence of human poverty and misery, the staggering growth of human population, and ever increasing human demands, the possibilities of further stress and permanent damage to the planet's resource base are very real.

Such statements have been duly broadcast by the media despite the facts, which tell a quite different story.

In the first place, world food production has increased considerably faster than population in recent decades. The increase in per capita food output between 1950 and 1977 amounted to either 28 percent or 37 percent, depending on whether United Nations or United States Department of Agriculture figures are used, as Julian Simon has shown. Clearly, this is a very substantial increase. More recent United Nations and U.S. Department of Agriculture data show that world food output has continued to match or outstrip population growth in the years since 1977. Some of the most dramatic increases have occurred in the poorest countries, those designated for "triage" by the apostles of doom. For example, rice and wheat production in India in 1983 was almost three-and-a-half times as great as in 1950. This was considerably more than twice the percentage increase in the population of India in the same period.[8]

In a recent article written at the Harvard Center for Population Studies, Nick Eberstadt calls attention to the great increases in the world food supply in recent decades. He points out that only about 2 percent of the world's population suffers from serious hunger, in contrast to the much larger estimates publicized by the Food and Agricultural Organization of the United Nations in its applications for grants to continue its attempts to "solve" the world hunger problem. Eberstadt notes that the improving world food situation is probably reflected by the fact that "in the past thirty years, life expectancy in the less developed countries, excluding China, has risen by more than a third," and that "in the past twenty years in these same nations, death rates for one-to-four-year-olds, the age group most vulnerable to nutritional setback, have dropped by nearly half."

He points out that the much-decried increase in food imports by some less-developed countries is not a cause for alarm, but actually requires a smaller proportion of their export earnings to finance than in 1960.

In 1980, according to Eberstadt, even the poorest of the less-developed countries had to use less than 10 percent of their export earnings to pay for their food imports. The good news is underscored by the fact that these countries have been able to export their manufactured and other nonfood items so much in recent years that it is profitable—it is the efficient choice—for them to export these products in exchange for food, just as developed countries do.

The recent famine in Africa may seem to belie these optimistic findings. Africa, however, is a continent torn by war; farmers cannot cultivate and reap in battle zones, and enemy troops often seize or burn crops. Collectivist governments, also endemic in Africa, often seize crops and farm animals without regard for farmers' needs. War and socialism are two great destroyers of the food supply in Africa, as they have been in other continents.

The impressive increases in food production that have occurred in recent decades have barely scratched the surface of the available food-raising resources, according to the best authorities. Farmers use less than half of the earth's arable land and only a minute part of the water available for irrigation. Indeed, three-fourths of the world's available cropland requires no irrigation.

How large a population could the world's agricultural resources support using presently known methods of farming? Colin Clark, former director of the Agricultural Economic Institute at Oxford University, classified world land-types by their food-raising capabilities and found that if all farmers were to use the best methods, enough food could be raised to provide an American-type diet for 35.1 billion people, more than seven times the present population. Since the American diet is a very rich one, Clark found that it would be possible to feed three times as many again, or more than twenty-two times as many as now exist, at a Japanese standard of food intake. Clark's estimate assumed that nearly half of the earth's land area would remain in conservation areas, for recreation and the preservation of wildlife.

Roger Revelle, former director of the Harvard Center for Population Studies, estimated that world agricultural resources are capable of providing an adequate diet (2,500 kilocalories per day), as well as fiber, rubber, tobacco, and beverages, for 40 billion people, or eight times the present number.

This, he thought, would require the use of less than one-fourth—compared with one-ninth today—of the earth's ice-free land area. He presumed that average yields would be about one-half those presently produced in the United States Midwest. Clearly, better yields and/or the use of a larger share of the land area would support over 40 billion persons.

Revelle has estimated that the less-developed continents, those whose present food supplies are most precarious, are capable of feeding 18 billion people, or six times their present population. He has estimated that the continent of Africa alone is capable of feeding 10 billion people, which is twice the amount of the present world population and more than twenty times the 1980 population of Africa. He sees "no known physical or biological reason" why agricultural yields in Asia should not be greatly increased. In a similar vein, the Indian economist Raj Krishna has written that

> … the amount of land in India that can be brought under irrigation can still be doubled … Even in Punjab, the Indian state where agriculture is most advanced, the yield of wheat can be doubled. In other states it can be raised three to seven times. Rice yields in the monsoon season can be raised three to 13 times, rice yields in the dry season two to three-and-a-half times, jowar (Indian millet) yields two to 11 times, maize yields two to 10 times, groundnut yields three-and-a-half to five-and-a-half times and potato yields one-and-a-half to five-and-a-half times.[9]

What Mr. Krishna is, in fact, saying is that Indian agriculture is potentially capable of feeding not only the people of India but the entire population of the world!

Revelle sums up his conclusions and those of other experts by quoting Dr. David Hopper, another well-known authority on agriculture:

> The world's food problem does not arise from any physical limitation on potential output or any danger of unduly stressing the environment. The limitations on abundance are to be found in the social and political structures of nations and in the economic relations among them. The unexploited global food resource is there, between Cancer and Capricorn. The successful husbandry of that resource depends on the will and actions of men.[10]

Obviously, such great expansions of output would require large inputs of fertilizer, energy, and human labor, as Revelle puts it:

> Most of the required capital facilities can be constructed in densely populated poor countries by human labor, with little modern machinery: in the process much rural unemployment and under-employment can be alleviated.

In other words, as Clark has noted, future generations can and will build their own farms and houses, just as in the past.

> With regard to fertilizer, Clark has pointed out that the world supply of the basic ingredients, potash and sulphates, is adequate for several centuries, while the third major ingredient, nitrogen, is freely available in the atmosphere, though requiring energy for extraction. Since the world's coal supply is adequate for some 2,000 years, this should pose no great problem. Revelle states that in principle … most—perhaps all—of the energy needed in modern high-yielding agriculture could be provided by the farmers themselves. For every ton of cereal grain there are one to two tons of humanly inedible crop residues with an energy content considerably greater than the food energy in the grain.

Surprisingly, in view of the recurrent alarms about desertification, urban encroachment, and other forces supposedly reducing the amount of world agricultural land, it is actually increasing.

Julian Simon has drawn attention to the data indicating this trend:

> A demographer, Joginder Kumar, found in a study at the University of California at Berkeley that there was 9 percent more total arable land in 1960 than in 1950 in 87 countries for which data were available and which constituted 73 percent of the world's total land area. And United Nations data show a 6 percent rise in the world's arable, permanent cropland from around 1963 to 1977 (the last date for which data are available).[11]

And UN data show a further increase of almost 1 percent between 1977 and 1980. Simon also notes that

> there are a total of 2.3 billion acres in the United States. Urban areas plus highways, nonagricultural roads, railroads, and airports total 61 million acres—just 2.7 percent of the total. Clearly, there is little competition between agriculture and cities and roads.

And that,

> furthermore, between 1.25 million and 1.7 million acres of cropland are being created yearly with irrigation, swamp drainage, and other reclamation techniques. This is a much larger quantity of new farmland than the amount that is converted to cities and highways each year.

Simon's point is significant: a very small share of the total land area is used for urban purposes—less than 3 percent in the United States. This is probably a high percentage by world standards since the United States has a peculiarly sprawling type of development. Doxiadis and Papaioannou have estimated that only three-tenths of 1 percent of the land surface of the earth is used for "human settlements."

Similarly, the biologist Francis P. Felice has shown that all the people in the world could be put into the state of Texas, forming one giant city with a population density less than that of many existing cities, and leaving the rest of the world empty. Each man, woman, and child in the 1984 world population could be given more than 1,500 square feet of land space in such a city (the average home in the United States ranges between 1,400 and 1,800 square feet). If one-third of the space of this city were devoted to parks and one-third to industry, each family could still occupy a single-story dwelling of average U.S. size.

In like vein, R. L. Sassone has calculated that there would be standing room for the entire population of the world within one-quarter of the area of Jacksonville, Florida.

Evidently, if the people of the world are floating in a lifeboat, it is a mammoth one quite capable of carrying many times its present passengers. An observer, in fact, would get the impression that he was looking at an empty boat, since the present occupants take up only a fraction of 1 percent of the boat's space and use less than one-ninth of its ice-free land area to raise their food and other agricultural products. The feeling of the typical air passenger that he is looking down on a mostly empty earth is correct.

On the extremely unlikely assumption that no improvements take place in technology and that population growth continues at its present rate, it will be more than a century and a quarter before world population will approach the limit of the support capacity estimated by Revelle, and almost two centuries before the limit estimated by Clark is reached. And, again on these wild surmises, what will the world be like then? At least one-half of the world's land area will still be in conservation and wildlife areas; and human settlements will occupy no more than 8 percent of the land. In a word, although by our assumptions, average living standards will no longer be able to rise, the boat will still be mostly empty.

Yet despite the optimism for human life in agriculture, and although most of the people in the less-developed world are still engaged in such work, we do live in the industrial age. Among the roughly one-third of the people who live in industrial countries, only a small proportion are farmers. In the

United States, for example, one out of thirty people in the labor force is a farmer.

Even the most superficial view of the industrial economy shows how vastly it differs from the economy of agriculture. It uses a high proportion of fossil fuels and metal inputs; it is relatively independent of climate and seasons; a high proportion of its waste products are "nonbiodegradable"; and it requires clustering rather than dispersal of its productive units, which encourages urbanization. While depending on agriculture for much of its resources, including its initial stock of capital, it has contributed greatly to the productivity and security of agriculture by providing energy, labor-saving machinery, and chemical fertilizers. Above all, perhaps, it has provided agriculture with cheap, fast transportation, so that local crop failures no longer mean famine.

It is generally agreed that industrialization has been important in reducing mortality and hence increasing population. And concerns regarding the limits of industry match those over the capacity of agriculture. How far can we go with the industrial process before we run out of the minerals and energy that are essential to it? How much "disruption" of nature does the industrial system create and how much can the earth and its inhabitants endure?

It is quite evident that, with few exceptions, intellectuals have never much liked the industrial process. Its noise, smoke—its obliteration of natural beauty—have never endeared it to the more genteel classes, or perhaps to anybody. But where its unattractive characteristics were once regarded as an unavoidable cost, given the benefits for human beings, now there is a growing conviction—especially among environmentalists—that these costs are unendurable and could be avoided by simply dispensing with part of the population. This is a simple choice from a set of complex alternatives, which raises much more far-reaching questions than whether we are simply "running out of everything."

First, though, the question: Are we running out of everything? If we are, the industrialization process, as well as all the benefits and problems it creates, will soon be at an end. (For those who

dislike industry this should be good news indeed, though they shy away from the argument.)

On this score, the signs are clear. There is very little probability of running out of anything essential to the industrial process at any time in the foreseeable future. Over the past decades there have been recurrent predictions of the imminent exhaustion of all energy and basic metals, none of which has come about. And properly so, because it is a familiar chemical principle that nothing is ever "used up." Materials are merely changed into other forms. Some of these forms make subsequent recycling easier, others less so. It is cheaper to retrieve usable metals from the city dump than from their original ore, but once gasoline has been burned it cannot be reused as gasoline. Economists gauge the availability of basic materials by measuring their price changes over time. A material whose price has risen over time (allowing for changes in the average value of money) is becoming more scarce, while one whose price has fallen is becoming more abundant, relative to the demand for it. Two major economic studies of the availability of basic metals and fuels found no evidence of increasing scarcity over the period 1870–1972. And in 1984 a group of distinguished resource experts reported that the cost trends of non-fuel minerals for the period 1950–1980 "fail to support the increasing scarcity hypothesis."

> Julian Simon has recently noted the trend of decreasing scarcity for all raw materials:
> An hour's work in the United States has bought increasingly more of copper, wheat, and oil (representative and important raw materials) from 1800 to the present. And the same trend has almost surely held throughout human history. Calculations of expenditures for raw materials as a proportion of total family budgets make the same point even more strongly. These trends imply that the raw materials have been getting increasingly available and less scarce relative to the most important and most fundamental element of life, human work-time. The prices of

raw materials have even been falling relative to consumer goods and the Consumer Price Index. All the items in the Consumer Price Index have been produced with increasing efficiency in terms of labor and capital over the years, but the decrease in cost of raw materials has been even greater than that of other goods, a very strong demonstration of progressively decreasing scarcity and increasing availability of raw materials.[12]

Simon also noted that the real price of electricity had fallen at the end of the 1970s to about one-third its level in the 1920s.

Even the Carter administration's gloomy *Global 2000* report admitted that "the real price of most mineral commodities has been constant or declining for many years," indicating less scarcity. Yet the report, in the face of all the evidence of a historical decline in industrial resource scarcity, trumpets an imminent reversal of the trend and an abrupt increase in the prices and scarcity of raw materials.

Other analysts disagree. As Ansley Coale points out, metals exist in tremendous quantities at lower concentrations. Geologists know that going from a concentration of 6 percent to 5 percent multiplies the available quantities by factors of ten to a thousand, depending on the metal.

Ridker and Cecelski of Resources for the Future are equally reassuring, concluding, "in the long run, most of our metal needs can be supplied by iron, aluminum, and magnesium, all of which are extractable from essentially inexhaustible sources."[13]

Even should scarcities of such materials develop, the economic impact would be small:

metals … are only a small fraction of the cost of finished goods. The same is true with energy…. In the United States, for example, non-fuel minerals account for less than one-half of one percent of the total output of goods and services, and energy costs comprise less than one percent.

In the case of fuels, the United States has currently reduced its own sources of low-cost petroleum. This can hardly be described as a "crisis," since higher-cost petroleum supplies are still available here while large reserves of low-cost petroleum remain and are being discovered in other parts of the world, though cartel influences are presently affecting prices. Extremely large deposits of coal remain in the United States and throughout the world, enough for a thousand years, possibly more than twice that, at foreseeable rates of increase in demand.

Summarizing the conclusions of a group of energy experts in 1984, Simon and Kahn wrote:

Barring extraordinary political problems, we expect the price of oil to go down … there is no basis to conclude … that humankind will ever face a greater shortage of oil in economic terms than it does now; rather, decreasing shortage is the more likely …

Speaking of all kinds of energy, they concluded:

The prospect of running out of energy is purely a bogeyman. The availability of energy has been increasing, and the meaningful cost has been decreasing, over the entire span of humankind's history. We expect this benign trend to continue at least until our sun ceases to shine in perhaps 7 billion years….

Furthermore, the United States has tremendous, unexploited opportunities to economize on energy. Because energy has been so cheap, Americans drive their cars more than any other people and, in some parts of the United States, heat their houses without insulation and even with open windows. A reduction in U.S. energy consumption by one-half would put us on a par with the people of western Europe, whose living standards are as high as ours.

Although history teaches that we can expect great technological changes in the future, the nature of these changes is unknown. To attempt, then, to determine the safe capacity of our lifeboat, it seems the better part of wisdom not to anticipate any miraculous rescues, such as breakthroughs in the use of solar or nuclear power. Old-fashioned as it may seem, the coal on board alone will provide us with energy for at least a millennium, to say nothing of the petroleum and natural gas—and solar and nuclear possibilities—all of which remain substantial.

The message is clear. The boat is extremely well stocked. The industrial system will not grind to a halt for lack of supplies.

But what about the disruption (an obscure term, and so all the more dreaded) supposedly created by population growth and/or industrialization? As Heilbroner puts it: "The sheer scale of our intervention into the fragile biosphere is now so great that we are forced to proceed with great caution lest we inadvertently bring about environmental damage of an intolerable sort."

Man has, of course, been intervening in the biosphere for thousands of years. Perhaps the most massive human intervention was the invention of agriculture. It is not certain that modern industry, which is confined to much smaller areas, is having even an equal effect. Both humanity and the rest of the biosphere have apparently survived the agricultural intervention rather well; in fact, well enough so that our present anxiety is whether too many of us have survived.

"Too many for what?" springs to mind. The fact that more people are now living longer, healthier, better-fed, and more comfortable lives, and have been for many decades, rather suggests that the interventions have been the very opposite of intolerable. According to a number of authorities, the best overall index of environmental quality is life expectancy, which has been increasing throughout the world during this century. It is precisely because of this increase that population has grown even though birth rates have fallen. It is possible, of course, that what the population alarmists really mean is that there are too many *other* people for their taste, or for those who prefer solitude, which is quite another thing....

These and other economists have spelled out the case against the assumptions and teachings of the population-bombers: population growth permits the easier acquisition as well as the more efficient use of the economic infrastructure—the modern transportation and communications systems, and the education, electrification, irrigation, and waste disposal systems. Population growth encourages agricultural investment—clearing and draining land, building barns and fences, improving the water supply. Population growth increases the size of the market, encouraging producers to specialize and use cost-saving methods of large-scale production. Population growth encourages governments, as well as parents, philanthropists, and taxpayers, to devote more resources to education. If wisely directed, these efforts can result in higher levels of competence in the labor force. Larger populations not only inspire more ideas but more *exchanges,* or improvements, of ideas among people, in a ratio that is necessarily more than proportional to the number of additional people. (For example, if one person joins an existing couple, the possible number of exchanges does not increase by one-third but triples.) One of the advantages of cities, as well as of large universities, is that they are mentally stimulating, that they foster creativity.

The arguments and evidence that population growth does not lead to resource exhaustion, starvation, and environmental catastrophe fail to persuade the true believers in the population bomb. They have, after all, other rationalizations for their fears of doom. Another recurring theme of the doomsdayers is, in the words of a public affairs statement by the U.S. Department of State, that population growth increases the size of the "politically volatile age group—those 15–24 years," which contributes to political unrest. Ambassador Richard Elliot Benedick, coordinator of population affairs in the U.S. State Department, spelled out the concern for the Senate Foreign Relations Committee in 1980:

> Rapid population growth ... creates a large proportion of youth in the population. Recent experience, in Iran and other countries, shows that this younger age group—frequently unemployed and crowded into urban slums—is particularly susceptible to

extremism, terrorism, and violence as outlets for frustration.[14]

The ambassador went on to enumerate a long list of countries of economic and strategic importance to the United States where, he claimed, population growth was encouraging "political instability." The list included Turkey, Egypt, Iran, Pakistan, Indonesia, Mexico, Venezuela, Nigeria, Bolivia, Brazil, Morocco, the Philippines, Zimbabwe, and Thailand—countries of special importance to the United States because of their "strategic location, provision of military bases or support, and supply of oil or other critical raw materials." While he admitted that it is "difficult to be analytically precise in pinpointing exact causes of a given historical breakdown in domestic or international order," he nevertheless insisted that "unprecedented demographic pressures" were of great significance.

No results of scientific research support Benedick's belief; it is simply another one of those unverified *assumptions* that advocates of population control rely upon to make their case. It may be, of course, that Ambassador Benedick is right: that the young tend to be more revolutionary and that public bureaucracies who want to stay in power would be wise to encourage the aging of the population through lower birth rates. As public bureaucracies increase their power in this age of growth of government, we may see an increasing manipulation of the population so as to ensure an older and more docile citizenry. However, putting aside the ethical implications and the welfare of society, and speaking only of the self-interest of the ruling bureaucracy, the risks are obvious. Such policy could arouse a deep antagonism among those on the check list, especially if they are citizens of countries who perceive the policy as a tool of outside interference in their most intimate national affairs.

The question, then, is resolved in favor of the economic notion of scarcity rather than the lifeboat model of absolute limits being the more nearly correct. While resources are always scarce relative to the demands that human beings place upon them, there is no indication of imminent, absolute limits. The limits are so far beyond the levels of our present use of resources as to be nearly invisible, and are actually receding as new knowledge develops. Ironically, though, the perception of economic scarcity may increase along with increasing wealth and income. There is no evidence whatsoever that slower rates of population growth encourage economic growth or economic welfare; on the contrary, the developing countries with *higher* rates of population growth have had higher average rates of per-capita-output growth in the period since 1950. It may, of course, be in the interests of a ruling bureaucracy to rid itself of those people it finds troublesome, but the policy can hardly promote the general welfare, and it would prove very costly, even to the ruling elites.

NOTES

1. Projectbook for the Exhibition "Population: The Problem Is Us": A Book of Suggestions or Implementing the Exhibition in Your Own Institution (Washington: The Smithsonian Institution, undated, circulated in late 1970s), p. 9.

2. Armen A. Alchian and William R. Allen, *University Economics,* 3rd ed. (Belmont: Wadsworth Publishing Co., 1972), p. 7.

3. Paul A. Samuelson, *Economics,* 11th ed. (New York: McGraw Hill, 1980), p. 17.

4. George Leland Bach, *Economics: An Introduction to Analysis and Policy,* 10th ed. (Englewood Cliffs: Prentice-Hall, Inc., 1980), p. 3.

5. Richard B. McKenzie and Gordon Tullock, *Modern Political Economy* (New York: McGraw-Hill, 1978), p. 18.

6. John D. Rockefeller III, Letter to the President and Congress, transmitting the Final Report on the Commission on Population Growth and the American Future, dated March 27, 1972.

7. Select Committee on Population, Report, "World Population: Myths and Realities," U.S. House of Representatives, 95th Congress, 2nd Session (Washington: U.S. Government Printing Office, 1978), p. 5.

8. *The Global 2000 Report to the President: Global Future: Time to Act,* prepared by the Council on Environmental Quality and the U.S. Department of State (Washington: U.S. Government Printing Office, January 1981), p. ix.

9. Raj Krishna, "The Economic Development of India," *Scientific American,* vol. 243, no. 3. September 1980, pp. 173–174.

10. Revelle, "The World Supply of Agricultural Land," op. cit., p. 184, quoting W. David Hopper, "The Development of Agriculture in Developing Countries," *Scientific American,* September 1976, pp. 197–205.

11. Julian L. Simon, "Worldwide, Land for Agriculture Is Increasing, Actually," *New York Times,* October 7, 1980, p. 23.

12. Simon, "Global Confusion," op. cit., p. 11.

13. Ronald G. Ridker and Elizabeth W. Cecelski, "Resources, Environment, and Population: The Nature of Future Limits," *Population Bulletin,* vol. 34, no. 3, August 1979, p. 29.

14. Richard Elliot Benedick, Statement before the Senate Foreign Relations Committee, April 29, 1980, reprinted in *Department of State Bulletin,* vol. 80, no. 2042, September 1980, p. 58.

STUDY QUESTIONS

1. How strong is Kasun's case that the "Population Control Industry" is misleading us about the dangers of our present population growth?

2. According to Kasun, what is the truth about population growth in relation to scarcity of resources?

3. Compare Kasun's arguments with Hardin's. Which one has the stronger case, and why?

4. Evaluate the anthropocentric viewpoint in Kasun's essay.

5. Do you think Kasun ignores quality-of-life issues?

9

Lifeboat Ethics

GARRETT HARDIN

A biographical sketch of Garrett Hardin is found at the beginning of Reading 28.
He argues that the proper metaphor that characterizes our global ecological situation is
not "spaceship" but "lifeboat." The spaceship metaphor is misleading since Earth has no

Reprinted from *Bioscience,* Vol. 24, No. 10: 561–8 (October 1974) by permission.

captain to steer it through its present and future problems. Rather, each rich nation is like a lifeboat in an ocean in which the poor of the world are swimming and in danger of drowning. Hardin argues that affluent societies, like lifeboats, ought to ensure their own survival by preserving a safety factor of resources. For a society to give away its resources to needy nations or to admit needy immigrants is like taking on additional passengers who would threaten to cause the lifeboat to capsize. Under these conditions, it is our moral duty to refrain from aiding the poor.

No generation has viewed the problem of the survival of the human species as seriously as we have. Inevitably, we have entered this world of concern through the door of metaphor. Environmentalists have emphasized the image of the earth as a spaceship—Spaceship Earth. Kenneth Boulding ... is the principal architect of this metaphor. It is time, he says, that we replace the wasteful "cowboy economy" of the past with the frugal "spaceship economy" required for continued survival in the limited world we now see ours to be. The metaphor is notably useful in justifying pollution control measures.

Unfortunately, the image of a spaceship is also used to promote measures that are suicidal. One of these is a generous immigration policy, which is only a particular instance of a class of policies that are in error because they lead to the tragedy of the commons. ... These suicidal policies are attractive because they mesh with what we unthinkably take to be the ideals of "the best people." What is missing in the idealistic view is an insistence that rights and responsibilities must go together. The "generous" attitude of all too many people results in asserting inalienable rights while ignoring or denying matching responsibilities.

For the metaphor of a spaceship to be correct the aggregate of people on board would have to be under unitary sovereign control. ... A true ship always has a captain. It is conceivable that a ship could be run by a committee. But it could not possibly survive if its course were determined by bickering tribes that claimed rights without responsibilities.

What about Spaceship Earth? It certainly has no captain, and no executive committee. The United Nations is a toothless tiger, because the signatories of its charter wanted it that way. The spaceship metaphor is used only to justify spaceship demands on common resources without acknowledging corresponding spaceship responsibilities.

An understandable fear of decisive action leads people to embrace "incrementalism"—moving toward reform by tiny stages. As we shall see, this strategy is counterproductive in the area discussed here if it means accepting rights before responsibilities. Where human survival is at stake, the acceptance of responsibilities is a precondition to the acceptance of rights, if the two cannot be introduced simultaneously.

LIFEBOAT ETHICS

Before taking up certain substantive issues let us look at an alternative metaphor, that of a lifeboat. In developing some relevant examples the following numerical values are assumed. Approximately two-thirds of the world is desperately poor, and only one-third is comparatively rich. The people in poor countries have an average per capita GNP (Gross National Product) of about $200 per year; the rich, of about $3,000. (For the United States it is nearly $5,000 per year.) Metaphorically, each rich nation amounts to a lifeboat full of comparatively rich people. The poor of the world are in other, much more crowded lifeboats. Continuously, so to speak, the poor fall out of their lifeboats and swim for a while in the water outside, hoping to be admitted to a rich lifeboat, or in some other way to benefit from the "goodies" on board. What should the passengers on a rich lifeboat do? This is the central problem of "the ethics of a lifeboat."

First we must acknowledge that each lifeboat is effectively limited in capacity. The land of every nation has a limited carrying capacity. The exact limit is a matter for argument, but the energy crunch is convincing more people every day that we have already exceeded the carrying capacity of the land. We have been living on "capital"—stored petroleum and coal—and soon we must live on income alone.

Let us look at only one lifeboat—ours. The ethical problem is the same for all, and is as follows. Here we sit, say 50 people in a lifeboat. To be generous, let us assume our boat has a capacity of 10 more, making 60. (This, however, is to violate the engineering principle of the "safety factor." A new plant disease or a bad change in the weather may decimate our population if we don't preserve some excess capacity as a safety factor.)

The 50 of us in the lifeboat see 100 others swimming in the water outside, asking for admission to the boat, or for handouts. How shall we respond to their calls? There are several possibilities.

One. We may be tempted to try to live by the Christian ideal of being "our brother's keeper," or by the Marxian ideal ... of "from each according to his abilities, to each according to his needs." Since the needs of all are the same, we take all the needy into our boat, making a total of 150 in a boat with a capacity of 60. The boat is swamped, and everyone drowns. Complete justice, complete catastrophe.

Two. Since the boat has an unused excess capacity of 10, we admit just 10 more to it. This has the disadvantage of getting rid of the safety factor, for which action we will sooner or later pay dearly. Moreover, *which* 10 do we let in? "First come, first served?" The best 10? The neediest 10? How do we *discriminate?* And what do we say to the 90 who are excluded?

Three. Admit no more to the boat and preserve the small safety factor. Survival of the people in the lifeboat is then possible (though we shall have to be on our guard against boarding parties).

The last solution is abhorrent to many people. It is unjust, they say. Let us grant that it is.

"I feel guilty about my good luck," say some. The reply to this is simple: *Get out and yield your place to others.* Such a selfless action might satisfy the conscience of those who are addicted to guilt but it would not change the ethics of the lifeboat. The needy person to whom a guilt-addict yields his place will not himself feel guilty about his sudden good luck. (If he did he would not climb aboard.) The net result of conscience-stricken people relinquishing their unjustly held positions is the elimination of their kind of conscience from the lifeboat. The lifeboat, as it were, purifies itself of guilt. The ethics of the lifeboat persist, unchanged by such momentary aberrations.

This then is the basic metaphor within which we must work out our solutions. Let us enrich the image step by step with substantive additions from the real world.

REPRODUCTION

The harsh characteristics of lifeboat ethics are heightened by reproduction, particularly by reproductive differences. The people inside the lifeboats of the wealthy nations are doubling in numbers every 87 years; those outside are doubling every 35 years, on the average. And the relative difference in prosperity is becoming greater.

Let us, for a while, think primarily of the U.S. lifeboat. As of 1973 the United States had a population of 210 million people, who were increasing by 0.8% per year, that is, doubling in number every 87 years.

Although the citizens of rich nations are outnumbered two to one by the poor, let us imagine an equal number of poor people outside our lifeboat—a mere 210 million poor people reproducing at a quite different rate. If we imagine these to be the combined populations of Colombia, Venezuela, Ecuador, Morocco, Thailand, Pakistan, and the Philippines, the average rate of increase of the people "outside" is 3.3% per year. The doubling time of this population is 21 years.

Suppose that all these countries, and the United States, agreed to live by the Marxian ideal, "to each according to his needs," the ideal of most Christians as well. Needs, of course, are determined by population size, which is affected by reproduction. Every nation regards its rate of reproduction as a sovereign right. If our lifeboat were big enough in the beginning it might be possible to live *for a while* by Christian-Marxian ideals. *Might.*

Initially, in the model given, the ratio of non-Americans to Americans would be one to one. But consider what the ratio would be 87 years later. By this time Americans would have doubled to a population of 420 million. The other group (doubling every 21 years) would now have swollen to 3,540 million. Each American would have more than eight people to share with. How could the lifeboat possibly keep afloat?

All this involves extrapolation of current trends into the future, and is consequently suspect. Trends may change. Granted: but the change will not necessarily be favorable. If—as seems likely—the rate of population increase falls faster in the ethnic group presently inside the lifeboat than it does among those now outside, the future will turn out to be even worse than mathematics predicts, and sharing will be even more suicidal.

RUIN IN THE COMMONS

The fundamental error of the sharing ethic is that it leads to the tragedy of the commons. Under a system of private property the men (or group of men) who own property recognize their responsibility to care for it, for if they don't they will eventually suffer. A farmer, for instance, if he is intelligent, will allow no more cattle in a pasture than its carrying capacity justifies. If he overloads the pasture, weeds take over, erosion sets in, and the owner loses in the long run.

But if a pasture is run as a commons open to all, the right of each to use it is not matched by an operational responsibility to take care of it. It is no use asking independent herdsmen in a commons

to act responsibly, for they dare not. The considerate herdsman who refrains from overloading the commons suffers more than a selfish one who says his needs are greater. (As Leo Durocher says, "Nice guys finish last.") Christian-Marxian idealism is counterproductive. That it *sounds* nice is no excuse. With distribution systems, as with individual morality, good intentions are no substitute for good performance.

A social system is stable only if it is insensitive to errors. To the Christian-Marxian idealist a selfish person is a sort of "error." Prosperity in the system of the commons cannot survive errors. If *everyone* would only restrain himself, all would be well; but it takes *only one less than everyone* to ruin a system of voluntary restraint. In a crowded world of less than perfect human beings—and we will never know any other—mutual ruin is inevitable in the commons. This is the core of the tragedy of the commons.

WORLD FOOD BANKS

In the international arena we have recently heard a proposal to create a new commons, namely an international depository of food reserves to which nations will contribute according to their abilities, and from which nations may draw according to their needs. Nobel laureate Norman Borlaug has lent the prestige of his name to this proposal.

A world food bank appeals powerfully to our humanitarian impulses. We remember John Donne's celebrated line, "Any man's death diminishes me." But before we rush out to see for whom the bell tolls let us recognize where the greatest political push for international granaries comes from, lest we be disillusioned later. Our experience with Public Law 480 clearly reveals the answer. This was the law that moved billions of dollars worth of U.S. grain to food-short, population-long countries during the past two decades. When P.L. 480 first came into being, a headline in the business magazine *Forbes* … revealed the power behind it: "Feeding the World's Hungry Millions: How It Will Mean Billions for U.S. Business."

And indeed it did. In the years 1960 and to 1970 a total of $7.9 billion was spent on the "Food for Peace" program as P.L. 480 was called. During the years 1948 to 1970 an additional $49.9 billion were extracted from American taxpayers to pay for other economic aid programs, some of which went for food and food-producing machinery. (This figure does *not* include military aid.) That P.L. 480 was a give-away program was concealed. Recipient countries went through the motions of paying for P.L. 480 food—with IOU's. In December 1973 the charade was brought to an end as far as India was concerned when the United States "forgave" India's $3.2 billion debt.... Public announcement of the cancellation of the debt was delayed for two months: one wonders why.

The search for a rational justification can be short-circuited by interjecting the word "emergency." Borlaug uses this word. We need to look sharply at it. What is an "emergency"? It is surely something like an accident, which is correctly defined as *an event that is certain to happen, though with a low frequency....* A well-run organization prepares for everything that is certain, including accidents and emergencies. It budgets for them. It saves for them. It expects them—and mature decision-makers do not waste time complaining about accidents when they occur.

What happens if some organizations budget for emergencies and others do not? If each organization is solely responsible for its own well-being, poorly managed ones will suffer. But they should be able to learn from experience. They have a chance to mend their ways and learn to budget for infrequent but certain emergencies. The weather, for instance, always varies and periodic crop failures are certain. A wise and competent government saves out of the production of the good years in anticipation of bad years that are sure to come. This is not a new idea. The Bible tells us that Joseph taught this policy to Pharaoh in Egypt more than 2,000 years ago. Yet it is literally true that the vast majority of the governments of the world today have no such policy. They lack either the wisdom or the competence, or

both. Far more difficult than the transfer of wealth from one country to another is the transfer of wisdom between sovereign powers or between generations.

"But it isn't their fault! How can we blame the poor people who are caught in an emergency? Why must we punish them?" The concepts of blame and punishment are irrelevant. The question is, what are the operational consequences of establishing a world food bank? If it is open to every country every time a need develops, slovenly rulers will not be motivated to take Joseph's advice. Why should they? Others will bail them out whenever they are in trouble.

Some countries will make deposits in the world food bank and others will withdraw from it: there will be almost no overlap. Calling such a depository-transfer unit a "bank" is stretching the metaphor of *bank* beyond its elastic limits. The proposers, of course, never call attention to the metaphorical nature of the word they use.

THE RATCHET EFFECT

An "international food bank" is really, then, not a true bank but a disguised one-way transfer device for moving wealth from rich countries to poor. In the absence of such a bank, in a world inhabited by individually responsible sovereign nations, the population of each nation would repeatedly go through a cycle of the sort shown in Figure 1. P_2 is greater than P_1, either in absolute numbers or because a deterioration of the food supply has removed the safety factor and produced a dangerously low ratio of resources to population. P_2 may be said to represent a state of overpopulation, which becomes obvious upon the appearance of an "accident," e.g., a crop failure. If the "emergency" is not met by outside help, the population drops back to the "normal" level—the "carrying capacity" of the environment—or even below. In the absence of population control by a sovereign, sooner or later the population grows to P_2 again and the cycle repeats. The long-term population curve ... is an irregularly fluctuating one, equilibrating more or less about the carrying capacity.

A demographic cycle of this sort obviously involves great suffering in the restrictive phase, but such a cycle is normal to any independent country with inadequate population control. The third-century theologian Tertullian ... expressed what must have been the recognition of many wise men when he wrote: "The scourges of pestilence, famine, wars, and earthquakes have come to be regarded as a blessing to overcrowded nations, since they serve to prune away the luxuriant growth of the human race."

Only under a strong and farsighted sovereign—which theoretically could be the people themselves, democratically organized—can a population equilibrate at some set point below the carrying capacity, thus avoiding the pains normally caused by periodic and unavoidable disasters. For this happy state to be achieved it is necessary that those in power be able to contemplate with equanimity the "waste" of surplus food in times of bountiful harvests. It is essential that those in power resist the temptation to convert extra food into extra babies. On the public relations level it is necessary that the phrase "surplus food" be replaced by "safety factor."

But wise sovereigns seem not to exist in the poor world today. The most anguishing problems are created by poor countries that are governed by rulers insufficiently wise and powerful. If such countries can draw on a world food bank in times of "emergency," the population *cycle* of Figure 1 will be replaced by the population *escalator* of Figure 2. The input of food from a food bank acts as the pawl of a ratchet, preventing the population from retracing its steps to a lower level. Reproduction pushes the population upward, inputs from the world bank prevent its moving downward. Population size escalates, as does the absolute magnitude of "accidents" and "emergencies." The process is brought to an end only by the total collapse of the whole system, producing a catastrophe of scarcely imaginable proportions.

Such are the implications of the well-meant sharing of food in a world of irresponsible reproduction.

All this is terribly obvious once we are acutely aware of the pervasiveness and danger of the commons. But many people still lack this awareness and the euphoria of the "benign demographic transition" ... interferes with the realistic appraisal of pejoristic mechanisms. As concerns public policy, the deductions drawn from the benign demographic transition are these:

1. If the per capita GNP rises the birth rate will fall; hence, the rate of population increase will fall, ultimately producing ZPG (Zero Population Growth).

2. The long-term trend all over the world (including the poor countries) is of a rising per capita GNP (for which no limit is seen).

3. Therefore, all political interference in population matters is unnecessary; all we need to do is

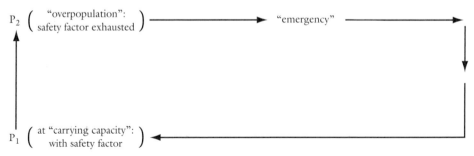

FIGURE 1 The population cycle of a nation that has no effective, conscious population control, and which receives no aid from the outside. P$_2$ is greater than P$_1$.

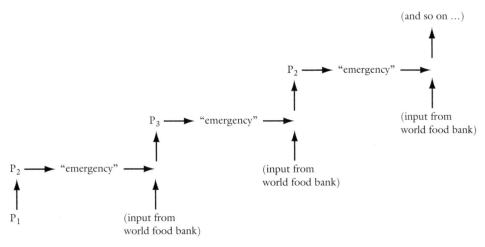

FIGURE 2 The Population Escalator. Note that input from a world food bank acts like the pawl of a ratchet, preventing the normal population cycle shown in Figure 1 from being completed. P_{n+1} is greater than P_n and the absolute magnitude of the "emergencies" escalates. Ultimately the entire system crashes. The crash is not shown, and few can imagine it.

foster economic "development"—*note the metaphor*—and population problems will solve themselves.

Those who believe in the benign demographic transition dismiss the pejoristic mechanism of Figure 2 in the belief that each input of food from the world fosters development within a poor country, thus resulting in a drop in the rate of population increase. Foreign aid has proceeded on this assumption for more than two decades. Unfortunately it has produced no indubitable instance of the asserted effect. It has, however, produced a library of excuses. The air is filled with plaintive calls for more massive foreign aid appropriations so that the hypothetical melioristic process can get started.

The doctrine of demographic laissez-faire implicit in the hypothesis of the benign demographic transition is immensely attractive. Unfortunately there is more evidence against the melioristic system than there is for it.... On the historical side there are many counterexamples. The rise in per capita GNP in France and Ireland during the past century has been accompanied by a rise in population growth. In the 20 years following the Second World War the same positive correlation was noted almost everywhere in the world. Never in world history before 1950 did the worldwide population growth reach 1% per annum. Now the average population growth is over 2% and shows no signs of slackening.

On the theoretical side, the denial of the pejoristic scheme of Figure 2 probably springs from the hidden acceptance of the "cowboy economy" that Boulding castigated. Those who recognize the limitations of a spaceship, if they are unable to achieve population control at a safe and comfortable level, accept the necessity of the corrective feedback of the population cycle shown in Figure 1. No one who knew in his bones that he was living on a true spaceship would countenance political support of the population escalator shown in Figure 2.

ECO-DESTRUCTION VIA THE GREEN REVOLUTION

The demoralizing effect of charity on the recipient has long been known. "Give a man a fish and he will eat for a day: teach him how to fish and he will eat for the rest of his days." So runs an ancient Chinese proverb. Acting on this advice the Rockefeller and Ford Foundations have financed a multipronged program for improving agriculture in the hungry nations. The result, known as the "Green Revolution," has been quite remarkable. "Miracle wheat" and "miracle rice" are splendid technological achievements in the realm of plant genetics.

Whether or not the Green Revolution can increase food production is doubtful …, but in any event not particularly important. What is missing in this great and well-meaning humanitarian effort is a firm grasp of fundamentals. Considering the importance of the Rockefeller Foundation in this effort it is ironic that the late Alan Gregg, a much-respected vice president of the Foundation, strongly expressed his doubts of the wisdom of all attempts to increase food production some two decades ago. (This was before Borlaug's work—supported by Rockefeller—had resulted in the development of "miracle wheat.") Gregg … likened the growth and spreading of humanity over the surface of the earth to the metastasis of cancer in the human body, wryly remarking that "Cancerous growths demand food; but, as far as I know, they have never been cured by getting it."

"Man does not live by bread alone"—the scriptural statement has a rich meaning even in the material realm. Every human being born constitutes a draft on all aspects of the environment—food, air, water, unspoiled scenery, occasional and optional solitude, beaches, contact with wild animals, fishing, hunting—the list is long and incompletely known. Food can, perhaps, be significantly increased: but what about clean beaches, unspoiled forests, and solitude? If we satisfy the need for food in a growing population we necessarily decrease the supply of other goods, and thereby increase the difficulty of equitably allocating scarce goods.…

The present population of India is 600 million, and it is increasing by 15 million per year. The environmental load of this population is already great. The forests of India are only a small fraction of what they were three centuries ago. Soil erosion, floods, and the psychological costs of crowding are serious. Every one of the net 15 million lives added each year stresses the Indian environment more severely. *Every life saved this year in a poor country diminishes the quality of life for subsequent generations.*

Observant critics have shown how much harm we wealthy nations have already done to poor nations through our well-intentioned but misguided attempts to help them.… Particularly reprehensible is our failure to carry out postaudits of these attempts.… Thus we have shielded our tender consciences from knowledge of the harm we have done. Must we Americans continue to fail to monitor the consequences of our external "dogooding"? If, for instance, we thoughtlessly make it possible for the present 600 million Indians to swell to 1,200 millions by the year 2001—as their present growth rate promises—will posterity in India thank us for facilitating an even greater destruction of *their* environment? Are good intentions ever a sufficient excuse for bad consequences?

IMMIGRATION CREATES A COMMONS

I come now to the final example of a commons in action, one for which the public is least prepared for rational discussion. The topic is at present enveloped by a great silence which reminds me of a comment made by Sherlock Holmes in A. Conan Doyle's story, "Silver Blaze." Inspector Gregory had asked, "Is there any point to which you would wish to draw my attention?" To this Holmes responded:

> "To the curious incident of the dog in the nighttime."
>
> "The dog did nothing in the night-time," said the Inspector.
>
> "That was the curious incident," remarked Sherlock Holmes.

By asking himself what would repress the normal barking instinct of a watchdog Holmes realized that it must be the dog's recognition of his master as the criminal trespasser. In a similar way we should ask ourselves, what repression keeps us from discussing something as important as immigration?

It cannot be that immigration is numerically of no consequence. Our government acknowledges a *net* flow of 400,000 a year. Hard data are understandably lacking on the extent of illegal entries, but a not implausible figure is 600,000 per year.... The natural increase of the resident population is now about 1.7 million per year. This means that the yearly gain from immigration is at least 19%, and may be 37%, of the total increase. It is quite conceivable that educational campaigns like that of Zero Population Growth, Inc., coupled with adverse social and economic factors—inflation, housing shortage, depression, and loss of confidence in national leaders—may lower the fertility of American women to a point at which all of the yearly increase in population would be accounted for by immigration. Should we not at least ask if that is what we want? How curious it is that we so seldom discuss immigration these days!

Curious, but understandable—as one finds out the moment he publicly questions the wisdom of the status quo in immigration. He who does so is promptly charged with *isolationism, bigotry, prejudice, ethnocentrism, chauvinism,* and *selfishness.* These are hard accusations to bear. It is pleasanter to talk about other matters, leaving immigration policy to wallow in the cross-currents of special interests that take no account of the good of the whole—*or of the interests of posterity.*

We Americans have a bad conscience because of things we said in the past about immigrants. Two generations ago the popular press was rife with references to *Dagos, Wops, Pollacks, Japs, Chinks,* and *Krauts*—all pejorative terms which failed to acknowledge our indebtedness to Goya, Leonardo, Copernicus, Hiroshige, Confucius, and Bach. Because the implied inferiority of foreigners was *then* the justification for keeping them out, it is *now* thoughtlessly assumed that restrictive policies can only be based on the assumption of immigrant inferiority. *This is not so.*

Existing immigration laws exclude idiots and known criminals; future laws will almost certainly continue this policy. But should we also consider the quality of the average immigrant, as compared with the quality of the average resident? Perhaps we should, perhaps we shouldn't. (What is "quality" anyway?) But the quality issue is not our concern here.

From this point on, *it will be assumed that immigrants and native-born citizens are of exactly equal quality,* however quality may be defined. The focus is only on quantity. The conclusions reached depend on nothing else, so all charges of ethnocentrism are irrelevant.

World food banks move food to the people, thus facilitating the exhaustion of the environment of the poor. By contrast, unrestricted immigration moves people to the food, thus speeding up the destruction of the environment in rich countries. Why poor people should want to make this transfer is no mystery: but why should rich hosts encourage it? This transfer, like the reverse one, is supported by both selfish interests and humanitarian impulses.

The principal selfish interest in unimpeded immigration is easy to identify; it is the interest of the employers of cheap labor, particularly that needed for degrading jobs. We have been deceived about the forces of history by the lines of Emma Lazarus inscribed on the Statue of Liberty:

> *Give me your tired, your poor*
> *Your huddled masses yearning to breathe free,*
> *The wretched refuse of your teeming shore,*
> *Send these, the homeless, tempest-tossed, to me:*
> *I lift my lamp beside the golden door.*

The image is one of an infinitely generous earth-mother, passively opening her arms to hordes of immigrants who come here on their own initiative. Such an image may have been adequate for the early days of colonization, but by the time these lines were written (1886) the force for immigration was largely manufactured inside our own borders by factory and mine owners who sought cheap labor not to be found among laborers already here. One group of foreigners after another was thus enticed into the United States to work at wretched jobs for wretched wages.

At present, it is largely the Mexicans who are being so exploited. It is particularly to the advantage of certain employers that there be many illegal immigrants. Illegal immigrant workers dare not complain about their working conditions for fear of being repatriated. Their presence reduces the bargaining power of all Mexican-American laborers. Cesar Chavez has repeatedly pleaded with congressional committees to close the doors to more Mexicans so that those here can negotiate effectively for higher wages and decent working conditions. Chavez understands the ethics of a lifeboat.

The interests of the employers of cheap labor are well served by the silence of the intelligentsia of the country. WASPs—White Anglo-Saxon Protestants—are particularly reluctant to call for a closing of the doors to immigration for fear of being called ethnocentric bigots. It was, therefore, an occasion of pure delight for this particular WASP to be present at a meeting when the points he would like to have made were made better by a non-WASP speaking to other non-WASPS. It was in Hawaii, and most of the people in the room were second-level Hawaiian officials of Japanese ancestry. All Hawaiians are keenly aware of the limits of their environment, and the speaker had asked how it might be practically and constitutionally possible to close the doors to more immigrants to the islands. (To Hawaiians, immigrants from the other 49 states are as much of a threat as those from other nations. There is only so much room in the islands, and the islanders know it. Sophistical arguments that imply otherwise do not impress them.)

Yet the Japanese-Americans of Hawaii have active ties with the land of their origin. This point was raised by a Japanese-American member of the audience who asked the Japanese-American speaker: "But how can we shut the doors now? We have many friends and relations in Japan that we'd like to bring to Hawaii some day so that they can enjoy this beautiful land."

The speaker smiled sympathetically and responded slowly: "Yes, but we have children now and someday we'll have grandchildren. We can bring more people here from Japan only by giving away some of the land that we hope to pass on to our grandchildren some day. What right do we have to do that?"

To be generous with one's own possessions is one thing; to be generous with posterity's is quite another. This, I think, is the point that must be gotten across to those who would, from a commendable love of distributive justice, institute a ruinous system of the commons, either in the form of a world food bank or that of unrestricted immigration. Since every speaker is a member of some ethnic group it is always possible to charge him with ethnocentrism. But even after purging an argument of ethnocentrism the rejection of the commons is still valid and necessary if we are to save at least some parts of the world from environmental ruin. Is it not desirable that at least some of the grandchildren of people now living should have a decent place in which to live?

Plainly many new problems will arise when we consciously face the immigration question and seek rational answers. No workable answers can be found if we ignore population problems. And—if the argument of this essay is correct—so long as there is no true world government to control reproduction everywhere it is impossible to survive in dignity if we are to be guided by Spaceship ethics. Without a world government that is sovereign in reproductive matters mankind lives, in fact, on a number of sovereign lifeboats. For the foreseeable future survival demands that we govern our actions by the ethics of a lifeboat. Posterity will be ill served if we do not.

STUDY QUESTIONS

1. What is Hardin's case against helping poor, needy countries? What is the significance of the lifeboat metaphor?

2. What is the relationship of population policies to world hunger?

3. Explain the "ratchet effect." Is Hardin right that in bringing aid to countries who do not control their population we act immorally?

10

Population and Food: A Critique of Lifeboat Ethics

WILLIAM W. MURDOCH AND ALLAN OATEN

William Murdoch is professor of biological science at the University of California at Santa Barbara and is the author of Environment: Resources, Pollution and Society *(2nd ed., 1975). Allan Oaten is also a biologist who has taught at the University of California at Santa Barbara and specializes in mathematical biology and statistics.*

Murdoch and Oaten begin by attacking Hardin's metaphors of "lifeboat," "commons," and "ratchet" as misleading. They then argue that other factors are needed to understand the population and hunger problem, including parental confidence in the future, low infant mortality rates, literacy, health care, income and employment, and an adequate diet. They claim that once the socioeconomic conditions are attended to, population size will take care of itself. Nonmilitary foreign aid to Third World countries is both just and necessary if we are to prevent global disaster.

MISLEADING METAPHORS

[Hardin's] "Lifeboat" Article actually has two messages. The first is that our immigration policy is too generous. This will not concern us here. The second, and more important, is that by helping poor nations we will bring disaster to rich and poor alike:

Metaphorically, each rich nation amounts to a lifeboat full of comparatively rich people. The poor of the world are in other, much more crowded lifeboats. Continuously, so to speak, the poor fall out of their lifeboats and swim for a while in the water outside, hoping to be admitted to a rich lifeboat, or in some other way to benefit from the "goodies" on board. What should the passengers on a rich lifeboat do? This is the central problem of "the ethics of a lifeboat." (Hardin)

Among these so-called "goodies" are food supplies and technical aid such as that which led to the Green Revolution. Hardin argues that we should withhold such resources from poor nations on the grounds that they help to maintain high rates of population increase, thereby making the problem worse. He foresees the continued supplying and increasing production of food as a process that will be "brought to an end only by the total collapse of the whole system, producing a catastrophe of scarcely imaginable proportions."

Turning to one particular mechanism for distributing these resources, Hardin claims that a world food bank is a commons—people have more motivation to draw from it than to add to it; it will have a ratchet or escalator effect on population because inputs from it will prevent population declines in over-populated countries. Thus "wealth can be steadily moved in one direction only, from the slowly-breeding rich to the rapidly-breeding poor, the process finally coming to a halt only when all countries are equally and miserably poor." Thus our help will not only bring ultimate disaster to poor countries, but it will also be suicidal for us.

As for the "benign demographic transition" to low birth rates, which some aid supporters have predicted, Hardin states flatly that the weight of evidence is against this possibility.

Finally, Hardin claims that the plight of poor nations is partly their own fault: "wise sovereigns seem not to exist in the poor world today. The most anguishing problems are created by poor countries that are governed by rulers insufficiently wise and powerful." Establishing a world food bank will exacerbate this problem: "slovenly rulers" will escape the consequences of their incompetence—"Others will bail them out whenever they are in trouble"; "Far more difficult than the transfer of wealth from one country to another is the transfer of wisdom between sovereign powers or between generations."

What arguments does Hardin present in support of these opinions? Many involve metaphors: lifeboat, commons, and ratchet or escalator. These metaphors are crucial to his thesis, and it is, therefore, important for us to examine them critically.

The lifeboat is the major metaphor. It seems attractively simple, but it is in fact simplistic and obscures important issues. As soon as we try to use it to compare various policies, we find that most relevant details of the actual situation are either missing or distorted in the lifeboat metaphor. Let us list some of these details.

Most important, perhaps, Hardin's lifeboats barely interact. The rich lifeboats may drop some handouts over the side and perhaps repel a boarding party now and then, but generally they live their own lives. In the real world, nations interact a great deal, in ways that affect food supply and population size and growth, and the effect of rich nations

on poor nations has been strong and not always benevolent.

First, by colonization and actual wars of commerce, and through the international marketplace, rich nations have arranged an exchange of goods that has maintained and even increased the economic imbalance between rich and poor nations. Until recently we have taken or otherwise obtained cheap raw material from poor nations and sold them expensive manufactured goods that they cannot make themselves. In the United States, the structure of tariffs and internal subsidies discriminates selectively against poor nations. In poor countries, the concentration on cash crops rather than on food crops, a legacy of colonial times, is now actively encouraged by western multinational corporations.... Indeed, it is claimed that in famine-stricken Sahelian Africa, multinational agribusiness has recently taken land out of food production for cash crops.... Although we often self-righteously take the "blame" for lowering the death rates of poor nations during the 1940s and 1950s, we are less inclined to accept responsibility for the effects of actions that help maintain poverty and hunger. Yet poverty directly contributes to the high birth rates that Hardin views with such alarm.

Second, U.S. foreign policy, including foreign aid programs, has favored "pro-Western" regimes, many of which govern in the interests of a wealthy elite and some of which are savagely repressive. Thus, it has often subsidized a gross maldistribution of income and has supported political leaders who have opposed most of the social changes that can lead to reduced birth rates. In this light, Hardin's pronouncements on the alleged wisdom gap between poor leaders and our own, and the difficulty of filling it, appear as a grim joke: our response to leaders with the power and wisdom Hardin yearns for has often been to try to replace them or their policies as soon as possible. Selective giving and withholding of both military and nonmilitary aid has been an important ingredient of our efforts to maintain political leaders we like and to remove those we do not. Brown ..., after noting that the withholding of U.S. food aid in 1973 contributed to the downfall of the Allende government in

Chile, comments that "although Americans decry the use of petroleum as a political weapon, calling it 'political blackmail,' the United States has been using food aid for political purposes for twenty years—and describing this as 'enlightened diplomacy.'"

Both the quantity and the nature of the supplies on a lifeboat are fixed. In the real world, the quantity has strict limits, but these are far from having been reached (University of California Food Task Force 1974). Nor are we forced to devote fixed proportions of our efforts and energy to automobile travel, pet food, packaging, advertising, corn-fed beef, "defense" and other diversions, many of which cost far more than foreign aid does. The fact is that enough food is now produced to feed the world's population adequately. That people are malnourished is due to distribution and to economics, not to agricultural limits (United Nations Economic and Social Council 1974).

Hardin's lifeboats are divided merely into rich and poor, and it is difficult to talk about birth rates on either. In the real world, however, there are striking differences among the birth rates of the poor countries and even among the birth rates of different parts of single countries. These differences appear to be related to social conditions (also absent from lifeboats) and may guide us to effective aid policies.

Hardin's lifeboat metaphor not only conceals facts, but misleads about the effects of his proposals. The rich lifeboat can raise the ladder and sail away. But in real life, the problem will not necessarily go away just because it is ignored. In the real world, there are armies, raw materials in poor nations, and even outraged domestic dissidents prepared to sacrifice their own and others' lives to oppose policies they regard as immoral.

No doubt there are other objections. But even this list shows the lifeboat metaphor to be dangerously inappropriate for serious policy making because it obscures far more than it reveals. Lifeboats and "lifeboat ethics" may be useful topics for those who are shipwrecked; we believe they are worthless—indeed detrimental—in discussions of food-population questions.

The ratchet metaphor is equally flawed. It, too, ignores complex interactions between birth rates and social conditions (including diets), implying as it does that more food will simply mean more babies. Also, it obscures the fact that the decrease in death rates has been caused at least as much by developments such as DDT, improved sanitation, and medical advances, as by increased food supplies, so that cutting out food aid will not necessarily lead to population declines.

The lifeboat article is strangely inadequate in other ways. For example, it shows an astonishing disregard for recent literature. The claim that we can expect no "benign demographic transition" is based on a review written more than a decade ago. … Yet, events and attitudes are changing rapidly in poor countries: for the first time in history, most poor people live in countries with birth control programs; with few exceptions, poor nations are somewhere on the demographic transition to lower birth rates …; the population-food squeeze is now widely recognized, and governments of poor nations are aware of the relationship. Again, there is a considerable amount of evidence that birth rates can fall rapidly in poor countries given the proper social conditions (as we will discuss later); consequently, crude projections of current populations growth rates are quite inadequate for policy making.

THE TRAGEDY OF THE COMMONS

Throughout the lifeboat article, Hardin bolsters his assertions by reference to the "commons." … The thesis of the commons, therefore, needs critical evaluation.

Suppose several privately owned flocks, comprising 100 sheep altogether, are grazing on a public commons. They bring in an annual income of $1.00 per sheep. Fred, a herdsman, owns only one sheep. He decides to add another. But 101 is too many: the commons is overgrazed and produces less food. The sheep lose quality and income drops to 90¢ per sheep. Total income is now $90.90 instead of $100.00. Adding the sheep has brought an overall loss. But Fred has gained: *his* income is $1.80 instead of $1.00. The gain from the additional sheep, which is his alone, outweighs the loss from overgrazing, which he shares. Thus he promotes his interest at the expense of the community.

This is the problem of the commons, which seems on the way to becoming an archetype. Hardin, in particular, is not inclined to underrate its importance: "One of the major tasks of education today is to create such an awareness of the dangers of the commons that people will be able to recognize its many varieties, however disguised" … and "All this is terribly obvious once we are acutely aware of the pervasiveness and danger of the commons. But many people still lack this awareness…."

The "commons" affords a handy way of classifying problems: the lifeboat article reveals that sharing, a generous immigration policy, world food banks, air, water, the fish populations of the ocean, and the western range lands are, or produce, a commons. It is also handy to be able to dispose of policies one does not like and "only a particular instance of a class of policies that are in error because they lead to the tragedy of the commons."

But no metaphor, even one as useful as this, should be treated with such awe. Such shorthand can be useful, but it can also mislead by discouraging and obscuring important detail. To dismiss a proposal by suggesting that "all you need to know about this proposal is that it institutes a commons and is, therefore, bad" is to assert that the proposed commons is worse than the original problem. This might be so if the problem of the commons were, indeed, a tragedy—that is, if it were insoluble. But it is not.

Hardin favors private ownership as the solution (either through private property or the selling of pollution rights). But, of course, there are solutions other than private ownership; and private ownership itself is no guarantee of carefully husbanded resources.

One alternative to private ownership of the commons is communal ownership of the sheep— or, in general, of the mechanisms and industries that exploit the resource—combined with communal

planning for management. (Note, again, how the metaphor favors one solution: perhaps the "tragedy" lay not in the commons but in the sheep. "The Tragedy of the Privately Owned Sheep" lacks zing, unfortunately.) Public ownership of a commons has been tried in Peru to the benefit of the previously privately owned anchovy fishery…. The communally owned agriculture of China does not seem to have suffered any greater overexploitation than that of other Asian nations.

Another alternative is cooperation combined with regulation. For example, Gulland … has shown that Antarctic whale stocks (perhaps the epitome of a commons since they are internationally exploited and no one owns them) are now being properly managed, and stocks are increasing. This has been achieved through cooperation in the International Whaling Commission, which has by agreement set limits to the catch of each nation.

In passing, Hardin's private ownership argument is not generally applicable to nonrenewable resources. Given discount rates, technology substitutes, and no more than an average regard for posterity, privately owned nonrenewable resources, like oil, coal and minerals, are mined at rates that produce maximum profits, rather than at those rates that preserve them for future generations….

BIRTH RATES: AN ALTERNATIVE VIEW

Is the food-population spiral inevitable? A more optimistic, if less comfortable, hypothesis, presented by Rich and Brown, is increasingly tenable: contrary to the "ratchet" projection, population growth rates are affected by many complex conditions besides food supply. In particular, a set of socioeconomic conditions can be identified that motivate parents to have fewer children; under these conditions, birth rates can fall quite rapidly, sometimes even before birth control technology is available. Thus, population growth can be controlled more effectively by intelligent human intervention that sets up the appropriate conditions than by doing nothing and trusting to "natural population cycles."

These conditions are parental confidence about the future, an improved status of women, and literacy. They require low infant mortality rates, widely available rudimentary health care, increased income and employment, and an adequate diet above subsistence levels. Expenditure on schools (especially elementary schools), appropriate health services (especially rural para-medical services), and agriculture reform (especially aid to small farmers) will be needed, and foreign aid can help here. It is essential that these improvements be spread across the population; aid can help here, too, by concentrating on the poor nations' poorest people, encouraging necessary institutional and social reforms, and making it easier for poor nations to use their own resources and initiative to help themselves. It is *not* necessary that per capita GNP be very high, certainly not as high as that of the rich countries during their gradual demographic transition. In other words, low birth rates in poor countries are achievable long before the conditions exist that were present in the rich countries in the late 19th and early 20th centuries.

Twenty or thirty years is not long to discover and assess the factors affecting birth rates, but a body of evidence is now accumulating in favor of this hypothesis. Rich and Brown show that at least 10 developing countries have managed to reduce their birth rates by an average of more than one birth per 1,000 population per year for periods of 5 to 16 years. A reduction of one birth per 1,000 per year would bring birth rates in poor countries to a rough replacement level of about 16/1,000 by the turn of the century, though age distribution effects would prevent a smooth population decline. We have listed these countries in Table 1, together with three other nations, including China, that are poor and yet have brought their birth rates down to 30 or less, presumably from rates of over 40 a decade or so ago.

These data show that rapid reduction in birth rates is possible in the developing world. No doubt it can be argued that each of these cases is in some way special. Hong Kong and Singapore are relatively rich; they, Barbados, and Mauritius are also tiny. China is able to exert great social pressure on its citizens; but China is particularly significant. It is enormous; its per capita GNP is almost as low as India's; and it started out in 1949 with a terrible health system. Also, Egypt, Chile, Taiwan, Cuba, South Korea, and Sri Lanka are quite large, and they are poor or very poor (Table 1). In fact, these examples represent an enormous range of religion, political systems, and geography and suggest that such rates of decline in the birth rate can be achieved whenever the appropriate conditions are met. "The common factor in these countries is that the *majority* of the population has shared in the economic and social benefits of significant national progress. ... [M]aking health, education and jobs more broadly available to lower income groups in poor countries contribute[s] significantly toward the motivation for smaller families that is the prerequisite of major reduction in birth rates." ...

The converse is also true. In Latin America, Cuba (annual per capita income $530), Chile ($720), Uruguay ($820), and Argentina ($1,160) have moderate to truly equitable distribution of goods and services and relatively low birth rates (27, 25, 23, and 22, respectively). In contrast, Brazil ($420), Mexico ($670), and Venezuela ($980) have very unequal distribution of goods and services and high birth rates (38, 42, and 41, respectively). Fertility rates in poor and relatively poor nations seem unlikely to fall as long as the bulk of the population does not share in increased benefits....

... As a disillusioning quarter-century of aid giving has shown, the obstacles of getting aid to those segments of the population most in need of it are enormous. Aid has typically benefited a small rich segment of society, partly because of the way aid programs have been designed but also because of human and institutional factors in the poor nations themselves.... With some notable exceptions, the distribution of income and services in poor nations is extremely skewed—much more uneven than in rich countries. Indeed, much of the population is essentially outside the economic system. Breaking this pattern will be extremely difficult. It will require not only aid that is designed specifically to benefit the rural poor, but also important institutional changes such as decentralization of decision making and the development of greater

T A B L E 1   **Declining Birth Rates and Per Capita Income in Selected Developing Countries. (These Are Crude Birth Rates, Uncorrected for Age Distribution.)**

Country	Time Span	Births/1,000/year		
		Average Annual Decline in Crude Birth Rate	Crude Birth Rate 1972	$ Per Capita Per Year 1973
Barbados	1960–69	1.5	22	570
Taiwan	1955–71	1.2	24	390
Tunisia	1966–71	1.8	35	250
Mauritius	1961–71	1.5	25	240
Hong Kong	1960–72	1.4	19	970
Singapore	1955–72	1.2	23	920
Costa Rica	1963–72	1.5	32	560
South Korea	1960–70	1.2	29	250
Egypt	1966–70	1.7	37	210
Chile	1963–70	1.2	25	720
China			30	160
Cuba			27	530
Sri Lanka			30	110

autonomy and stronger links to regional and national market for local groups and industries such as cooperative farms.

Thus, two things are being asked of rich nations and of the United States in particular: to increase nonmilitary foreign aid, including food aid, and to give it in ways, and to governments, that will deliver it to the poorest people and will improve their access to national economic institutions. These are not easy tasks, particularly the second, and there is no guarantee that birth rates will come down quickly in all countries. Still, many poor countries have, in varying degrees, begun the process of reform, and recent evidence suggests that aid and reform together can do much to solve the twin problems of high birth rates and economic underdevelopment. The tasks are far from impossible. Based on the evidence, the policies dictated by a sense of decency are also the most realistic and rational.

STUDY QUESTIONS

1. What are the criticisms leveled against Hardin's arguments?

2. What is Murdoch and Oaten's view on the question of population growth? What is the gradual demographic transition theory? Is their view plausible?

3. Compare Hardin's arguments with Murdoch and Oaten's response. Where does the evidence lie?

4. What are the disanalogies between a lifeboat and the United States?

Chapter 4

Pollution: Soil Air Water

IN 1962, Rachel Carson published *Silent Spring* in which she documented the effects of DDT and other pesticides on human health. She charged that these "elixirs of death" were causing widespread cancer and genetic mutations as well as wreaking havoc on birds, fish, and wildlife. Her famous opening words not only mark the beginning of the modern environmental movement but also set its tone.

> There was once a town in the heart of America where all life seemed to live in harmony with its surroundings. The town lay in the midst of a checkerboard of prosperous farms, with fields of grain and hillsides of orchards where, in spring, white clouds of bloom drifted above the green fields. In autumn, oak and maple and birch set up a blaze of color that flamed and flickered across a backdrop of pines. Then foxes barked in the hills and deer silently crossed the fields, half hidden in the mists of the fall mornings....
>
> Then a strange blight crept over the area and everything began to change. Some evil spell had settled on the community: mysterious maladies swept the flocks of chickens; the cattle and sheep sickened and died. Everywhere was a shadow of death. The farmers spoke of much illness among their families. In the town the doctors had become more and more puzzled by new kinds of sickness appearing among their patients. There had been several sudden and unexplained deaths, not only among adults but even among children, who would be stricken suddenly while at play and die within a few hours.

It took ten years before DDT was banned from agricultural use. Meanwhile it was discovered that we were releasing hosts of other toxins into our air, water, and soil. Although governments now regulate toxins, they are still used in enormous quantities in both agriculture and industry.

In 1989, the oil tanker *Exxon Valdez* ran aground off the Alaskan Coast, spilling 1.26 million barrels of oil into Prince William Sound. It was the worst oil spill in history. The pristine beauty of the Alaskan Coast with its wealth of birds, fish, and wildlife was degraded. Five hundred square miles of the Sound were polluted. Millions of fish, birds, and wildlife were killed, and fishermen lost their means of livelihood. The fishing industry, which earns $100 million annually in Prince William Sound, ground to an abrupt halt. The Exxon Corporation was unprepared for an accident of such magnitude. It had only 69 barrels of oil dispersant on hand in Alaska, when nearly 10,000 barrels were needed to clean up the spill. The ship's captain, Joseph Hazelwood, was found guilty of negligence and operating the tanker under the influence of alcohol, and Exxon was fined $100 million. Greenpeace put an ad in newspapers, showing Joseph Hazelwood's face, with the caption: "It wasn't his driving that caused the Alaskan oil spill. It was yours. The spill was caused by a nation drunk on oil. And a government asleep at the wheel."

This spill has just been exceeded by the British Petroleum Deep Water spill in the Gulf of Mexico. An explosion on April 20, 2010, on off shore drilling rig killed eleven workers and triggered a massive leak at the sea bed level. It is still disputed what exactly the series of failures was; BP claims that Halliburton Energy Services, which had installed infrastructure on the sea bed, shares blame. Over 2 million (some estimates reported numbers closer to 2.5 million) gallons of crude oil leaked into the Gulf of Mexico every day for almost 4 months. The spill was capped on July 15, but the ecological consequences, though it is still assessed, are obviously enormous. Mainstream environmentalism has been remarkably passive about this issue, and the story has already mostly dropped out of the media. There are around 3,500 other offshore rigs in the Gulf of Mexico, though only a small number are deep wells.

Pollution may be broadly defined as any unwanted state or change in the properties of air, water, soil, liquid, or food that can have a negative impact on the health, well-being, or survival of human beings or other living organisms. Most pollutants are undesirable chemicals that are produced as by-products when a resource is converted into energy or a commodity. Types of pollution include contaminated water, chemically polluted air (such as smog), toxic waste in the soil, poisoned food, high

levels of radiation, and noise. They also include acid rain and second-hand cigarette smoke because these can have a deleterious effect on our health.

Three factors determine the severity of a pollutant: its chemical nature (how harmful it is to various types of living organisms), its concentration (the amount per volume of air, water, soil, or body weight), and its persistence (how long it remains in the air, water, soil, or body).

A pollutant's persistence can be divided into three types: degradable, slowly degradable, and nondegradable. Degradable pollutants, such as human sewage and contaminated soil, are usually broken down completely or reduced to acceptable levels by natural chemical processes. Slowly degradable pollutants, such as DDT, plastics, aluminum cans, and chlorofluorocarbons (CFCs), often take decades to degrade to acceptable levels. Nondegradable pollutants, such as lead and mercury, are not broken down by natural processes.

We know little about the short- and long-range harmful potential, for people and for the environment, of most of the more than 70,000 synthetic chemicals in commercial use. The Environmental Protection Agency (EPA) estimates that 80% of cancers are caused by pollution. We know that half of our air pollution is caused by the internal combustion engines of motor vehicles and that coal-burning stationary power plants produce unacceptable amounts of sulfur dioxide (SO_2). The World Health Organization (WHO) estimates that about 1 billion urban people (about one-fifth of humanity) are being exposed to health hazards from air pollution and that emphysema, an incurable lung disease, is rampant in our cities. Studies tell us that smog is hazardous to our health and that it has caused thousands of deaths in such cities as London, New York, and Los Angeles.

In the United States, 80% of freshwater aquifers are in danger, so a large percentage (estimates are more than 30%) of the U.S. population is drinking contaminated water. By 1991 the EPA had listed 1211 hazardous waste sites for cleanup, at an estimated cost of $26 million per site. Acid rain is killing our forests and lakes.

In our first reading, Hilary French documents the dire consequences of air pollution. Her essay provides hard data around which rational discussion can take place.

Our second reading contains a sharp indictment of corporate capitalism by George Bradford. Reacting to what he perceived to be a condoning of the tragedy of Bhopal, India (where a Union Carbide factory exploded, killing 3,000 people in 1984) by the *Wall Street Journal,* Bradford lashes out at the whole economic and social philosophy that permitted and is responsible for this and many other threats to humanity. In the Third World, businesses cut costs by having lax safety standards. Chemicals that are banned in the United States and Europe are produced overseas. Even in the United States and Europe, our industrial culture continues to endanger our lives. We must throw "off this Modern Way of Life," argues Bradford, for it only constitutes a "terrible burden" that threatens to crush us all.

Our third reading, "People or Penguins: The Case for Optimal Pollution" by William Baxter, explores the relationship between resources and pollution, showing that we cannot have the good of resource use without the bad of pollution. The point is to decide on the proper balance. Those like Baxter, who take a decidedly anthropocentric point of view, argue that we ought to risk pollution that might endanger other species (as DDT does) if it promotes human advantage.

In our fourth reading, entomologist David Pimentel assesses the progress and problems of pesticide use since *Silent Spring* was written. On the one hand, much progress has been made so that the poisons in pesticides affect humans and wildlife less directly. But unfortunately, pesticide-resistant insects have replaced their less damaging ancestors. Furthermore, pesticides have destroyed some of the natural enemies of certain pests, so more crops are now lost to insects than they were when *Silent Spring* was written. However, because of better overall agricultural techniques and fertilizers, the total picture is positive.

11

You Are What You Breathe

HILARY FRENCH

Hilary French is a staff researcher for the Worldwatch Institute.

In this essay, French provides a detailed, documented account of the devastating global effects of air pollution. Because the wind carries the polluted air from one nation to another, this problem requires international as well as national action and cooperation. If we are to solve the problem, our lifestyles will have to change.

Asked to name the world's top killers, most people wouldn't put air pollution high on their lists.

A nuisance, at best, but not a terribly serious threat to health.

From *The Worldwatch Reader,* ed. Lester R. Brown (New York: W. W. Norton & Co., 1991). Copyright © 1991 Worldwatch Institute. Reprinted by permission of The Worldwatch Institute.

The facts say otherwise. In greater Athens, for example, the number of deaths rises sixfold on heavily polluted days. In Hungary, the government attributes 1 in 17 deaths to air pollution. In Bombay, breathing the air is equivalent to smoking 10 cigarettes a day. And in Beijing, air-pollution-related respiratory distress is so common that it has been dubbed the "Beijing Cough."

Air pollution is truly a global public health emergency. United Nations statistics show that more than one billion people—a fifth of humanity—live in areas where the air is not fit to breathe. Once a local phenomenon primarily affecting city dwellers and people living near factories, air pollution now reaches rural as well as urban dwellers. It's also crossing international borders.

In the United States alone, roughly 150 million people live in areas whose air is considered unhealthy by the Environmental Protection Agency (EPA). According to the American Lung Association, this leads to as many as 120,000 deaths each year.

A century ago, air pollution was caused primarily by the coal burned to fuel the industrial revolution. Since then, the problem and its causes have become more complex and widespread. In some parts of the world, including much of Eastern Europe and China, coal continues to be the main source of pollution. Elsewhere, automobiles and industries are now the primary cause.

Adding to the miasma, industries are emitting pollutants of frightening toxicity. Millions of tons of carcinogens, mutagens, and poisons pour into the air each year and damage health and habitat near their sources and, via the winds, sometimes thousands of miles away. Many regions that have enjoyed partial success combating pollution are finding their efforts overwhelmed as populations and economies grow and bring in more power plants, home furnaces, factories, and motor vehicles.

Meanwhile, global warming has arisen as the preeminent environmental concern; this sometimes conveys the misleading impression that conventional air pollution is yesterday's problem. But air pollutants and greenhouse gases stem largely from fossil fuels burned in energy, transportation, and industrial systems. Having common roots, the two problems can also have common solutions. Unfortunately, policymakers persist in tackling them separately, which runs the risk of lessening one while exacerbating the other.

Air pollution has proven so intractable a phenomenon that a book could be written about the history of efforts to combat it. Law has followed law. As one problem has largely been solved, a new one has frequently emerged to take its place. Even some of the solutions have become part of the problem: The tall smokestacks built in the 1960s and 1970s to disperse emissions from huge coal-burning power plants became conduits to the upper atmosphere for the pollutants that form acid rain.

Turning the corner on air pollution requires moving beyond patchwork, end-of-the-pipe approaches to confront pollution at its sources. This will mean reorienting energy, transportation, and industrial structures toward prevention.

CHEMICAL SOUP

Although air pollution plagues countries on all continents and at all levels of development, it comes in many different varieties. The burning of fossil fuels—predominantly coal—by power plants, industries, and home furnaces was the first pollution problem recognized as a threat to human health. The sulfur dioxide and particulate emissions associated with coal burning—either alone or in combination—can raise the incidence of respiratory diseases such as coughs and colds, asthma, bronchitis, and emphysema. Particulate matter (a general term for a complex and varying mixture of pollutants in minute solid form) can carry toxic metals deep into the lungs.

Pollution from automobiles forms a second front in the battle for clean air. One of the worst auto-related pollutants is ozone, the principal ingredient in urban smog. Formed when sunlight causes hydrocarbons (a by-product of many industrial processes and engines) to react with nitrogen oxides (produced by cars and power plants), ozone can cause serious respiratory distress. Recent U.S. research

TABLE 1   **Health Effects of Pollutants from Automobiles**[1]

Pollutant	Health Effect
Carbon monoxide	Interferes with blood's ability to absorb oxygen; impairs perception and thinking; slows reflexes; causes drowsiness; and so can cause unconsciousness and death; if inhaled by pregnant women, may threaten growth and mental development of fetus.
Lead	Affects circulatory, reproductive, nervous, and kidney systems; suspected of causing hyperactivity and lowered learning ability in children; hazardous even after exposure ends.
Nitrogen oxides	Can increase susceptibility to viral infections such as influenza. Can also irritate the lungs and cause bronchitis and pneumonia.
Ozone	Irritates mucous membranes of respiratory system; causes coughing, choking, and impaired lung function; reduces resistance to colds and pneumonia; can aggravate chronic heart disease, asthma, bronchitis, and emphysema.
Toxic emissions	Suspected of causing cancer, reproductive problems, and birth defects. Benzene is a known carcinogen.

[1] Automobiles are a primary source, but not the only source, of these pollutants.

SOURCE: National Clean Air Coalition and the U.S. Environmental Protection Agency.

suggests that ground-level ozone causes temporary breathing difficulty and long-term lung damage at lower concentrations than previously believed.

Other dangerous pollutants spewed by automobiles include nitrogen dioxide, carbon monoxide, lead, and such toxic hydrocarbons as benzene, toluene, xylene, and ethylene dibromide (see Table 1).

At elevated levels, nitrogen dioxide can cause lung irritation, bronchitis, pneumonia, and increased susceptibility to viral infections such as influenza. Carbon monoxide can interfere with the blood's ability to absorb oxygen; this impairs perception and thinking, slow reflexes, and causes drowsiness and—in extreme cases—unconsciousness and death. If inhaled by a pregnant woman, carbon monoxide can threaten the fetus's physical and mental development.

Lead affects the circulatory, reproductive, nervous, and kidney systems. It is suspected of causing hyperactivity and lowered learning ability in children. Because it accumulates in bone and tissue, it is hazardous long after exposure ends.

Concern is growing around the world about the health threat posed by less common but extremely harmful airborne toxic chemicals such as benzene, vinyl chloride, and other volatile organic chemicals produced by automobiles and industries. These chemicals can cause a variety of illnesses, such as cancer and genetic and birth defects, yet they have received far less regulatory attention around the world than have "conventional" pollutants.

WHERE THE BREATHING ISN'T EASY

With the aid of pollution control equipment and improvements in energy efficiency, many Western industrialized countries have made significant strides in reducing emissions of sulfur dioxide and particulates. The United States, for example, cut sulfur oxide emissions by 28 percent between 1970 and 1987 and particulates by 62 percent (see Figure 1). In Japan, sulfur dioxide emissions fell by 39 percent from 1973 to 1984.

The same cannot be said for Eastern Europe and the Soviet Union, where hasty industrialization after World War II, powered by abundant high-sulfur brown coal, has led to some of the worst air pollution ever experienced. Pollution control technologies have been virtually nonexistent. And,

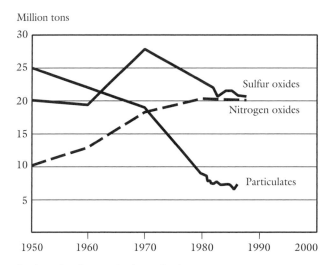

Million tons

FIGURE 1 Emissions of Selected Pollutants in the United States, 1950–1987.
SOURCE: Worldwatch Institute, based on Summers and Heston.

because of heavily subsidized fuel prices and the absence of market forces governing production, these countries never made the impressive gains in energy efficiency registered in the West after the oil shocks of the 1970s.

Many developing countries also confront appalling air pollution problems. The lack of adequate pollution control technologies and regulations, plus plans to expand energy and industrial production, translates into worsening air quality in many cities. Urbanization in much of the Third World means that increasing numbers of people are exposed to polluted city air.

A 1988 report by the United Nations' Environment Program (UNEP) and the World Health Organization (WHO) gives the best picture to date of the global spread of sulfur dioxide and particulate pollution (see Table 2). Of the 54 cities with data available on sulfur dioxide pollution for 1980 to 1984, 27 were on the borderline or in violation of the WHO health standard.

High on the list were Shenyang, Tehran, and Seoul, as well as Milan, Paris, and Madrid; this indicates that sulfur dioxide problems have by no means been cured in industrial countries. Though conditions are gradually improving in most of the

TABLE 2   **Violations of Sulfur Dioxide and Suspended Particulate Matter Standards, Selected Cities[1]**

City	Sulfur Dioxide	Particulates[2]
	(number of days above WHO standard)	
New Delhi	6	294
Xian	71	273
Beijing	68	272
Shenyang	146	219
Tehran	104	174
Bangkok	0	97
Madrid	35	60
Kuala Lampur	0	37
Zagreb	30	34
Sao Paulo	12	31
Paris	46	3
New York	8	0
Milan	66	n.a.
Seoul	87	n.a.

[1] Averages of readings at a variety of monitoring sites from 1980 to 1984.
[2] For Madrid, Sao Paulo, and Paris, the reading is of smoke rather than particulates.
SOURCE: United Nations' Environment Program and World Health Organization, Assessment of Urban Air Quality (Nairobi: Global Environment Monitoring System, 1988).

cities surveyed, several in the Third World reported a worsening trend.

Suspended particulate matter poses an even more pervasive threat, especially in the developing world, where the appropriate control technologies have not been installed and conditions are frequently dusty. Fully 37 of the 41 cities monitored for particulates averaged either borderline or excessive levels. Annual average concentrations were as much as five times the WHO standard in both New Delhi and Beijing.

Ozone pollution, too, has become a seemingly intractable health problem in many parts of the world. In the United States, 1988 ushered in one of the hottest and sunniest years on record, and also one of the worst for ground-level ozone in more than a decade. According to the Natural Resources Defense Council, the air in New York City violated the federal health standard on 34 days—two to three times a week, all summer long. In Los Angeles, ozone levels surged above the federal standard on 172 days. At last count 382 counties, home to more than half of all Americans, were out of compliance with the EPA ozone standard.

Ozone is becoming a problem elsewhere, too. In Mexico City, the relatively lenient government standard of a one-hour ozone peak of 0.11 parts per million not to be exceeded more than once daily is topped more than 300 days a year—nearly twice as often as Los Angeles violates its much stricter standard.

The other automobile-related pollutants also constitute a far-flung health threat. The WHO/UNEP report estimates that 15 to 20 percent of urban residents in North America and Europe are exposed to unacceptably high levels of nitrogen dioxide, 50 percent to unhealthy carbon monoxide concentrations, and a third to excessive lead levels. In a study in Mexico City, lead levels in the blood of 7 out of 10 newborns were found to exceed WHO standards. "The implication for Mexican society, that an entire generation of children will be intellectually stunted, is truly staggering," says Mexican chemist and environmental activist Manuel Guerra.

Airborne toxic chemical emissions present no less of a danger. In the United States, the one country that has begun to tally total emissions, factories reported 1.3 million tons of hazardous emissions in 1987, including 118,000 tons of carcinogens. According to the EPA, these emissions cause about 2,000 cancer deaths a year.

These deaths fall disproportionately on certain communities. For example, in West Virginia's Kanawha Valley—home to a quarter of a million people and 13 major chemical plants—state health department records show that, between 1968 and 1977, the incidence of respiratory cancer was more than 21 percent above the national average. According to EPA statistics, a lifetime of exposure to the airborne concentrations of butadiene, chloroform, and ethylene oxide in this valley could cause cancer in 1 resident in 1,000.

Unfortunately, data are not so extensive for other countries. Wherever uncontrolled polluting industries such as chemical plants, smelters, and paper mills exist, however, emission levels are undoubtedly high. Measurements of lead and cadmium in the soil of the upper Silesian towns of Olkosz and Slawkow in Poland, for instance, are among the highest recorded anywhere in the world.

The health damage inflicted by air pollution comes at great human cost; it also carries an economic price tag. The American Lung Association estimates that air pollution costs the United States $40 billion annually in health care and lost productivity.

CLEARING THE AIR

In the Western industrial world, the last 20 years has been a period of intense political and scientific activity aimed at restoring clean air. The approaches to date, however, have tended to be technological Band-Aids rather than efforts to address the roots of the problem.

Scrubbers, nitrogen-oxides control technologies, and new cleaner-burning coal technologies can all reduce emissions dramatically, but they are not the ultimate solutions. For one, they can create environmental problems of their own, such as the need to dispose of scrubber ash, a hazardous waste. Second, they do little if anything to reduce carbon dioxide emissions, so make no significant contribution to slowing global warming.

For these reasons, technologies of this kind are best viewed as a bridge to the day when energy-efficient societies are the norm and pollution-free sources such as solar, wind, and water power provide the bulk of the world's electricity.

Improving energy efficiency is a clean air priority. Such measures as more-efficient refrigerators and lighting can markedly and cost-effectively reduce electricity consumption; this will in turn reduce emissions. Equally important, the savings that results from not building power plants because demand has been cut by efficiency can more than offset the additional cost of installing scrubbers at existing plants.

Using conservative assumptions, the Washington, D.C.–based American Council for an Energy Efficient Economy concluded that cutting sulfur dioxide emissions steeply with a scrubbers/conservation combination could actually save consumers in the Midwest up to $8 billion.

Similar rethinking can help reduce auto emissions. To date, modifying car engines and installing catalytic converters have been the primary strategies employed to lower harmful emissions. These devices reduce hydrocarbon emissions by an average of 87 percent, carbon monoxide by an average of 85 percent, and nitrogen oxides by 62 percent over the life of a vehicle. Although catalytic converters are sorely needed in countries that don't require them, they alone are not sufficient. Expanding auto fleets are overwhelming the good they do, even in countries that have mandated their use.

Alternative fuels, such as methanol, ethanol, natural gas, hydrogen, and electricity, are being pushed by many governments as the remedy for the air pollution quagmire. Although these fuels may have some role to play eventually, they can by no means be viewed as a panacea.

Reducing air pollution in cities is likely to require a major shift away from automobiles as the cornerstone of urban transportation systems. As congestion slows traffic to a crawl in many cities, driving to work is becoming unattractive anyway. Convenient public transportation, car pooling, and measures that facilitate bicycle commuting are the cheapest, most effective ways for metropolitan areas to proceed.

Driving restrictions already exist in many of the world's cities. For example, Florence has turned its downtown into a pedestrian mall during daylight hours. Budapest bans motor traffic from all but two streets in the downtown area during particularly polluted spells. In Mexico City and Santiago, one-fifth of all vehicles are kept off the streets each weekday based on their license-plate numbers.

As with power plant and auto emissions, efforts to control airborne toxic chemicals will be most successful if they focus on minimizing waste rather than simply on controlling emissions. Such a strategy also prevents waste from being shifted from one form to another. For instance, control technologies such as scrubbers and filters produce hazardous solid wastes that must be disposed on land.

The Congressional Office of Technology Assessment has concluded it is technically and economically feasible for U.S. industries to lower production of toxic wastes and pollutants by up to 50 percent within the next few years. Similar possibilities exist in other countries.

Freedom of environmental information can also be a powerful regulatory tool. In the United States, "right-to-know" legislation requiring industries to release data on their toxic emissions has been instrumental in raising public awareness of the threat and spurring more responsible industrial behavior. The Monsanto Company, a major chemical producer, was so embarrassed by the enormous pollution figures it was required to release in 1989 that it simultaneously announced its intention to cut back emissions 90 percent by 1992.

Few European countries have released information about emissions from industrial plants, although that may change if the European Economic Community (EEC) issues a directive now in draft form on freedom of information regarding environmental matters. The recent political transformation in Eastern Europe and the Soviet Union are gradually improving the environmental data flow, although much progress in this area remains to be made.

SOLUTION FROM SMOG CITY

In most parts of the world, air pollution is now squarely on the public policy agenda. This is a promising sign. Unfortunately, the public's desire for clean air has not yet been matched with the political leadership needed to provide it. Recent developments at the national and international levels, though constituting steps forward, remain inadequate to the task.

In the United States, for example, recent major amendments to the Clean Air Act of 1970 will cut acid rain emissions in half, tighten emissions standards for automobiles significantly, and require much stricter control of toxic air pollutants.

Almost any legislation would be an improvement. Twenty years after the act became law, 487 counties still are not in compliance. But the legislation fails to address the problem at a fundamental level by not encouraging energy efficiency, waste reduction, and a revamping of transportation systems and urban designs.

Los Angeles—with the worst air quality in the United States—is one of the first regions in the world to really understand that lasting change will not come through mere tinkering. Under a bold new air-quality plan embracing the entire region, the city government will discourage automobile use, boost public transportation, and control household and industrial activities that contribute to smog.

For example, paints and solvents will have to be reformulated to produce fewer ozone-forming fumes; gasoline-powered lawn mowers and lighter fluid will be banned; carpooling will be mandated; and the number of cars per family limited. Even though the plan has been approved by all of the relevant state and federal agencies, implementing it at the local level will be a challenge.

Most of Europe, though quicker than the United States to cut back sharply on the emissions that cause acid rain, has been slower to tackle urban air quality. Non-EEC countries such as Austria, Norway, Sweden, and Switzerland have had strong auto emissions control legislation in place for several years, but until recently the EEC had been unable to agree on its own stringent standards.

This finally changed in June 1989, when the EEC Council of Environmental Ministers ended a nearly four-year debate and approved new standards for small cars. These will be as tough as those now in effect in the United States. To meet them, small cars will have to be equipped with catalytic converters. Although an important step forward, it's somewhat ironic that Europe sees its adoption of U.S. standards as a major victory at the same time the United States realizes these regulations don't go far enough.

In Eastern Europe and the Soviet Union, air pollution emerged as a pressing political issue as *glasnost* and the revolutions of 1989 opened up public debate. Air pollution in much of the region is taking a devastating toll on human health. Fledgling governments in Eastern Europe are under pressure to show some improvements.

A HELPFUL HAND

To make a dent in their pollution, Eastern Europe and the Soviet Union will need Western technologies and a dose of domestic economic and environmental reform. Given current economic conditions in these countries, money for purchasing pollution control, energy efficiency, renewable energy, and waste reduction technologies will have to come in part in the form of environmental aid from the West.

Aid of this kind can be classified as enlightened philanthropy, since stemming pollution in Eastern Europe, where even rudimentary controls are still lacking, can yield a far greater return on the investment than taking further incremental steps at home. To illustrate this point, Sweden receives 89 percent of the sulfur that contributes to the acid rain poisoning its lakes and forests from other countries. Because much of this is of Eastern European origin, anything Sweden does to combat emissions there helps at home.

Air pollution is beginning to emerge on the political agenda in the Third World as well. In Cubatão, Brazil, a notoriously polluted industrial city known as "the Valley of Death," a five-year-old government cleanup campaign is starting to make a dent in the problem. Total emissions of particulates, for instance, were cut from 521,600 pounds a day in 1984 to 156,000 in 1989.

Mexico City, too, is embarking on an ambitious cleanup. With the support of the World Bank, Japan, the United States, and West Germany, the municipal government is introducing a package of measures aimed at cutting automotive pollution dramatically over the next two to three years. As part of the plan, driving will be restricted on certain days. In March 1991, Mexican President Carlos Salinas de Gortari ordered the shutdown of a large oil refinery on the outskirts of Mexico City that has long been a major contributor to the city's pollution problem.

Industrial countries are involved in a variety of efforts to assist developing countries with air pollution problems. The International Environmental Bureau in Switzerland and the World Environment Center in New York City help facilitate transfer of pollution control information and technology to the Third World. The World Bank is exploring ways to step up its air pollution control activities. One proposed project involving the World Bank and the UN Development Program would help Asian governments confront urban air pollution, among other environmental problems.

Legislation passed by the U.S. Congress requires the Agency for International Development to encourage energy efficiency and renewable energy through its programs in the interests of slowing global warming. This step will reduce air pollution at the same time.

While the means are available to clear the air, it will be a difficult task. In the West, powerful businesses such as auto manufacturers and electric utilities will strongly resist measures that appear costly. In Eastern Europe, the Soviet Union, and the developing world, extreme economic problems coupled with shortages of hard currency mean that money for pollution prevention and control is scarce.

Overcoming these barriers will require fundamental modifications of economic systems. As long as air pollution's costs remain external to economic accounting systems, utilities, industries, and individuals will have little incentive to reduce the amount of pollution they generate. Taxes, regulations, and public awareness can all be harnessed to bring the hidden costs of air pollution out into the open.

On the promising side, faced with mounting costs to human health and the environment, people on every continent are beginning to look at pollution prevention through a different economic lens. Rather than a financial burden, they're seeing that it is a sound investment. The old notion that pollution is the price of progress seems finally to be becoming a relic of the past.

STUDY QUESTIONS

1. What conclusions should we come to after reading French's assessment of the hazards of air pollution? What does the data signify for the future?

2. If you were to propose a plan to solve the problem of air pollution, how would you begin? What sort of measures would you take both locally and nationally? How would you deal with other nations who are polluting the atmosphere?

3. Is air pollution an area that the United Nations should be involved in? Explain your reasoning.

12

We All Live in Bhopal

GEORGE BRADFORD

George Bradford is an editor of The Fifth Estate.

In this essay, Bradford argues that in the Third World, as well as in Europe and the United States, industrial capitalism is harming hundreds of thousands of people and imposing a frightful risk on millions more through unsafe practices that pollute our air, water, soil, and food. Taking the tragic explosion of the Union Carbide insecticide plant in Bhopal, India as his point of departure, he recounts a tale of corporate negligence and moral culpability. Calling these large corporations "corporate vampires," Bradford accuses them of turning industrial civilization into "one vast, stinking extermination camp."

Our modern way of life, dependent on dangerous industrial institutions, reeks with harmful pollution. We must rid ourselves of it before we are crushed by it.

The cinders of the funeral pyres at Bhopal are still warm, and the mass graves still fresh, but the media prostitutes of the corporations have already begun their homilies in defense of industrialism and its uncounted horrors. Some 3,000 people were slaughtered in the wake of the deadly gas cloud, and 20,000 will remain permanently disabled. The poison gas left a 25 square mile swath of dead and dying, people and animals, as it drifted southeast away from the Union Carbide factory. "We thought it was a plague," said one victim. Indeed it was: a chemical plague, an *industrial plague.*

Ashes, ashes, all fall down!

A terrible, unfortunate, "accident," we are reassured by the propaganda apparatus for Progress, for History, for "Our Modern Way of Life." A price, of course, has to be paid—since the risks are necessary to ensure a higher Standard of Living, a Better Way of Life.

The *Wall Street Journal,* tribune of the bourgeoisie, editorialized, "It is worthwhile to remember that the Union Carbide insecticide plant and the people surrounding it were where they were for compelling reasons. India's agriculture has been thriving, bringing a better life to millions of rural people, and partly because of the use of modern agricultural technology that includes applications of insect killers." The indisputable fact of life, according to this sermon, is that universal recognition that India, like everyone else, "needs technology. Calcutta-style scenes of human deprivation

George Bradford, "We All Live in Bhopal," in *Fifth Estate* (4632 Second, Detroit, MI 48201) (Winter 1985): Vol. 19, No. 4 (319). Reprinted in J. Zerzan and Alice Carnes, *Questioning Technology* (Santa Cruz, CA: Freedom Press, 1988). Reprinted by permission.

can be replaced as fast as the country imports the benefits of the West's industrial revolution and market economics." So, despite whatever dangers are involved, "the benefits outweigh the costs" (December 13, 1984).

The *Journal* was certainly right in one regard— the reasons for the plant and the people's presence there are certainly compelling: capitalist market relations and technological invasion are as compelling as a hurricane to the small communities from which those people were uprooted. It conveniently failed to note, however, that countries like India do not import the *benefits* of industrial capitalism; those benefits are *exported* in the form of loan repayments to fill the coffers of the bankers and corporate vampires who read the *Wall Street Journal* for the latest news of their investments. The Indians only take the risks and pay the costs; in fact, for them, as for the immiserated masses of people living in the shantytowns of the Third World, there are no risks, only certain hunger and disease, only the certainty of death squad revenge for criticizing the state of things as they are.

GREEN REVOLUTION
A NIGHTMARE

In fact, the Calcutta-style misery is the result of Third World industrialization and the so called industrial "Green Revolution" in agriculture. The Green Revolution, which was to revolutionize agriculture in the "backward" countries and produce greater crop yields, has only been a miracle for the banks, corporations and military dictatorships who defend them. The influx of fertilizers, technology, insecticides and bureaucratic administration exploded millennia-old rural economies based on subsistence farming, creating a class of wealthier farmers dependent upon western technologies to produce cash crops such as coffee, cotton and wheat for export, while the vast majority of farming communities were destroyed by capitalist market competition and sent like refugees into the

growing cities. These victims, paralleling the destroyed peasantry of Europe's Industrial Revolution several hundred years before, joined either the permanent underclass of unemployed and underemployed slumdwellers eking out a survival on the tenuous margins of civilization, or became proletarian fodder in the Bhopals, Sao Paulos and Djakartas of an industrializing world—an industrialization process, like all industrialization in history, paid for by the pillage of nature and human beings in the countryside.

Food production goes up in some cases, of course, because the measure is only quantitative— some foods disappear while others are produced year round, even for export. *But subsistence is destroyed.* Not only does the rural landscape begin to suffer the consequences of constant crop production and use of chemicals, but the masses of people—laborers on the land and in the teeming hovels growing around the industrial plants—go hungrier in a vicious cycle of exploitation, while the wheat goes abroad to buy absurd commodities and weapons.

But subsistence is culture as well: culture is destroyed with subsistence, and people are further trapped in the technological labyrinth. The ideology of progress is there, blared louder than ever by those with something to hide, a cover-up for plunder and murder on levels never before witnessed.

INDUSTRIALIZATION OF
THE THIRD WORLD

The industrialization of the Third World is a story familiar to anyone who takes even a glance at what is occurring. The colonial countries are nothing but a dumping ground and pool of cheap labor for capitalist corporations. Obsolete technology is shipped there along with the production of chemicals, medicines and other products banned in the developed world. Labor is cheap, there are few if any safety standards, and *costs are cut*. But the formula of cost–benefit still stands: the costs are simply borne by others, by the victims of Union Carbide, Dow, and Standard Oil.

Chemicals found to be dangerous and banned in the US and Europe are produced instead overseas—DDT is a well-known example of an enormous number of such products, such as the unregistered pesticide Leptophos exported by the Velsicol Corporation to Egypt which killed and injured many Egyptian farmers in the mid-1970s. Other products are simply dumped on Third World markets, like the mercury-tainted wheat which led to the deaths of as many as 5,000 Iraqis in 1972, wheat which had been imported from the US. Another example was the wanton contamination of Nicaragua's Lake Managua by a chlorine and caustic soda factory owned by Pennwalt Corporation and other investors, which caused a major outbreak of mercury poisoning in a primary source of fish for the people living in Managua.

Union Carbide's plant at Bhopal did not even meet US safety standards according to its own safety inspector, but a UN expert on international corporate behavior told the *New York Times,* "A whole list of factors is not in place to insure adequate industrial safety" throughout the Third World. "Carbide is not very different from any other chemical company in this regard." According to the *Times,* "In a Union Carbide battery plant in Jakarta, Indonesia, more than half the workers had kidney damage from mercury exposure. In an asbestos cement factory owned by the Manville Corporation 200 miles west of Bhopal, workers in 1981 were routinely covered with asbestos dust, a practice that would never be tolerated here." (12/9/84)

Some 22,500 people are killed every year by exposure to insecticides—a much higher percentage of them in the Third World than use of such chemicals would suggest. Many experts decried the lack of an "industrial culture" in the "underdeveloped" countries as a major cause of accidents and contamination. But where an "industrial culture" thrives, is the situation really much better?

INDUSTRIAL CULTURE AND INDUSTRIAL PLAGUE

In the advanced industrial nations an "industrial culture" (and little other) exists. Have such disasters been avoided as the claims of these experts would lead us to believe?

Another event of such mammoth proportions as those of Bhopal would suggest otherwise—in that case, industrial pollution killed some 4,000 people in a large population center. That was London, in 1952, when several days of "normal" pollution accumulated in stagnant air to kill and permanently injure thousands of Britons.

Then there are the disasters closer to home or to memory, for example, the Love Canal (still leaking into the Great Lakes water system), or the massive dioxin contaminations at Seveso, Italy and Times Creek, Missouri, where thousands of residents had to be permanently evacuated. And there is the Berlin and Farro dump at Swartz Creek, Michigan, where C-56 (a pesticide by-product of Love Canal fame), hydrochloric acid and cyanide from Flint auto plants had accumulated. "They think we're not scientists and not even educated," said one enraged resident, "but anyone who's been in high school knows that cyanide and hydrochloric acid is what they mixed to kill the people in the concentration camps."

A powerful image: industrial civilization as one vast, stinking extermination camp. We all live in Bhopal, some closer to the gas chambers and to the mass graves, but all of us close enough to be victims. And Union Carbide is obviously not a fluke—the poisons are vented in the air and water, dumped in rivers, ponds and streams, fed to animals going to market, sprayed on lawns and roadways, sprayed on food crops, every day, everywhere. The result may not be as dramatic as Bhopal (which then almost comes to serve as a *diversion,* a deterrence machine to take our minds off the pervasive reality which Bhopal truly represents), but it is as deadly. When ABC News asked

University of Chicago professor of public health and author of *The Politics of Cancer,* Jason Epstein, if he thought a Bhopal-style disaster could occur in the US, he replied: "I think what we're seeing in America is far more slow—not such large accidental occurrences, but a slow, gradual leakage with the result that you have excess cancers or reproductive abnormalities."

In fact, birth defects have doubled in the last 25 years. And cancer is on the rise. In an interview with the *Guardian,* Hunter College professor David Kotelchuck described the "Cancer Atlas" maps published in 1975 by the Department of Health, Education and Welfare. "Show me a red spot on these maps and I'll show you an industrial center of the US," he said. "There aren't any place names on the maps but you can easily pick out concentrations of industry. See, it's not Pennsylvania that's red it's just Philadelphia, Erie and Pittsburgh. Look at West Virginia here, there's only two red spots, the Kanawha Valley, where there are nine chemical plants including Union Carbide's, and this industrialized stretch of the Ohio River. It's the same story wherever you look."

There are 50,000 toxic waste dumps in the United States. The EPA admits that *ninety per cent* of the 90 billion pounds of toxic waste produced annually by US industry (70 per cent of it by chemical companies) is disposed of "improperly" (although we wonder what they would consider "proper" disposal). These deadly products of industrial civilization—arsenic, mercury, dioxin, cyanide, and many others—are simply dumped, "legally" and "illegally," wherever convenient to industry. Some 66,000 different compounds are used in industry. Nearly a billion tons of pesticides and herbicides comprising 225 different chemicals were produced in the US last year, and an additional 79 million pounds were imported. Some two per cent of chemical compounds have been tested for side effects. There are 15,000 chemical plants in the United States, daily manufacturing mass death.

All of the dumped chemicals are leaching into our water. Some three to four thousand wells, depending on which government agency you ask, are

contaminated or closed in the US. In Michigan alone, 24 municipal water systems have been contaminated, and a thousand sites have suffered major contamination. According to the Detroit *Free Press,* "The final toll could be as many as 10,000 sites" in Michigan's "water wonderland" alone (April 15, 1984).

And the coverups go unabated here as in the Third World. One example is that of dioxin; during the proceedings around the Agent Orange investigations, it came out that Dow Chemical had lied all along about the effects of dioxin. Despite research findings that dioxin is "exceptionally toxic" with "a tremendous potential for producing chlor-acne and systemic injury," Dow's top toxicologist, V. K Rowe, wrote in 1965, "We are not in any way attempting to hide our problems under a heap of sand. But we certainly do not want to have any situations arise which will cause the regulatory agencies to become restrictive."

Now Vietnam suffers a liver cancer epidemic and a host of cancers and health problems caused by the massive use of Agent Orange there during the genocidal war waged by the US. The sufferings of the US veterans are only a drop in the bucket. And dioxin is appearing everywhere in our environment as well, in the form of recently discovered "dioxin rain."

GOING TO THE VILLAGE

When the Indian authorities and Union Carbide began to process the remaining gases in the Bhopal plant, thousands of residents fled, despite the reassurances of the authorities. The *New York Times* quoted one old man who said, "They are not believing the scientists or the state government or anybody. They only want to save their lives."

The same reporter wrote that one man had gone to the train station with his goats, "hoping that he could take them with him—anywhere, as long as it was away from Bhopal" (December 14, 1984). The same old man quoted above told the reporter, "All the public has gone to the village."

The reporter explained that "going to the village" is what Indians do when trouble comes.

A wise and age-old strategy for survival by which little communities always renewed themselves when bronze, iron and golden empires with clay feet fell to their ruin. But subsistence has been and is everywhere being destroyed, and with it, culture. What are we to do when there is no village to go to? When we all live in Bhopal, and Bhopal is everywhere? The comments of two women, one a refugee from Times Creek, Missouri, and another from Bhopal, come to mind. The first woman said of her former home, "This was a nice place once. Now we have to bury it." The other woman said, "Life cannot come back. Can the government pay for the lives? Can you bring those people back?"

The corporate vampires are guilty of greed, plunder, murder, slavery, extermination and devastation. And we should avoid any pang of sentimentalism when the time comes for them to pay for their crimes against humanity and the natural world. But we will have to go beyond them, to ourselves: subsistence, and with it culture, has been destroyed. We have to find our way back to the village, out of industrial civilization, out of this exterminist system.

The Union Carbides, the Warren Andersons, the "optimistic experts" and the lying propagandists all must go, but with them must go the pesticides, the herbicides, the chemical factories and the chemical way of life which is nothing but death.

Because this is Bhopal, and it is all we've got. This "once nice place" can't be simply buried for us to move on to another pristine beginning. The empire is collapsing. We must find our way back to the village, or as the North American natives said, "back to the blanket," and we must do this not by trying to save an industrial civilization which is doomed, but in that renewal of life which must take place in its ruin. By throwing off this Modern Way of Life, we won't be "giving things up" or sacrificing, but throwing off a terrible burden. Let us do so soon before we are crushed by it.

STUDY QUESTIONS

1. Does Bradford make his case that Western industrial society is dangerous to humanity and nature and needs to be rejected? What are the implications of Bradford's indictment? What sort of world do you think that he would want us to live in? Is Bradford a "Luddite"? (Luddites were people in England in the early nineteenth century who went around destroying machines because they believed that the Industrial Revolution was evil.)

2. Is the anger that comes through in this article justified? Is modern industrial practice really morally irresponsible? Explain your answer.

3. How might someone in the business community respond to Bradford's essay? Can our industrial practices be defended?

13

People or Penguins:
The Case for Optimal Pollution

WILLIAM F. BAXTER

William Baxter is professor of law at Stanford University and the author of People or
Penguins: The Case for Optimal Pollution *(1974) from which this selection is taken.*

*In this essay, Baxter aims at clarifying the relationship between resource use and
pollution. They are the opposite sides of the same coin, the privilege and its price, the good
and the bad. Baxter argues that we cannot have a pollution-free society without harming
humans. If we are humanists, committed to promoting the human good above all else, as he
is, we should be willing to allow pollution where it harms animals and trees if overall benefits
accrue to human beings.*

I start with the modest proposition that, in dealing
with pollution, or indeed with any problem, it is
helpful to know what one is attempting to accomplish. Agreement on how and whether to pursue a
particular objective, such as pollution control, is not
possible unless some more general objective has
been identified and stated with reasonable preci-
sion. We talk loosely of having clean air and clean
water, of preserving our wilderness areas, and so
forth. But none of these is a sufficiently general
objective: each is more accurately viewed as a
means rather than as an end.

With regard to clean air, for example, one may
ask, "how clean?" and "what does clean mean?" It
is even reasonable to ask, "why have clean air?"
Each of these questions is an implicit demand that
a more general community goal be stated—a goal
sufficiently general in its scope and enjoying sufficiently general assent among the community of

actors that such "why" questions no longer seem
admissible with respect to that goal.

If, for example, one states as a goal the proposition that "every person should be free to do whatever he wishes in contexts where his actions do not
interfere with the interests of other human beings,"
the speaker is unlikely to be met with a response of
"why." The goal may be criticized as uncertain in
its implications or difficult to implement, but it is so
basic a tenet of our civilization—it reflects a cultural
value so broadly shared, at least in the abstract—that
the question "why" is seen as impertinent or im-
ponderable or both.

I do not mean to suggest that everyone would
agree with the "spheres of freedom" objective just
stated. Still less do I mean to suggest that a
society could subscribe to four or five such general
objectives that would be adequate in their coverage
to serve as testing criteria by which all other

Reprinted with permission of Columbia University Press from William F. Baxter, *People or Penguins: The Case for Optimal Pollution* (1974).

disagreements might be measured. One difficulty in the attempt to construct such a list is that each new goal added will conflict, in certain applications, with each prior goal listed; and thus each goal serves as a limited qualification on prior goals.

Without any expectation of obtaining unanimous consent to them, let me set forth four goals that I generally use as ultimate testing criteria in attempting to frame solutions to problems of human organization. My position regarding pollution stems from these four criteria. If the criteria appeal to you and any part of what appears hereafter does not, our disagreement will have a helpful focus: which of us is correct, analytically, in supposing that his position on pollution would better serve these general goals. If the criteria do not seem acceptable to you, then it is to be expected that our more particular judgments will differ, and the task will then be yours to identify the basic set of criteria upon which your particular judgments rest.

My criteria are as follows:

1. The spheres of freedom criterion stated above.
2. Waste is a bad thing. The dominant feature of human existence is scarcity—our available resources, our aggregate labors, and our skill in employing both have always been, and will continue for some time to be, inadequate to yield to every man all the tangible and intangible satisfactions he would like to have. Hence, none of those resources, or labors, or skills, should be wasted—that is, employed so as to yield less than they might yield in human satisfactions.
3. Every human being should be regarded as an end rather than as a means to be used for the betterment of another. Each should be afforded dignity and regarded as having an absolute claim to an evenhanded application of such rules as the community may adopt for its governance.
4. Both the incentive and the opportunity to improve his share of satisfactions should be preserved to every individual. Preservation of

incentive is dictated by the "no-waste" criterion and enjoins against the continuous, totally egalitarian redistribution of satisfactions, or wealth; but subject to that constraint, everyone should receive, by continuous redistribution if necessary, some minimal share of aggregate wealth so as to avoid a level of privation from which the opportunity to improve his situation becomes illusory.

The relationship of these highly general goals to the more specific environmental issues at hand may not be readily apparent, and I am not yet ready to demonstrate their pervasive implications. But let me give one indication of their implications. Recently scientists have informed us that use of DDT in food production is causing damage to the penguin population. For the present purposes let us accept that assertion as an indisputable scientific fact. The scientific fact is often asserted as if the correct implication—that we must stop agricultural use of DDT—followed from the mere statement of the fact of penguin damage. But plainly it does not follow if my criteria are employed.

My criteria are oriented to people, not penguins. Damage to penguins, or sugar pines, or geological marvels is, without more, simply irrelevant. One must go further, by my criteria, and say: Penguins are important because people enjoy seeing them walk about rocks; and furthermore, the well-being of people would be less impaired by halting use of DDT than by giving up penguins. In short, my observations about environmental problems will be people-oriented, as are my criteria. I have no interest in preserving penguins for their own sake.

It may be said by way of objection to this position, that it is very selfish of people to act as if each person represented one unit of importance and nothing else was of any importance. It is undeniably selfish. Nevertheless I think it is the only tenable starting place for analysis for several reasons. First, no other position corresponds to the way most people really think and act—i.e., corresponds to reality.

Second, this attitude does not portend any massive destruction of nonhuman flora and fauna, for people depend on them in many obvious ways, and they will be preserved because and to the degree that humans do depend on them.

Third, what is good for humans is, in many respects, good for penguins and pine trees—clean air for example. So that humans are, in these respects, surrogates for plant and animal life.

Fourth, I do not know how we could administer any other system. Our decisions are either private or collective. Insofar as Mr. Jones is free to act privately, he may give such preferences as he wishes to other forms of life: he may feed birds in winter and do less with himself, and he may even decline to resist an advancing polar bear on the ground that the bear's appetite is more important than those portions of himself that the bear may choose to eat. In short my basic premise does not rule out private altruism to competing life-forms. It does rule out, however, Mr. Jones' inclination to feed Mr. Smith to the bear, however hungry the bear, however despicable Mr. Smith.

Insofar as we act collectively on the other hand, only humans can be afforded an opportunity to participate in the collective decisions. Penguins cannot vote now and are unlikely subjects for the franchise—pine trees more unlikely still. Again each individual is free to cast his vote so as to benefit sugar pines if that is his inclination. But many of the more extreme assertions that one hears from some conservationists amount to tacit assertions that they are specially appointed representatives of sugar pines, and hence that their preferences should be weighted more heavily than the preferences of other humans who do not enjoy equal rapport with "nature." The simplistic assertion that agricultural use of DDT must stop at once because it is harmful to penguins is of that type.

Fifth, if polar bears or pine trees or penguins, like men, are to be regarded as ends rather than means, if they are to count in our calculus of social organization, someone must tell me how much each one counts, and someone must tell me how these life-forms are to be permitted to express their preferences, for I do not know either answer. If the

answer is that certain people are to hold their proxies, then I want to know how those proxy-holders are to be selected: self-appointment does not seem workable to me.

Sixth, and by way of summary of all the foregoing, let me point out that the set of environmental issues under discussion—although they raise very complex technical questions of how to achieve any objective—ultimately raise a normative question: what ought we to do. Questions of ought are unique to the human mind and world—they are meaningless as applied to a nonhuman situation.

I reject the proposition that we ought to respect the "balance of nature" or to "preserve the environment" unless the reason for doing so, express or implied, is the benefit of man.

I reject the idea that there is a "right" or "morally correct" state of nature to which we should return. The word "nature" has no normative connotation. Was it "right" or "wrong" for the earth's crust to heave in contortion and create mountains and seas? Was it "right" for the first amphibian to crawl up out of the primordial ooze? Was it "wrong" for plants to reproduce themselves and alter the atmospheric composition in favor of oxygen? For animals to alter the atmosphere in favor of carbon dioxide both by breathing oxygen and eating plants? No answers can be given to these questions because they are meaningless questions.

All this may seem obvious to the point of being tedious, but much of the present controversy over environment and pollution rests on tacit normative assumptions about just such nonnormative phenomena: that it is "wrong" to impair penguins with DDT, but not to slaughter cattle for prime rib roasts. That it is wrong to kill stands of sugar pines with industrial fumes, but not to cut sugar pines and build housing for the poor. Every man is entitled to his own preferred definition of Walden Pond, but there is no definition that has any moral superiority over another, except by reference to the selfish needs of the human race.

From the fact that there is no normative definition of the natural state, it follows that there is no normative definition of clean air or pure water—hence no definition of polluted air—or of pollution—except by reference to the needs of man. The "right" composition of the atmosphere is one which has some dust in it and some lead in it and some hydrogen sulfide in it—just those amounts that attend a sensibly organized society thoughtfully and knowledgeably pursuing the greatest possible satisfaction for its human members.

The first and most fundamental step toward solution of our environmental problems is a clear recognition that our objective is not pure air or water but rather some optimal state of pollution. That step immediately suggests the question: How do we define and attain the level of pollution that will yield the maximum possible amount of human satisfaction?

Low levels of pollution contribute to human satisfaction but so do food and shelter and education and music. To attain ever lower levels of pollution, we must pay the cost of having less of these other things. I contrast that view of the cost of pollution control with the more popular statement that pollution control will "cost" very large numbers of dollars. The popular statement is true in some senses, false in others; sorting out the true and false senses is of some importance. The first step in that sorting process is to achieve a clear understanding of the difference between dollars and resources. Resources are the wealth of our nation; dollars are merely claim checks upon those resources. Resources are of vital importance; dollars are comparatively trivial.

Four categories of resources are sufficient for our purposes: At any given time a nation, or a planet if you prefer, has a stock of labor, of technological skill, of capital goods, and of natural resources (such as mineral deposits, timber, water, land, etc.). These resources can be used in various combinations to yield goods and services of all kinds—in some limited quantity. The quantity will be larger if they are combined efficiently, smaller if combined inefficiently. But in either event the resource stock is limited, the goods and services that they can be made to yield are limited; even the most efficient use of them will yield less than our population, in the aggregate, would like to have.

If one considers building a new dam, it is appropriate to say that it will be costly in the sense that it will require x hours of labor, y tons of steel and concrete, and z amount of capital goods. If these resources are devoted to the dam, then they cannot be used to build hospitals, fishing rods, schools, or electric can openers. That is the meaningful sense in which the dam is costly.

Quite apart from the very important question of how wisely we can combine our resources to produce goods and services, is the very different question of how they get distributed—who gets how many goods? Dollars constitute the claim checks which are distributed among people and which control their share of national output. Dollars are nearly valueless pieces of paper except to the extent that they do represent claim checks to some fraction of the output of goods and services. Viewed as claim checks, all the dollars outstanding during any period of time are worth, in the aggregate, the goods and services that are available to be claimed with them during that period—neither more nor less.

It is far easier to increase the supply of dollars than to increase the production of goods and services—printing dollars is easy. But printing more dollars doesn't help because each dollar then simply becomes a claim to fewer goods, i.e., becomes worth less.

The point is this: many people fall into error upon hearing the statement that the decision to build a dam, or to clean up a river, will cost $X million. It is regrettably easy to say: "It's only money. This is a wealthy country, and we have lots of money." But you cannot build a dam or clean a river with $X million—unless you also have a match, you can't even make a fire. One builds a dam or cleans a river by diverting labor and steel and trucks and factories from making one kind of goods to making another. The cost in dollars is merely a shorthand way of describing the extent of the diversion necessary. If we build a dam for $X million, then we must recognize that we will have $X million less housing and food and medical care and electric can openers as a result.

Similarly, the costs of controlling pollution are best expressed in terms of the other goods we will have to give up to do the job. This is not to say the job should not be done. Badly as we need more housing, more medical care, and more can openers, and more symphony orchestras, we could do with somewhat less of them, in my judgment at least, in exchange for somewhat cleaner air and rivers. But that is the nature of the trade-off, and analysis of the problem is advanced if that unpleasant reality is kept in mind. Once the trade-off relationship is clearly perceived, it is possible to state in a very general way what the optimal level of pollution is. I would state it as follows:

People enjoy watching penguins. They enjoy relatively clean air and smog-free vistas. Their health is improved by relatively clean water and air. Each of these benefits is a type of good or service. As a society we would be well advised to give up one washing machine if the resources that would have gone into that washing machine can yield greater human satisfaction when diverted into pollution control. We should give up one hospital if the resources thereby freed would yield more human satisfaction when devoted to elimination of noise in our cities. And so on, trade-off by trade-off, we should divert our productive capacities from the production of existing goods and services to the production of a cleaner, quieter, more pastoral nation up to—and no further than—the point at which we value more highly the next washing machine or hospital that we would have to do without than we value the next unit of environmental improvement that the diverted resources would create.

Now this proposition seems to me unassailable but so general and abstract as to be unhelpful—at least unadministerable in the form stated. It assumes we can measure in some way the incremental units of human satisfaction yielded by very different types of goods.... But I insist that the proposition stated describes the result for which we should be striving—and again, that it is always useful to know what your target is even if your weapons are too crude to score a bull's eye.

STUDY QUESTIONS

1. Evaluate the four tenets of Baxter's environmental philosophy.

    a. Which do you agree with, and which do you disagree with? Explain why.

    b. Is human benefit the only morally relevant criterion with regard to our behavior to animals and the environment?

    c. Do penguins and sugar pine trees have intrinsic value? Or is their value entirely instrumental, derived from benefits to humans?

2. Do you agree with Baxter that pollution is just the opposite side of the coin of resource use? Do you also agree that on the principle that "waste is a bad thing" we are led to use resources for human good and thus bring about some level of pollution?

3. Compare Baxter's analysis with those of Bradford and French. What are their similarities and differences? Does Baxter shed any light on the matter?

FOR FURTHER READING

Bernards, Neal, ed. *The Environmental Crisis*. San Diego, CA: Greenhaven Press, 1991.

Bogard, William. The Bhopal Tragedy: Language, Logic and Politics in the Production of a Hazard. Boulder, CO: Westview, 1989.

Brown, Lester. *The Twenty Ninth Day*. New York: Norton, 1978.

———, ed. *The Worldwatch Reader*. Washington, DC: Worldwatch Institute, 1991.

Brown, Michael. *The Toxic Cloud*. New York: Harper & Row, 1987.

Gore, Albert. *Earth in the Balance*. Boston: Houghton Mifflin, 1992.

Keeble, John. *Out of the Channel: The Exxon Valdez Spill.* New York: HarperCollins, 1991.

Lomborg, Bjorn. *The Skeptical Environmentalist.* New York: Routledge, 2001.

McKibbern, Bill. *The End of Nature.* New York: Random House, 1989.

Postel, Sandra. *Defusing the Toxic Threat: Controlling Pesticides and Industrial Waste.* Washington, DC: Worldwatch Institute, 1987.

Ray, Dixy Lee, and Lou Guzzo. *Trashing the Planet.* Washington, DC: Regnery Gateway, 1990.

Silver, Cheryl Pollack. *Protecting Life on Earth: Steps to Save the Ozone Layer.* Washington, DC: Worldwatch Institute, 1988.

Simon, Julian. *The Ultimate Resource.* Princeton, NJ: Princeton University Press, 1981.

Wellburn, Alan. *Air Pollution and Acid Rain.* New York: Wiley, 1988.

14

Is *Silent Spring* Behind Us?

DAVID PIMENTEL

David Pimentel is professor of entomology at Cornell University and the author of Ecological Effects of Pesticides on Nontarget Species *(1971).*

In this selection, Pimentel assesses the progress of the pesticide problem since Rachel Carson's Silent Spring. *Assembling an array of information, he details the ways in which the situation has improved and the ways in which it has deteriorated.*

Is *silent spring* behind us? Have environmental problems associated with pesticide use improved? The answer is a qualified "yes."

Rachel Carson's warning in 1962 generated widespread concern, but many years elapsed before action was taken to halt some of the environmental damage being inflicted by pesticides on our sensitive natural biota. More than 20 years later we still have not solved all the pesticide environmental problems, although some real progress has been made.

FEWER PESTICIDE PROBLEMS DURING THE PAST TWO DECADES

Chlorinated insecticides, such as DDT, dieldrin, and toxaphene, are characterized by their spread and persistence in the environment. The widespread use of chlorinated insecticides from 1945 to 1972 significantly reduced the populations of predatory birds such as eagles, peregrine falcons, and ospreys. Trout, salmon, and other fish populations were seriously

Reprinted from *Silent Spring Revisited*, ed. G. J. Marco, R. M. Hollingsworth, and W. Durham (Washington, D.C.: American Chemical Society, 1987) by permission. Notes deleted.

reduced, and their flesh was contaminated with pesticide residues. Snakes and other reptile populations, as well as certain insect and other invertebrate populations that were highly sensitive to the chlorinated insecticides, were reduced.

Since the restriction on the use of chlorinated insecticides went into effect in 1972, the quantities of these residues in humans and in terrestrial and aquatic ecosystems have slowly declined. From 1970 to 1974, for example, DDT residues in human adipose tissue declined by about one-half in Caucasians who were 0–14 years of age (see Table 1). The declines in other Caucasian age groups and in blacks have not been as great. In agricultural soils, DDT residues have declined by about one-half or from 0.015 parts per million (ppm) in 1968 to 0.007 ppm in 1973. The decline of DDT in soil led to a decline in the amount of DDT running into aquatic ecosystems and resulted in a significant decline in DDT residues found in various fish. For example, in lake trout caught in the Canadian waters of eastern Lake Superior, DDT residues declined from 1.04 ppm in 1971 to only 0.05 ppm in 1975. In aquatic birds that feed on fish, DDT residues also declined. For example, DDT residues in brown pelican eggs collected in South Carolina declined from 0.45 ppm in 1968 to only 0.004 ppm in 1975.

Because DDT and other organochlorine residues in terrestrial ecosystems have declined, various populations of birds, mammals, fishes, and reptiles have started to recover and increase in number. For example, peregrine falcons have been bred in the laboratory and then successfully released in the environment. Limited data do exist on the recoveries of a few animal species, but we do not know the recovery rates for those animal populations that were seriously affected by chlorinated insecticides. Those species with short generation times and high reproductive rates, like insects, have probably recovered best.

New pesticide regulations established in the early 1970s restricted the use of highly persistent pesticides, which include chlorinated insecticides. DDT, toxaphene, and dieldrin, for example, persist in the environment for 10 to 30 years. Two major problems are associated with the use of highly persistent pesticides. Annual applications of chlorinated insecticides add to the total quantity of insecticides in the environment because they degrade slowly. This persistence in the environment increases the chances for the chemicals to move out of the target area into the surrounding environment.

The amount of chlorinated insecticide residues in the environment since most of the chlorinated insecticides were banned has been declining. But because these insecticides are relatively stable, some will persist 30 years or more, and some will be present in the U.S. environment until the end of this century. Fortunately these residues are relatively low, so their effect on most organisms should be minimal.

Persistence of chlorinated insecticides in the environment is only one of the problems created by these chemicals. Their solubility in fats and oils resulted in their accumulation in the fatty tissues of animals, including humans. Thus, bioaccumulation of chlorinated insecticides is a serious environmental problem. Organisms like water fleas and fish, for example, concentrated DDT and other chlorinated insecticides from a dosage of 1 part per billion (ppb) in the environment to

TABLE 1   Total DDT Equivalent Residues in Human Adipose Tissue from General U.S. Population by Race

Age (years)	1970	1971	1972	1973	1974
Caucasians					
0–14	4.16	3.32	2.79	2.59	2.15
15–44	6.89	6.56	6.01	5.71	4.91
45 and above	8.01	7.50	7.00	6.63	6.55
Blacks					
0–14	5.54	7.30		4.68	3.16
15–44	10.88	13.92	11.32	9.97	9.18
45 and above	16.56	19.57	15.91	14.11	11.91

Note: All residues are measured in parts per million lipid weight.

levels in their tissues of 100,000 times that. Bioaccumulation continues in the environment with several pesticides (e.g., parathion and 2,4–D), but restricting the use of chlorinated insecticides has reduced this environmental problem.

Movement and magnification of pesticides in the food chain also occurs, but must be carefully documented. Some organisms concentrate pesticides in their bodies 100,000-fold over levels in the ambient environment, and this condition might mistakenly be interpreted as a case of biomagnification in the food chain. Biomagnification in the food chain has been documented with birds like osprey and gulls that feed on fish and has proven to be a serious problem to these predaceous birds.

INCREASED PESTICIDE PROBLEMS DURING THE PAST TWO DECADES

Although restricted use of chlorinated insecticides has relieved some environmental problems, the escalation of pesticide use since 1970 has intensified several other environmental and social problems. Pesticide production and use has increased 2.3-fold since 1970, from around 1.0 to nearly 1.5 billion pounds annually.

Recent research has documented the fact that certain pesticide use may actually increase pest problems. For example, herbicides like 2,4-D used at recommended dosages on corn increased the susceptibility of corn to both insects and plant pathogens. Also the reproduction of certain insects can be stimulated by low dosages of certain insecticides, as occurred in the Colorado potato beetle. For example, sublethal doses of parathion increase egg production by 65%. In addition, most of the insecticides that replaced the chlorinated insecticides are more toxic per unit weight than the chlorinated insecticides.

If one pesticide is more toxic and more biologically active than another, it is not necessarily hazardous to the environment. Risk depends on the dosage and method of application of the specific pesticide. If one pesticide's per-unit weight is more toxic than another, the more toxic chemical is usually applied at a lower dosage that will cause about a 90% kill in the pest population. Thus, a highly toxic material used at a low dosage can achieve about the same mortality as a low-toxicity material. Both high- and low-toxicity pesticides affect pests and nontarget organisms in a similar manner, but the risks to humans handling highly toxic pesticides are far greater than when handling pesticides with a low toxicity. Humans handling highly toxic pesticides like parathion are more likely to be poisoned than those handling pesticides of low toxicity like DDT. If one spills DDT and wipes the pesticide off the skin, no harm is done. However, a similar accident with parathion often leads to poisoning severe enough to require hospitalization.

Human Poisonings

Humans are exposed to pesticides by handling and applying them, by contacting them on treated vegetation, and, to a lesser extent, from their presence in food and water supplies. The number of annual human pesticide poisonings has been estimated at about 45,000; about 3000 of these are sufficiently severe to require hospitalization. The number of annual accidental deaths caused by pesticides is about 50. Accurate data on human pesticide poisonings still are not available 20 years after *Silent Spring*.

Furthermore, detecting the causes of cancer from pesticides is exceedingly difficult because of the long lag time prior to illness and the wide variety of cancer-producing factors that humans are exposed to in their daily activities. No one knows if less human cancer is caused by pesticides now than 20 years ago. Probably less than 1% of human cancers today are caused by pesticides.

We are constantly exposed to pesticides. Despite efforts to keep pesticides out of our food and water, about 50% of U.S. foods sampled by the

Food and Drug Administration (FDA) contain detectable levels of pesticides. Improvements in analytical chemical procedures are helping us detect smaller and smaller quantities of pesticides in food and water. These extremely low dosages should have little or no public health effect.

Domestic Animal Poisonings

Because domestic animals are present on farms and near homes where pesticides are used, many of these animals are poisoned. Dogs and cats are most frequently affected because they often wander freely about the home and farm and have ample opportunity to come in contact with pesticides.

A major loss of livestock products (about $3 million annually) occurs when pesticide residues are found in these products. This problem will probably continue as the quantity of pesticides used continues to rise.

Bee Poisonings

Honeybees and wild bees are essential to the pollination of fruits, vegetables, forage crops, and natural plants. Pesticides kill bees, and the losses to agriculture from bee kills and the related reduction of pollination are estimated to be $135 million each year. Evidence suggests that bee poisonings are probably greater now than in 1962 for several reasons. More highly toxic insecticides are being used, and greater quantities of insecticides are being dispensed. In addition, more pesticide is being applied by aircraft, and aircraft applications are employing ultra low volume (ULV) application equipment. ULV applications require smaller droplets for coverage, and this practice tends to increase pesticide drift problems.

Crop Losses

Although pesticides are employed to protect crops from pests, some crops are damaged as a result of pesticidal treatments. Heavy pesticide use damages crops and causes declines in yields because: (1) herbicide residues that remain in the soil after use on one crop injure chemically sensitive crops planted in rotation, (2) certain desired crops cannot be planted in rotation because of knowledge of potential hazard injury, (3) excessive residues of pesticides remain on the harvested crop and result in its destruction or devaluation, (4) pesticides that are applied improperly or under unfavorable environmental conditions result in drift and other problems, and (5) pesticides drift from a treated crop to nearby crops and destroy natural enemies or the crop itself.

Although an accurate estimate of the negative impact of pesticides on crops in agriculture is extremely difficult to obtain, a conservative estimate is about $70 million annually. The problem is probably worse today than in Carson's time because 7 times more pesticide is being applied today than 20 years ago, and its use is more widespread. This statement is especially true of herbicides.

Reduced Populations of Natural Enemies

In undisturbed environments, most insect and mite populations remain at low densities because a wide array of factors, including natural enemies, control them. When insecticides or other pesticides are applied to crops to control one or more pest species, natural enemy populations are sometimes destroyed, and subsequently pest outbreaks occur.

For example, before the synthetic pesticide era (1945) the major pests of cotton in the United States were the boll weevil and cotton leafworm. When extensive insecticide use began in 1945, several other insect and mite species became serious pests. These include the cotton bollworm, tobacco budworm, looper, cotton aphid, and spider mites. In some regions where pesticides are used to control the boll weevil, as many as five additional treatments have to be made to control bollworms and budworms because their natural enemies have been destroyed. This cycle has meant more pesticide use, more natural enemies destroyed, greater pest populations, and more pesticides used.

Pesticide Resistance

In addition to destroying natural enemies, the widespread use of pesticides often causes pest populations to develop resistance and pass it on to their progeny. More than 420 species of insects and mites and several weed species have developed resistance to pesticides. Pesticide resistance in pests results in additional sprays of some pesticides or the use of alternative and often more expensive pesticides. Again the process of pest control escalates the cycle of pesticide use and the development of resistance.

An estimated $133 million worth of added sprays or more expensive pesticides has been employed to deal with the resistance problem annually. This dollar cost, of course, does not include the side effects apparent in the environment and in public health from using more pesticides and more toxic pesticides.

Fishery Losses

Pesticides in treated cropland often run off and move into aquatic ecosystems. Water-soluble pesticides are easily washed into streams and lakes, whereas other pesticides are carried with soil sediments into aquatic ecosystems. Each year several million tons of soil, and with it, pesticides, are washed into streams and lakes.

At present only a small percentage of fish kills are reported because of the procedures used in reporting fish losses. For example, 20% of the reported fish kills give no estimate of the number of dead fish because fish kills often cannot be investigated quickly enough to determine the primary cause. Also, fast-moving waters rapidly dilute all pollutants, including pesticides, and thus make the cause of the kill difficult to determine. Dead fish are washed away or sink to the bottom, so accurate counts are not possible.

Samples of water recently confirmed a steadily decreasing concentration of pesticides found in surface waters and streams from 1964 to 1978. This reduction is apparently related to the replacement of persistent pesticides with less persistent materials. Despite the reduced pesticide residues in streams, an estimated $800,000 or more in fish is lost annually (each fish was calculated to have a value of 40 cents). This estimate of nearly $1 million probably is several times too low and does not confirm that *Silent Spring* is behind us.

Impacts on Wildlife and Microorganisms

Too little information exists to make even a conservative estimate of the populations of vertebrates, invertebrates, and microorganisms that are adversely affected by pesticides. Most invertebrates and microorganisms perform many essential functions to agriculture, forestry, and other segments of human society; such as preventing the accumulation of water, cleaning water or soil of pollutants, recycling vital chemical elements within the ecosystem, and conserving soil and water. An estimated 200,000 species of plants and animals exist in the United States and, at best, we have information on the effects of pesticides on less than 1000 species. Most of these data are based on "safe concentration" tests conducted in the laboratory. This situation confirms that little is known about pesticide effects on the natural environment. At present evaluation must be based on indicator species.

STATUS OF INTEGRATED PEST MANAGEMENT

Integrated pest management (IPM), introduced more than a decade ago, aimed to reduce pesticide use by monitoring pest populations and using pesticides only when necessary as well as augmenting pest control with alternative nonchemical strategies. What happened? IPM has not been successful, and in fact, more of all kinds of pesticides are being used in the United States and throughout the world than ever before.

The reasons for the poor performance of IPM are complex. First, IPM technology, even if it is simply monitoring pest and natural enemy populations, requires a great deal more basic information than scientists now have. This fact signals the pressing need for basic research on the ecology of pests, their natural enemies, and their environment. Also, the use of this basic information to develop control programs is much more sophisticated than routine application of pesticides. Because this technology is more sophisticated, trained manpower is needed, and often the farmer is not trained and cannot be expected to carry out effective IPM programs.

Pesticides are unquestionably simple and quick to use. They have a significant psychological advantage over IPM and especially over nonchemical controls like biological control. Biological controls gradually bring pest populations under control, but do not give the immediate satisfaction of direct kill like pesticides do. However, as research continues and greater ecological knowledge of pests and agroecosystems increases, IPM has the potential to improve pest control.

WHY ARE LOSSES DUE TO PESTS GREATER TODAY THAN 40 YEARS AGO?

Currently, an estimated 37% of all crops is lost annually to pests (13% to insects, 12% to plant pathogens, and 12% to weeds) in spite of the combined use of pesticidal and nonchemical controls. According to a survey of data collected from 1942 to the present, crop losses from weeds declined slightly from 13.8% to 12% because of a combination of improved herbicidal, mechanical, and cultural weed control practices. During the same period, losses from plant pathogens increased slightly from 10.5% to 12%.

On average, however, crop losses due to insects have increased nearly twofold (from 7% to about 13%) from the 1940s to the present in spite of a 10-fold increase in insecticide use. Thus far the impact of this loss in terms of production has been effectively offset through the use of higher yielding varieties and increased use of fertilizers.

The substantial increase in crop losses caused by insects can be accounted for by some of the major changes that have taken place in U.S. agriculture since the 1940s. These changes include

- planting of crop varieties that are increasingly susceptible to insect pests;

- destruction of natural enemies of certain pests, which in turn creates the need for additional pesticide treatments;

- increase in the development of pesticide resistance in insects;

- reduced crop rotations and crop diversity and an increase in the continuous culture of a single crop;

- reduced FDA tolerance and increased cosmetic standards of processors and retailers for fruits and vegetables;

- reduced field sanitation including less destruction of infected fruit and crop residues;

- reduced tillage, leaving more crop remains on the land surface to harbor pests for subsequent crops;

- culturing crops in climatic regions where they are more susceptible to insect attack;

- use of pesticides that alter the physiology of crop plants and make them more susceptible to insect attack.

CONCLUSION

Progress has been made on pesticide problems, but *Silent Spring* is not entirely behind us. Pesticide use continues, and the quantities of pesticides applied grow annually despite support for IPM control. In future decades, as the world population grows rapidly and agricultural production is stretched to meet food needs, we should not forget Carson's warnings.

Pesticides will continue to be effective pest controls, but the challenge now is to find ways to use them judiciously to avoid many of the environmental hazards and human poisonings that exist today. With this goal for research and development we can achieve effective, relatively safe pest control programs.

STUDY QUESTIONS

1. Go over Pimentel's discussion and describe the ways the pesticide problem has improved and how it has deteriorated.

2. Can you suggest ways to improve our situation still further?

Chapter 5

Food Ethics

Hunger is a child with shriveled limbs and a swollen belly. It is the grief of parents, or a person gone blind for lack of vitamin A.[1]

The victim of starvation burns up his own body fats, muscles and tissues for fuel. His body quite literally consumes itself and deteriorates rapidly. The kidneys, liver and endocrine system often cease to function properly. A shortage of carbohydrates, which play a vital role in brain chemistry, affects the mind. Lassitude and confusion set in, so that starvation victims often seem unaware of their plight. The body's defenses drop; disease kills most famine victims before they have time to starve to death. An individual begins to starve when he has lost about a third of his normal body weight. Once this loss exceeds 40%, death is almost inevitable.[2]

TEN THOUSAND PEOPLE starve to death every day, another 2 billion (out of a global population of over 6 billion) are malnourished, and 460 million are permanently hungry. Almost half of these are children. More than one-third of the world goes to bed hungry each night. In recent years, devastating famines have occurred in Bangladesh (1974), Ethiopia (1972–74, 1984), Cambodia (1978), Chad and Sudan (1985), and in many of the other 43 countries making up the sub-Saharan region of Africa throughout the 1970s and 1980s, including the recent famine in Somalia. Since the 1960s conditions have deteriorated in many parts of the world.[3]

On the other hand, another third of the world lives in affluence. Imagine ten children eating at a table. The three healthiest eat the best food and throw much of it away or give it to their pets. Two other children get just enough to get by on. The other five do not get enough food. Three of them who are weak manage to stave off hunger pangs by eating bread and rice, but the other two are unable to do even that and die of hunger-related diseases, such as pneumonia and dysentery. Such is the plight of children in the world.

In the United States, enough food is thrown into the garbage each day to feed an entire nation, more money is spent on pet food than on aid to the world's starving, and many people are grossly overweight.

Problems of global scarcity, poverty, hunger, and famine are among the most urgent facing us. What is our duty to the hungry in our country and in other lands? What obligations do we have toward the poor abroad? What rights do the starving have against us? To what extent, if any, should hunger relief be tied to population control?

In our first reading, Mylan Engel, Jr. links world hunger with environmental integrity and animal rights and argues that by changing the way we eat, we could save millions of lives and feed the whole world. He argues that even by our present moral values we have a moral duty to become vegetarians. We then examine genetically modified foods, with Jonathon Rauch arguing that they are potentially the solution to world hunger and Mae-Wan Ho presenting evidence that they not only are dangerous for the environment but are also taking autonomy away from individual farmers. Finally, Tristam Coffin and Michael Allen Fox examine the impact of the meat industry upon the world's food supply and the environment.

NOTES

1. Arthur Simon, *Bread for the World* (New York: Paulist Press, 1975).
2. *Time Magazine*, November 11, 1974.
3. Statistics in this introduction come from the U.N. Food and Agriculture Organization. Some of the discussion is based on Arthur Simon, op. cit.

15

Hunger, Duty, and Ecology: On What We Owe Starving Humans

MYLAN ENGEL, JR.

Mylan Engel, Jr. is associate professor of philosophy at Northern Illinois University. His primary areas of interest include epistemology, philosophy of religion, and practical ethics. His current research centers on the following issues: personal and doxastic justification in epistemology; epistemic contextualism, skepticism, and closure; rational belief in the absence of reasons; human obligations toward nonhuman animals; and our duties to those living in absolute poverty. Engel has provided the following abstract of his article.

An argument is advanced for the moral obligatoriness of (O_1) supporting famine relief organizations through financial contributions and (O_2) refraining from squandering food in situations of food scarcity. Unlike other ethical arguments for the obligation to assist the world's absolutely poor, my argument is not predicated on any highly contentious ethical theory which can you reject. Rather, it is predicated on your own beliefs. The argument shows that the things you currently believe already commit you to the obligatoriness of helping to reduce malnutrition and famine-related diseases by sending a nominal percentage of your income to famine-relief organizations and by not squandering food that could be fed to them. Being consistent with your own beliefs implies that to do any less is to be profoundly immoral.

HUNGER, DUTY, AND ECOLOGY: ON WHAT WE OWE STARVING HUMANS

You probably remember many of the tragic events of September 11, 2001. Nineteen terrorists hijacked four commercial airliners, crashing two of them into the World Trade Center towers, one into the Pentagon, and one in a field in Pennsylvania. Approximately 3,200 innocent individuals died needlessly. People around the world stared at their television sets in horror and disbelief as the news media aired clips of the attack 'round the clock. The tragedy immediately roused President Bush to declare "war on terrorism." Volunteers from all across America traveled to New York at their own expense to aid in the rescue and clean-up efforts. Charitable contributions poured into the American Red Cross, which in turn wrote checks totaling $143.4 million in emergency aid (averaging $45,837 per family). The U.S. government put together a $5 billion relief package that will provide $1.6 million to each of the victim's families. The United States has spent billions more on its military efforts to root out Osama bin Laden and his al-Qaeda terrorist network. As the dust from the 9/11 attacks has finally settled, it is safe to say that Americans are now taking terrorism seriously.

Here are some of the tragic events that took place on 9/11 that you probably don't recall. On that infamous day, more than 33,000 innocent children under the age of five died *senseless, needless* deaths—18,000 died from malnutrition and another

15,300 died of untreated poverty-related diseases. It must be stressed that almost all of these deaths were *unnecessary.* They could have *easily been prevented.* The United States alone grows enough grain and soybeans to feed the world's human population several times over. Given this overabundance of food, the lives of those children who starved to death on 9/11 could have easily been saved, had we only diverted a relatively modest portion of this food to them. As for the disease-related deaths, 19% of the 33,000 children who lost their lives on 9/11 died from the dehydrating effects of chronic diarrhea. Almost all of these 6,350 diarrheal dehydration deaths could have been prevented by administering each child a single packet of oral rehydration salts (cost per packet: 15 cents). Another 19% of these children died from acute respiratory infections. Most of them could have been saved with a course of antibiotics (cost: 25 cents). Most of the 2,300 children who died from measles could have been saved with vitamin A therapy (cost per capsule: less than 10 cents). What makes the deaths of these children particularly tragic is that virtually all of them were readily preventable. They occurred only because otherwise good people did nothing to prevent them.

Despite the fact that the number of innocent children who died needlessly on 9/11 was ten times greater than the number of innocent people who lost their lives in the 9/11 terrorist attack, compassionate conservative President Bush did not declare war on hunger or on poverty. The U.S. government did not immediately institute a multibillion dollar relief package for the world's absolutely poor. People did not make out generous checks to famine-relief organizations. The media did not so much as mention the tragedy of so many innocent young lives lost. And, as if 9/11 wasn't enough for us to deal with, on 9/12 another 33,000 innocent children under the age of five died unnecessarily, and another 33,000 on 9/13. In the 22 months that have transpired since the 9/11 tragedy, more than 22 million innocent children under the age of five have died needlessly. By any objective measure, the tragedy of the 9/11 attack pales in comparison with the tragedy of world hunger and famine-related disease. Each year the latter claims 3,800 times more innocent lives than the 9/11 attack. Despite the magnitude of the tragedy of global hunger and childhood malnutrition, the overwhelming majority of affluent and moderately affluent people, including most philosophers, send no money to famine-relief organizations. Of the 4 million people who receive solicitations from UNICEF each year, less than 1% donate anything at all. For most of us, world hunger doesn't even register a blip on our moral radar screens, much less present itself as a serious moral problem requiring action on our part.

My aim in the present paper is an ambitious one. I hope to convince you (and others) to *take hunger seriously*. How? By showing you that your beliefs already commit you to the view that global hunger and *absolute poverty*[1] impose serious moral obligations on moderately affluent people. Starting with your beliefs as premises, I shall argue that affluent and moderately affluent people, like you and me, are morally obligated:

(O₁) to provide modest financial support for famine-relief organizations and/or other humanitarian organizations working to reduce the amount of unnecessary pain, suffering, and death in the world, and

(O₂) to refrain from squandering food that could be fed to the world's absolutely poor.

1. PRELIMINARIES

The central questions this essay addresses are not new: Is it morally permissible for moderately

affluent people who have the financial means to prevent some innocent children from starving to death to do nothing to reduce the number of children suffering from starvation? Are moderately affluent people morally obligated to send money to famine-relief organizations to help reduce world hunger and absolute poverty? If so, what is the extent of their obligation—i.e., just how much money must they send to these humanitarian organizations if they are to avoid being immoral?

These questions took center stage in the 1970s when a spate of philosophers offered arguments defending the view that affluent and moderately affluent people are morally required to provide financial support to organizations working to alleviate hunger, malnutrition, and absolute poverty around the world. Arguments from practically every theoretical perspective in normative ethics (except for libertarianism, which will be discussed later) were advanced: utilitarian arguments, Kantian arguments, human rights-based arguments, and ideal contractarian arguments. Working backwards, Jan Narveson (1977) rejects the libertarian "Nobody needs to help anybody" stance as unreasonable and, using a Rawlsean approach, he tentatively defends the view that one is free to acquire more property than one's neighbor, but only if one is "willing to contribute a certain amount of one's wealth to those in undeserved misfortune, once one gets beyond a certain minimal amount—a fraction which perhaps increases as one gets more and more." William Aiken (1977) argues that the moral right to be saved from starvation derives from the more general moral right to be saved from preventable death due to deprivation and that this latter right generates a stringent corresponding moral obligation on the part of those in a position to prevent such deaths. As Aiken puts it:

> Until it is true that I cannot help another without putting myself in an equivalent position of need (that is, dying of deprivation), I have a *prima facie* obligation to honor others' right to be saved from preventable death due to deprivation.[2]

The Kantian argument is predicated on Kant's claim that we have an imperfect duty to help those in dire need. As I interpret Kant, the duty is imperfect, since (i) there is no specific person to whom we owe it; (ii) since we owe it to persons generally and because we cannot possibly help *every* person in dire need, we are free to fulfill the duty in various ways as various opportunities to help present themselves; and (iii) the duty is a general duty that is never completely satisfied—i.e., no matter how many people in dire need we help, we are still obligated to help other people in dire need when we can do so. It is not a duty that we should fulfill *only* when some especially salient case presents itself. It is a duty that we should fulfill *whenever* we can, provided that doing so won't prevent us from our doing any of our other overriding duties. Most of us living in affluent nations have relatively few nearby opportunities to help people in dire need (because most of the people we regularly encounter are not in dire need). But there are millions of people elsewhere who are in dire need (of food, medicine, etc.), some of whom we can help by sending money to organizations like OXFAM, and so, on Kantian grounds, we ought to send money to these organizations whenever doing so will not prevent us from carrying out any of our other duties. Emphasizing consequentialist reasoning, Peter Unger (1996) argues that our *primary basic moral values* entail the following Pretty Demanding Dictate:

> (P₁) On pain of living a life that's seriously immoral, a typical well-off person, like you and me, must give away most of her financially valuable assets, and much of her income, directing the funds to lessen efficiently the serious suffering of others.

In his seminal article "Famine, Affluence, and Morality," Peter Singer (1972) offers a utilitarian argument to the effect that we ought to send famine-relief organizations "as much money as possible, that is, at least up to the point at which by giving more one would begin to cause serious suffering for oneself and one's dependents—perhaps even beyond this point to the point of marginal utility." Singer begins his argument with the following much-discussed example:

The Pond: Suppose that on my way to give a lecture I notice that a small child has fallen in [a pond] and is in danger of drowning. Would anyone deny that I ought to wade in and pull the child out? This will mean getting my clothes muddy and either canceling my lecture or delaying it until I can find something dry to change into, but compared with the avoidable death of the child this is insignificant.

The Pond example is supposed to motivate the following principle:

> (P₁) If it is in our power to prevent something very bad from happening, without thereby sacrificing anything of comparable moral significance, we ought to do it.[3]

Singer takes (P₂) to be uncontroversial and thinks it explains why we ought to pull the child from the pond. Given (P₂), Singer reasons as follows: Since absolute poverty is very bad, we ought to prevent as much absolute poverty as we can, without thereby sacrificing anything of comparable moral significance. Since most of the material possessions with which we surround ourselves pale in significance compared to an innocent child's life, we ought to forego such luxuries and save children instead.

These arguments taken together present us with a certain sort of puzzle. First, each of these arguments is initially quite compelling, at least if one accepts the normative framework within which the argument is couched. For example, it seems that any hedonistic or preference act-utilitarian is committed to Singer's principle (P₂), regardless whether The Pond justifies (P₂). Because the other premises in Singer's argument are uncontroversial, it looks as if any hedonistic or preference act-utilitarian must accept Singer's robust conclusion. In short, these arguments provide strong utilitarian, Kantian, rights-based, and contractarian reasons for thinking that we have a moral duty to assist those in absolute poverty. Second, utilitarianism, Kantian ethics, human rights-based ethics, and contractarianism are among the most widely accepted theories in normative ethics. Most philosophers working in ethics today claim to accept some version of one of these theories. Third, with the possible exception of Narveson's view, all of the arguments just considered draw highly demanding conclusions. These arguments (especially Singer's, Unger's, and Aiken's) conclude that we are morally obligated to send sizeable portions of our wealth and income to famine-relief organizations like CARE and that we should continue doing so up to the point where further contributions would reduce us to the same level of need as those we are trying to help. Fourth, few people, philosophers included, contribute anything to CARE, OXFAM, or UNICEF, and almost no people contribute sizeable portions of their income to these organizations, even after they have heard the arguments. What has gone wrong?

Perhaps such highly demanding views are psychologically overwhelming and hence counterproductive. Shelly Kagan considers such an objection. As he puts it:

> [I]f morality demands too much … then when people fall short of its requirements (as doubtless they will do) they will say to themselves that they might as well obey none of morality's requirements at all. Given this all-or-nothing attitude, it is important that morality's requirements not be too severe—for were they severe morality would fall into wide neglect.

Call this objection *Too Much*. According to Too Much, what has gone wrong is that the overly demanding moral principles advocated by Singer, Unger, and Aiken have generated a counterproductive kind of futility thinking: "If I can't live up to the ideal, I shouldn't even try to approximate it." But Too Much is a psychological thesis. Even if true, it has no bearing on what our *actual* moral duties are. It is only concerned with what moral duties and principles we should publicly espouse. In short, Too Much can be restated as follows: "There may be good consequentialist reasons for *understating* the extent of people's *actual* moral obligations, namely, that by doing so people will fulfill

more of their *actual* obligations than they otherwise would have." Such an observation tells us nothing about what our *actual* duties are nor does it do anything to *reduce* or *minimize* those actual duties. Plus, Too Much is probably false. It is highly doubtful that people engage in the sort of all-or-nothing thinking that Too Much predicts, for as Kagan observes:

> Many people disobey the speed limit; few consequently feel free to run down pedestrians. I see no reason why we couldn't teach people to think, "Well, I'm not doing all I should—but only a *monster* would fail to do at least … "

If all-or-nothing futility thinking isn't to blame, then our puzzle remains. Why have such seemingly compelling arguments been so ineffective in evoking behavioral change? I think the answer is more straightforward than Too Much. Moral arguments often tell people that they ought to do things they don't want to do. Typically, when people are presented with an argument telling them that they ought to do *X*—where *X* is something they would rather not do—they look for reasons to reject that argument. One of the most common reasons that I have heard philosophers give for rejecting the arguments of Singer and company runs roughly as follows:

> Singer's preference utilitarianism is irremediably flawed, as are Kant's ethics, Aiken's theory of human rights, and Rawlsean contractarianism. The literature is peppered with devastating objections to these views. Because all of the aforementioned arguments are predicated on flawed ethical theories, all these arguments are also flawed. Until someone can provide me with clear moral reasons grounded in a true moral theory for sending large portions of my income to famine-relief organizations, I will continue to spend my money on what I please.

Such a self-serving reply is both disingenuous and sophistical. It is disingenuous because, as noted earlier, utilitarianism, Kantian ethics, human rights-based ethics, and contractarianism are among the most widely accepted theories in normative ethics. In other contexts, philosophers typically embrace one of these four theoretical approaches to ethics. It is sophistical because a similar reply can be used to "justify" or rationalize virtually any behavior. Because no moral theory to date is immune to objection, one could, for example, "justify" rape on the grounds that all of the arguments against rape are predicated on flawed ethical theories.

The speciousness of such a "justification" of rape is obvious. No one who seriously considers the brutality of rape can think that it is somehow justified/permissible *simply because* all current ethical theories are flawed. But such specious reasoning is often used to "justify" allowing millions of innocent children to starve to death each year. I aim to block this spurious reply by providing an argument for the moral obligatoriness of (O_1) and (O_2), which does not rest on any particular, highly contentious ethical theory. Rather, it rests on beliefs you already hold.[4]

One caveat before we begin. Ethical arguments are often context-dependent, in that they presuppose a specific audience in a certain set of circumstances. Recognizing what that intended audience and context are can prevent confusions about the scope of the ethical claim being made. My argument is context-dependent in precisely this way. It is not aimed at those relatively few people in developed nations who are so impoverished that they couldn't contribute to famine relief without extreme sacrifice. Rather, it is directed at people like you who are relatively well-off and who could easily contribute to famine relief with minimal sacrifice. I intend to show that your beliefs commit you to the view that it is morally wrong not to support famine-relief organizations (or other organizations working to reduce unnecessary suffering) for anyone who is in the circumstances in which you typically find yourself and *a fortiori* that it is morally wrong for you not to support such organizations. Enough by way of preamble, on to your beliefs.

2. THE THINGS YOU BELIEVE

The beliefs attributed to you herein would normally be considered noncontentious. In most contexts, we would take someone who didn't hold these beliefs to be either morally defective or irrational. Of course, in most contexts, people aren't being asked to part with their hard-earned cash. Still, even with that two-week luxury cruise in the Bahamas on the line, you will, I think, readily admit to believing the following propositions:

(B$_1$) Other things being equal, a world with less (more) pain and suffering is better (worse) than a world with more (less) pain and suffering.

(B$_2$) A world with less (more) *unnecessary* suffering is better (worse) than a world with more (less) *unnecessary* suffering.[5]

For those who have doubts as to whether or not they really do believe these two propositions, compare our world α as it actually is—where millions of innocent children suffer slow painful deaths from starvation each year—with possible world W_1, where W_1 is like our world in all respects except for two, namely, in W_1 every child has sufficient food to eat and every country has instituted effective population measures that have reduced human population to sustainable levels. W_1 is clearly a better world than α, and you know that it is. After all, unnecessary suffering is intrinsically bad and α contains vastly more unnecessary suffering than W_1.

Unnecessary suffering isn't the only thing you disvalue, as is evidenced by your belief:

(B$_3$) A world with fewer (more) *unnecessary* childhood deaths is better (worse) than a world with more (fewer) *unnecessary* childhood deaths.

Because you believe (B$_3$) and also believe that *unnecessary* suffering is intrinsically bad, you no doubt believe both:

(B$_4$) It is bad when an innocent child under the age of 5 dies instantly in an automobile accident, and

(B$_5$) It is even worse when an innocent child under the age of 5 suffers a slow painful death from starvation.

These beliefs together commit you to the belief:

(B$_6$) Other things being equal, the world would be: (i) better if there were fewer children starving to death, (ii) much better if there were no children starving to death, and (iii) worse if there were more children starving to death.

Having reflected upon Singer's Pond, you surely believe:

(B$_7$) It is wrong to let an innocent child under age 5 *drown when one can easily save that child with no risk and with minimal cost to oneself.*

The fact that you accept (B$_7$) demonstrates that you believe that there are at least some positive duties—i.e., duties to benefit others. So, you probably believe:

(B$_8$) We ought to take steps to make the world a better place, *especially those steps that require little effort and minimal sacrifice on our part.*

But even if you reject (B$_8$) on the grounds that we have no positive duties (or very limited positive duties), you still think there are negative duties to do no harm, and so you believe:

(B$_{8'}$) One ought to avoid making the world a worse place, *at least whenever one can do so with minimal effort and negligible sacrifice.*

You also believe:

(B$_9$) A morally good person will take steps to make the world a better place and even stronger steps to avoid making the world a worse place, and

(B$_{10}$) Even a "minimally decent person"[6] would take steps to help reduce the amount of unnecessary pain, suffering, and death in the world *if s/he could do so with little effort on her/his part.*

You also have beliefs about the sort of person you are. You believe one of the following propositions when the reflexive pronoun is indexed to yourself:

(B$_{11}$) I am a morally good person; or

(B$_{12}$) I am at least a minimally decent person.

You also believe of yourself:

(B$_{13}$) I am the sort of person who certainly would take steps to help reduce the amount of unnecessary pain, suffering, and death in the world *if I could do so with little effort on my part,* and

(B$_{14}$) I am an intellectually honest individual.

Finally, like most people, you believe:

(B$_{15}$) It is wrong to kill an innocence person unjustly.

And so you believe:

(B$_{16}$) It is wrong to kill innocent children between the ages of 2 and 5 as a means of population control, when equally effective nonlethal means of population control are readily available.

Even where *unjust killing* is not involved, you believe:

(B$_{17}$) Other things being equal, it is better when a person lives out her natural lifespan than when she dies prematurely.

Because you believe (B$_7$), (B$_8$), (B$_{10}$), and (B$_{17}$), presumably you also believe:

(B$_{18}$) Other things being equal, it is wrong to let an innocent person die *when one can prevent that death with minimal effort and negligible sacrifice.*

Because (B$_{18}$) is completely general in its application, it commits you to the following belief as well:

(B$_{19}$) Other things being equal, it is wrong to let an innocent person die as a means of population control *when one can prevent that death with minimal effort and negligible sacrifice* and when equally effective nonlethal means of population control are readily available.

3. WHY YOU ARE COMMITTED TO THE MORAL OBLIGATORINESS OF (O_1)

The burden of the present section is to show that your beliefs (B_1)–(B_{19}) already commit you to obligation (O_1). Using different subsets of [(B_1), (B_2), …, (B_{19})], I will argue that anyone who believes (B_1)–(B_{19}) is committed to accepting two commonsensical, minimally demanding, normative principles and that these two principles entail that we are morally obligated (O_1) to send a modest portion of our income to famine-relief organizations and/or other organizations working to reduce unnecessary suffering. Because each of these normative principles independently entails obligation (O_1), you don't have to believe all of (B_1)–(B_{19}) for my argument to succeed. However, the more of these propositions you believe, the greater *your* commitment to the obligatoriness of (O_1).

Upon closer inspection, the arguments for demanding dictates like those advocated by Unger and Singer break down. For example, Unger's argument for his Pretty Demanding Dictate is predicated on *The Weak Principle of Ethical Integrity*:

> Other things being even nearly equal, if it's **all right** for you to impose losses on others with the result that there's a significant lessening in the serious losses suffered by others overall, then, if you're to avoid doing what's seriously wrong, *you **can't fail to impose*** much lesser losses on yourself, nor can you fail to accept such lesser losses, when the result's a much more significant lessening of such serious losses overall. (Unger's italics; bold emphasis mine)

But this principle is false. The fact that it would be *permissible* for you to impose certain losses on others does not entail that it is *obligatory* for you to impose lesser losses on yourself. It only entails that it would be *permissible* for you to impose such losses on yourself, and that has never been in doubt. What is at issue is whether or not we are *obligated* to impose such losses on ourselves. Because Unger's argument is predicated on a false normative principle, his argument for Pretty Demanding Dictate is unsound.

In order for Singer's argument for the obligation to assist to be sound, his principle (P_2) must be true, but is (P_2) true? Singer suggests that it is the truth of (P_2) that accounts for the wrongness of letting the child drown. To be sure, (P_2) entails that it is wrong to let the child drown, but so do many other weaker principles. Consider the following highly specific principle:

> (P_3) If one encounters a young child drowning in a shallow pond and one can save the child without personal risk and without ruining more than $400 worth of clothes, then one ought to save the child.

Like (P_2), (P_3) also entails that it is wrong to let the child drown. So, it is not clear that it is (P_2)'s truth that accounts for the wrongfulness of letting the child drown. Perhaps, it is the truth of (P_3) instead. To be sure, one can rightfully object that (P_3) is not couched at the appropriate level of generality for a normative principle. The point of mentioning (P_3) is just to show that there are considerably weaker principles than (P_2) that can account for the wrongness of letting the child drown. Because other weaker principles can account for the wrongfulness of letting the child drown, Singer's example does not show that (P_2) is true. Here is a more plausible principle:

> (P_4) Other things being equal, if you can prevent an innocent person from dying with minimal effort, with no noticeable reduction in your standard of living or the standard of living of your dependents, with no risk to yourself or others, and without thereby failing to fulfill any other more pressing obligation, then you ought to do so.

Unlike (P₃), (P₄) is sufficiently general to provide normative guidance in a wide variety of circumstances. Moreover, (P₄) also entails that it would be wrong of you to let the child drown. Granted, if you wade into the pond, you will ruin your cotton twill pants, your oxford cloth shirt, and your tweed jacket, but being a professor you have several tweed jackets, several pairs of Dockers, and numerous oxford cloth shirts. Even if the clothes you are wearing are completely ruined, there will be no noticeable difference in your standard of living. You will simply wear different clothes that are already hanging in your closet. My modest principle (P₄) has another thing going for it, as well. Anyone, like you, who believes (B₃), (B₈·), (B₁₀), (B₁₂), (B₁₇), and (B₁₈) is already committed to (P₄), on pain of inconsistency.

Your beliefs [(B₁), (B₂), (B₈), and (B₁₀)] also commit you to another minimalistic principle:

(P₅) If you can help to reduce the amount of unnecessary suffering in the world with minimal effort on your part, with no risk to yourself or others, with no noticeable reduction in your standard of living or the standard of living of your dependents, and without thereby failing to fulfill any other more pressing obligation, then you ought to do so.

Now here's the rub. Any affluent or moderately affluent person who is committed to (P₄) and (P₅) is already committed to the obligatoriness of sending a portion of her income to famine relief organizations and/or other organizations working to reduce unnecessary suffering. Consider the implications of your commitment to (P₄). According to (P₄), you ought to prevent a person from dying if you can do so with minimal effort and no noticeable reduction in your standard of living or that of your dependents, all else being equal. By sending a modest portion of your income to OXFAM, CARE, or UNICEF, you can prevent many innocent children from dying unnecessarily. Plus, you can do so with no noticeable reduction in your or your dependents' standards of living, and your doing so will not prevent you from fulfilling any more pressing

obligation. So, according to (P₄), you ought to do so. It is worth noting that your belief (B₁₈)—it is wrong to let an innocent person die *when one can prevent that death with minimal effort and minimal sacrifice on one's part*—entails the same result. By not sending money to famine-relief organizations like those listed above, you are letting numerous innocent children under the age of 5 die when you could have easily prevented their deaths with *little effort* (writing out a check) and *minimal sacrifice* on your part (no noticeable reduction in your standard of living). (B₁₈) entails that it is wrong of you to let these children die. Thus, your beliefs about the intrinsic badness of unnecessary childhood deaths and our duties to help prevent such deaths commit you to the obligatoriness of sending a portion of your income to organizations like OXFAM, CARE, and UNICEF to prevent some of those innocent children from dying.

Your beliefs about the intrinsic badness of unnecessary suffering [(B₁) and (B₂)] and your beliefs about our duties to minimize such suffering [(B₈), (B₁₀), (B₁₂), and (B₁₃)] together commit you to the view that you ought to help reduce the amount of unnecessary suffering in the world when you can do so with minimal effort, with no risk to yourself or others, and with no noticeable reduction in your standard of living [i.e., they commit you to (P₅)]. Children living in absolute poverty don't only *die* from starvation. They *suffer* terribly from unrelenting hunger and its attendant diseases, including impaired brain development, measles, chronic diarrhea, chronic fatigue, and wasting. Sending a modest portion of your income to OXFAM, CARE, or UNICEF will enable these organizations to provide food, clean water, and needed medications to numerous malnourished children, thereby alleviating their suffering and greatly reducing their risk of disease. Because you can easily do so (by making out a check) with no risk to yourself or to others, with no noticeable reduction in your standard of living, and without failing to perform any other more serious obligation, your beliefs, together with their concomitant, (P₅), entail that you ought to do so.

Your other beliefs support the same conclusion. You believe (B₉)—a morally good person will take steps to make the world a better place and even stronger steps to avoid making the world a worse place—and (B_{10})—even a "minimally decent person" would take steps to help reduce the amount of unnecessary pain, suffering, and death in the world *if s/he could do so with little effort on her/his part.* You also believe that you are a morally good person $[(B_{11})]$, or at least a minimally decent one $[(B_{12})]$, and that you are the kind of person who would take steps to help reduce the amount of pain, suffering, and death in the world *if you could do so with little effort on your part* $[(B_{13})]$. As we have already seen, *with minimal effort and negligible sacrifice,* you could take steps to help reduce both the number of unnecessary childhood deaths and the amount of unnecessary suffering experienced by these impoverished children just by writing out a modest check to OXFAM, CARE, UNICEF, or some other humanitarian organization working effectively to reduce the amount of unnecessary suffering in the world. Given (B_{10}), you ought to provide modest support to one (or more) of these organizations. Given (B_{12}) and (B_{13}), if you really are the kind of person you think you are, you will provide such support to one (or more) of these organizations.

We have just seen that consistency with your other beliefs requires that you send a portion of your income to famine-relief organizations and/or other organizations working to reduce unnecessary suffering and prevent unnecessary death. But how much of your money are you obligated to send to such worthy organizations? Here I must appeal to your belief (B_{14}). Because you take yourself to be an intellectually honest individual, you must honestly ask yourself how much can you afford to send to famine relief organizations with no noticeable reduction in your standard of living (or in the standard of living of your dependents). Granted, just how much money you can send without noticeably reducing your standard of living will depend on what stage of life you are in and on the extent of your financial resources. Even so, I submit that, like most moderately affluent people, you could easily divert 2% of your income to such worthy causes as famine relief and global population control without the slightest noticeable change in your current

standard of living. I arrived at this number in the following highly scientific manner. I asked my teaching assistant who makes $9,000 per year if he could send 1% of his income ($90 per year, $7.50 per month) to famine-relief organizations with no noticeable difference in his current standard of living, and he said, "Yes." Almost everyone reading this article, except for students who are being forced to read it for a class, makes considerably more money than my teaching assistant; and although it may be true that you have more financial obligations than my T.A. (your house payment, insurance, college tuition for your children, etc. versus his rent, insurance, student fees, etc.), still, given the law of marginal utility, if he can afford to send 1% of his income with no noticeable reduction in his standard of living, you can almost certainly afford to send 2% of your income without noticeably reducing your standard of living. As overpaid philosophy professors, many of you make $40,000 a year. Two percent of $40,000 is $800/year or $15/week. Sending $15/week to famine-relief organizations would prevent more than 250 innocent children under age 5 from dying annually, and your life wouldn't be worse off in any noticeable way. Did your standard of living change *in any noticeable way* when George "Read My Lips" Bush increased your taxes by 2% (while promising to cut them)? No. So, it is extremely doubtful that you would be able to notice a 2% reduction in your current income level, especially if you have your credit card billed automatically for $60 each month. It would be just another monthly payment that you wouldn't even notice.

Many of you could send an even greater percentage of your income (perhaps as much as 5% of your income) with no noticeable reduction in your standard of living. As I said earlier, this is where intellectual honesty comes in. You must honestly determine what percentage of your income you could send to famine-relief organizations without noticeably reducing your standard of living and without thereby failing to fulfill any other overriding obligations, for, according to your own beliefs, that percentage is the *minimum* amount that you are morally required to send to famine-relief organizations and/or other organizations working to reduce unnecessary suffering.

One thing seems reasonably clear: You could easily send 1% of your income to such worthy organizations as OXFAM, CARE, UNICEF, and IPPF with no noticeable difference in your standard of living or the standard of living of any of your dependents. Because your beliefs commit you to (P_4) and (P_5), your beliefs commit you to contributing at the very least 1% of your income, and probably 2% or more, to such important organizations. To do any less is seriously immoral, *by your own standards.*

What about students? Because students also accept (B_1)–(B_{19}), their beliefs likewise entail that if they can reduce the number of innocent children starving to death *with minimal effort and negligible sacrifice on their part,* then they ought to do so. The question is whether they can do so with minimal effort and sacrifice. If you're a student, money's tight, right? As a student struggling to pay your own bills, can you really be morally obligated to support organizations working to save the lives of innocent impoverished children? The answer will no doubt vary from student to student, but here again, intellectual honesty must play a role. Would your life really be any worse off, say, if you had one less beer ($2.00) or café latté ($2.50) per week, or one less pack of cigarettes ($4.00) per month? Or suppose you bought one less CD ($15.00) every two months. Would that really make your life noticeably worse off? (How many CDs sit unused on your shelf anyway?) If we are honest with ourselves, most of us, *including most students,* have to admit that we make lots of frivolous purchases. Reducing the number of these frivolous purchases ever so slightly won't make any noticeable difference in our quality of life, and, in some cases, reducing the number of these purchases would actually improve both our health and the quality of our lives—e.g., reducing the number of cigarettes one smokes or the number of high-fat café lattés one drinks. By way of illustration, suppose you drank one fewer café lattés per week. As a result, you would save $10 per month. By simply sending the $10 saved each month to OXFAM, you would, over the course of a year, prevent 40 children from dying soon, and your standard of living would remain essentially the same. If you are absolutely crazy about café lattés and feel your life wouldn't be complete

without a latté a day, then you must honestly ask yourself whether you could cut back on some other frivolous purchases without noticeably reducing the quality of your life. Even buying just one fewer CD *per year* and sending that $15.00 to UNICEF would prevent 5 children from dying soon. The point is simply this: By cutting out a frivolous purchase here or there, even students could help to reduce the number of innocent children suffering and dying from absolute poverty and malnutrition *with minimal effort and no noticeable reduction in their standards of living.*

The moral of the present section is clear: Consistency with your own beliefs forces you to admit: (i) that you are morally obligated to send a portion of your income to famine-relief organizations and/or other organizations working to reduce the amount of unnecessary pain, suffering, and death in the world and (ii) that the minimum you are obligated to send is whatever amount you could send with no noticeable reduction in your or your dependents' standards of living and without thereby failing to meet any of your other more stringent obligations. For most of us, that means sending 2% of our income to such organizations (which amounts to around 1.5% of your income after taxes). For most students, it means cutting back on a few frivolous purchases and sending the money saved to one of these organizations. To make fulfilling this obligation as easy and effortless as possible, I have provided the addresses and phone numbers for OXFAM, CARE, UNICEF, and IPPF at the end of this article.

4. WHY YOU ARE COMMITTED TO THE MORAL OBLIGATORINESS OF (O_2)

You have just seen that your beliefs entail that you are obligated:

(O_1) To send a modest portion of our income to humanitarian organizations working to reduce the amount of unnecessary suffering in the world.

But our duties to the world's absolutely poor don't stop with (O₁). As we shall presently see, your beliefs also entail that we are obligated:

(O₂) To refrain from squandering food that could be fed to the world's absolutely poor, especially when doing so involves no risk to ourselves or others.

A. Malnutrition

When we think of malnutrition, images of poor starving children wasting away in undeveloped nations quickly come to mind. We don't think of the obese people suffering from diabetes, hypertension, and heart disease that are all too common in developed countries. But these latter people are clearly malnourished, as well. The fact is that there are two kinds of malnutrition—undernutrition and overnutrition—and both of them result in preventable disease, unnecessary suffering, and premature death. *Undernutrition* arises when a person consumes insufficient calories and/or insufficient macro- and micro-nutrients to meet the basic energy and nutrient requirements for normal biological and metabolic function. Undernutrition causes a wide variety of deficiency diseases including: tissue wasting (due to protein deficiency); brain underdevelopment (due to inadequate fat consumption prior to age 2); blindness (vitamin A deficiency); scurvy (vitamin C deficiency), beriberi (thiamin deficiency), and pellagra (niacin and protein deficiency); and death from starvation (insufficient calories). These diseases, so common in undeveloped countries, are virtually nonexistent in developed nations. *Overnutrition* arises when one consumes too many calories, excess fat, excess saturated fat, excess protein, excess cholesterol, excess refined sugar, and excess sodium. Overnutrition gives rise to a wide variety of diseases of excess: coronary artery disease, stroke and other arteriosclerotic diseases (excess cholesterol, saturated fat, transfatty acids, and iron); obesity (excess fat and calories); hypertension (excess fat, calories, and sodium), diabetes mellitus (excess fat, calories, and refined sugar), some forms of cancer (excess fat), and osteoporosis (excess protein consumption,

coupled with inactivity). These diseases, rampant in developed countries, are practically unheard of in underdeveloped countries. As we shall see, both forms of malnutrition have the same root cause, a form of agriculture that (i) fosters overnutrition and (ii) systematically requires the overnourished to squander food that could have been made available to the undernourished.

B. Day-Old Bread: Why Squandering Food in a World of Scarcity Is Morally Wrong

Day-Old Bread: Suppose there is a small bakery in my neighborhood that sells its day-old bread at one-third of the regular price. The bakery doesn't want to run out of bread for its full-paying customers, so it typically bakes twelve more loaves of bread than it anticipates needing. Also suppose there is a small homeless shelter for battered women and children in the neighborhood. It can afford to buy only the discounted day-old bread. When there is no day-old bread available, these people go without bread for the day. Suppose I know all these facts, but I, nevertheless, start buying the remaining twelve loaves of bread (in addition to the loaf I regularly buy) right before the bakery closes each day just because I like the way it makes my kitchen smell. As a result, there is no longer any day-old bread available. Of course, I can't eat that much bread. So, the next day, when that fresh-baked smell is gone, I simply throw all twelve loaves of bread in the garbage. By squandering food in this way, I have knowingly caused the women and children in the shelter to go hungry, and I have done so just to satisfy my trivial desire to have my kitchen smell a certain way. Finally, suppose I keep up my bread-purchasing habit for so long that some of these women and children end up dying from hunger-related diseases.

Have I done anything wrong? Your beliefs entail that I have. You believe that a world with more *unnecessary* suffering is worse than a world with less *unnecessary* suffering [(B₂)], and you also believe that we ought to avoid making the world a worse place when we can do so with minimal effort and negligible sacrifice [$(B_{8'})$]. In Day-Old Bread, I have knowingly squandered food that these women and children would have been able to eat and have, thus, knowingly caused them to suffer unnecessarily just so that I could experience a certain olfactory sensation. I have knowingly made the world a worse place by increasing the amount of unnecessary suffering it contains for an entirely trivial reason. Here, I have actively and knowingly made others worse off. One thing I could have easily done to avoid making the world a worse place would have been to purchase only the bread I need, leaving the rest for others to consume. Perhaps, it would not be wrong of me to purchase vastly more bread than I need in a world where everyone's food needs were adequately met, but as your beliefs rightly reveal, it is wrong of me to waste food that could be fed to severely undernourished humans who desperately need that food. Simply put, your beliefs entail that we are obligated to (O_2)—to refrain from squandering food that could be fed to others who desperately need it.

Multi-Squanderer Scenario: Suppose I am not unique in my desire to smell fresh-baked bread. Suppose that there are people in every community in America who enjoy the smell of fresh-baked bread as much as I do and who, like me, buy up all the available bread at their local bakeries just before closing time so that there is no day-old bread available anywhere in the country. And suppose that, as a result, women and children in shelters all across North America are starving to death, just so lots of other North Americans can enjoy the smell of fresh-baked bread. Does the fact that lots of other people are squandering bread in this way make it any less wrong of me to squander the bread from my local bakery? Not one bit. The fact that other people are behaving immorally does not justify my doing so. Given your beliefs, the only difference between Day-Old Bread and Multi-Squanderer Scenario is that in the latter case lots of other people are just as morally culpable as I am.

C. Eating in a World of Scarcity: (O_2)'s Implications

Day-Old Bread illustrates that your beliefs commit you to the moral obligatoriness of not squandering food that could be fed to the world's absolutely poor. You are not alone in this commitment. Anyone who believes (B_1)–(B_{19}), and that includes almost everyone, is committed to the obligatoriness of (O_2). Even without appealing to (B_1)–(B_{19}), almost everyone would agree that it is wrong to knowingly throw away bread that could save other people's lives and that, therefore, we are obligated not to squander food in this way. What most people don't realize is that in order to fulfill obligation (O_2), they must radically change the way they eat.

If you are like most moderately affluent people, you eat meat and lots of it: Bacon or sausage for breakfast, one or two quarter-pound hamburgers for lunch, and steak, pork chops, or chicken for dinner. For most people in affluent nations, eating this way is normal—it's how they were raised to eat—and it seems not only permissible, but downright wholesome. But things are not always as they seem. The burden of the present section is to show that anyone who believes (B_1)–(B_{19}) is already committed, on pain of inconsistency, to the immorality of eating most meat. Elsewhere, I have argued that beliefs like (B_1), (B_2), (B_8), $(B_{8'})$, and (B_{10}) commit us to the immorality of eating meat and other animal products because of the enormous amount of unnecessary *animal* suffering modern animal factories generate.[7] Here, I am interested in the untold *human* suffering that such a system of agriculture produces.

The numbers used in Day-Old Bread were not chosen at random. They were chosen because it takes 12.9 pounds of grain to produce one pound of beef. This grain could be fed directly to the world's starving poor, but instead it is fed to intentionally bred cows—cows that would not have existed and, hence, would not have needed to be fed, had we not artificially inseminated their mothers. These cows, in turn, convert that grain to manure. By cycling grain through cattle to produce animal protein, we lose 90% of that grain's protein, 96% of its calories, 100% of its carbohydrates, and 100% of its fiber. By cycling grain through cattle so that affluent people can eat meat, starving *humans* are being deprived of that grain so that *cows* can be fed. As a result, while more than 1 billion humans experience chronic hunger, cows in feedlots never go hungry. Playing off our Day-Old Bread analogy, those 12.9 pounds of grain could have been converted to 12.9 loaves of bread that could have, in turn, been fed to the world's starving poor. Instead, that grain/bread is wasted, just so people in affluent nations can eat meat and other animal products. There is no way around it: Whenever one purchases a pound of beef, one is supporting a system of agriculture that effectively squanders 12.9 pounds of grain for every pound of beef produced.

Although beef production is one of the most inefficient means of food production, all forms of animal agriculture are highly inefficient. Of the 12 million tons of grain protein produced in the United States in 1991, 10 million tons were fed to livestock, leaving only 2 million tons for human consumption. Of the 9.2 million tons of legume protein produced in the United States that year, 9 million tons were fed to livestock, leaving only 0.2 million ton for human consumption. For the 21 million tons of plant protein fed to livestock, we received only 7 million tons of livestock protein in return (a 33% protein-conversion efficiency rate). The end result is a net loss of 14 million tons of protein, protein that could have saved the lives of starving children had it not been squandered on livestock production. And protein isn't the only macronutrient we lose by feeding grain to livestock. We also lose all of that grain's carbohydrates and fiber (meat contains no carbohydrates or fiber) and approximately 90% of its caloric energy. I noted at the outset that the United States grows more than enough grain and soybeans to feed the world's entire human population. Unfortunately, most of that grain is squandered on livestock production. Of the estimated 740 kg of grain grown in the United States per person per year, 663 kg are fed to livestock, leaving only 77 kg for human consumption.[8] Were we to forego foods of animal origin and eat that grain directly, there would be more than enough grain left over to feed the world's starving human population.

The irony is that the same system of agriculture that deprives starving humans of grain, thereby contributing to undernutrition in poor nations, is also one of the primary causes of overnutrition in affluent nations. It is now an established fact that diets high in saturated fat and cholesterol greatly increase the risk of several chronic degenerative diseases, including heart disease, hypertension, obesity, diabetes, and some forms of cancer. We also know that meat and animal products are the principal sources of saturated fat and cholesterol in standard Western diets. The evidence is so compelling that the American Dietetic Association, the leading nutritional organization in the United States, now maintains:

> Scientific data suggest positive relationships between a vegetarian diet and reduced risk for several chronic degenerative diseases and conditions, including obesity, coronary artery disease, hypertension, diabetes mellitus, and some types of cancer. *It is the position of The American Dietetic Association (ADA) that appropriately planned vegetarian diets are healthful, are nutritionally adequate, and provide health benefits in the prevention and treatment of certain diseases.*[9]

The ADA also holds:

> Well-planned vegan and lacto-ovo vegetarian diets are appropriate for all stages of the life cycle, including during pregnancy and lactation. Appropriately planned vegan and lacto-ovo vegetarian diets satisfy nutrient needs of infants, children, and adolescents and promote normal growth.

One result of feeding our children a meat-based diet—childhood obesity—is both ironic and sad. While children in underdeveloped countries are starving to death, more than one-fifth of U.S. children are obese. In addition, the damage to coronary arteries arising from a meat-based diet begins remarkably early. Dr. Spock points out: "Fatty deposits are now typically found in the coronary arteries of children on a typical American diet by the age of three. And by the age of twelve, they are found in 70% of children." As a result, Dr. Spock recommends vegan diets for all children over the age of 2. These last observations demonstrate that our duty not to squander food is not overridden by a biological need to consume meat and animal products. There is no such need. Neither adults nor children need to consume any animal products at all. As the ADA has averred, appropriately planned vegan diets—diets devoid of meat and animal products—are *nutritionally adequate* for all stages of the life cycle. If Dr. Spock is right, appropriately planned vegan diets are *nutritionally superior* to meat-based diets. Either way, we have no need for meat and animal products. We eat them only because we like the way they taste.

Does the desire for a particular taste sensation justify us in squandering food that could be fed to starving children? No. In Day-Old Bread, we saw that your beliefs entail the wrongness of squandering 12 loaves of bread just so one can experience a particular olfactory sensation. By doing so, one not only fails to benefit others, one actively makes others worse off. Of course, by purchasing meat because one likes its taste, one is squandering 12 pounds of grain, just to experience a particular gustatory sensation, and, in so doing, one is actively making others—those in desperate need of that grain—worse off. Surely, the fact that it is a *gustatory* sensation, rather than an *olfactory* sensation, is not morally relevant. Because your beliefs entail that it is wrong to squander bread in Day-Old Bread, your beliefs also entail that it is wrong to squander grain by purchasing meat. Hence, your commitment to the obligatoriness of not squandering grain commits you to the obligatoriness of adopting a predominantly plant-based diet devoid of meat and animal products obtained from grain-fed animals. Because virtually all commercially produced meat (including beef, pork, chicken, turkey, and farm-raised fish), dairy products, and eggs come from grain-fed animals, consistency with your own beliefs requires that you adopt a quasi-vegan diet devoid of beef,

pork, chicken, turkey, farm-raised fish, dairy products, and eggs.[10]

One might object that (O_2) does not entail that the obligatoriness of adopting such a diet on the grounds that the difficulty of planning a nutritionally balanced quasi-vegan diet for oneself and one's family simply makes such a diet too risky. Such an objection is entirely unfounded. It is extremely easy to eat a nutritionally balanced vegan diet. No special food combining is necessary. All one need do is eat sufficient calories centered around the Physicians Committee for Responsible Medicine's *new* four food groups: I. Whole Grains (5+ servings/day), II. Vegetables (3+ servings/day), III. Fruits (3+ servings/day), and IV. Legumes (2+ servings/day). Anyone who eats the recommended daily servings from these new four groups will be eating a nutritionally sound plant-based diet. And far from being risky, such a diet will reduce one's risk of heart disease, cancer, stroke, hypertension, obesity, and diabetes.

There is no justification for squandering precious grain reserves in a world of food scarcity. This conclusion is not derived from some highly contentious ethical theory you likely reject, but from beliefs you already hold. Consistency with your own beliefs entails that it's wrong to squander food that could be fed to the world's starving poor for trivial reasons like taste or smell. Because modern meat, dairy, and egg production necessarily squanders grain that could be fed directly to humans, *your own beliefs* entail that it is wrong to consume these products, which, in turn, entails that quasi-vegan diets are obligatory.

5. OBJECTIONS AND REPLIES

A. The Iteration Objection

In Section 3, after showing that Singer's and Unger's attempts to defend highly demanding dictates fail, I argued that your beliefs commit you to two *much less demanding* normative principles (P_4) and (P_5), which, in turn, entail that you are obligated to (O_1)—to send a modest portion of your income to famine-relief organizations and/or other organizations working to reduce unnecessary suffering. The present worry is that these two principles will ultimately reduce to the very same highly demanding dictate from which I was aiming to distance myself. Because *standards of living* are vague and lack precise boundaries, there can be a repeated series of non-noticeable reductions in one's standard of living, such that, before long, one is radically worse off than one's original starting position, and noticeably so.

My response is quite simple. Neither (P_4) nor (P_5) is intended to be iterated in this way. In fact, (P_4) and (P_5) are intended to be compatible with gradual increases in one's standard of living so as to enable one to do even more to help reduce the amount of unnecessary suffering down the road. To block the iteration objection and to make explicit the kinds of principles your beliefs clearly commit you to, (P_4) and (P_5)—as they apply to *moderately affluent* people—should be restricted as follows: The principles never require a moderately affluent person to have a standard of living *noticeably* lower than the highest standard of living she has ever enjoyed. Even with this restriction in place, (P_4) and (P_5) still entail that most of us are morally required to send at least 2% of our income to famine-relief organizations and/or other organizations working to reduce unnecessary suffering. The reason is this: Because standards of living typically continue to improve the longer people are in the workforce, most people are currently enjoying their highest standards of living. (P_4) and (P_5) require these people to provide whatever amount of financial assistance they can provide without noticeably lowering their standard of living from its current optimal level.

B. The Libertarian Objection: There Are No Positive Duties

Strict libertarians insist that although we have negative duties to do no harm, we have *no* positive duties to assist others. Thus, on the libertarian view, it would not be wrong of you to let the child drown in Singer's Pond. Libertarians maintain that even though you could save the child with minimal sacrifice and no risk to yourself, you have absolutely no positive obligation to assist the child in any way. Because they deny the existence of positive duties, libertarians contend that it also would *not* be wrong of you *not* to save the lives of numerous starving children by sending a modest portion of your income to famine-relief organizations. Granted, libertarians do think that it would be *good* of you to wade in and save the child. They also think it would be *good* of you to send money to such worthy causes as famine relief, but these actions would be entirely supererogatory on your part. Thus, the libertarian objection runs as follows: Because there are *no* positive duties, we have *no* obligation to send money to famine-relief organizations, even though that money would save the lives of numerous innocent children.

As noted earlier, Narveson claims that such a libertarian "nobody-needs-to-help-anybody" stance is unreasonable. A variation on the trolley problem suggests that he is right. Suppose that six innocent people are trapped on the tracks and a runaway trolley is barreling down on them. Fortunately, you just happen to be standing right next to a switch which, if flipped, will divert the trolley onto a second track. Even more fortunately, unlike typical trolley problems where three people are trapped on the second track and you have to decide between killing three and letting six die, in the present trolley case, no one is on the other track and so, if the switch is flipped, the train will be diverted to the second track where it will roll safely to a stop with no one being injured. The question is this: Are you morally required to flip the switch and save the six people? Not according to the libertarian. Even though you are standing right next to the switch and can flip the switch with little effort and no sacrifice on your part, with no risk to yourself or others, and without thereby violating any other obligations, the libertarian maintains that it would *not* be wrong of you to let the six die by not flipping the switch.

Such a position strikes most of us as morally outrageous. You *should* flip the switch, and it would be *clearly wrong* of you not to do so. And you, no doubt, agree. Because you believe that one should wade into the pond to save the child [(B₇)], you surely think it would be wrong not to flip the switch. I realize that a die-hard libertarian might remain unconvinced, but you are not a die-hard libertarian. You believe that there are both positive and negative duties. Thus, the libertarian objection under consideration gives *you* absolutely no reason to think that (O₁) is not obligatory.

C. Malthusian Musings

A common reason offered for not sending money to famine-relief organizations is that doing so will just exacerbate the problem. If lots more children under age 5 survive, then when they reach puberty and start having their own children, there will be even more mouths to feed, and as a result, there will be even more human suffering due to starvation. In short, it is better to let 12 million children starve to death each year than to save them and have two or three times that many children starving 15 years from now.

Couched in the more scientific language of ecology, the Malthusian objection runs as follows: Left unchecked, organisms will reproduce until they reach the carrying capacity K of their respective ecosystems. Once they exceed K, there will be a major crash in the population size of that organism. By feeding starving humans, the anti-assistance argument goes, we are simply speeding up the time at which we exceed the Earth's K for humans (hereafter K_h). Better to let 12 million children starve to death each year than to exceed K_h and have an even more devastating population crash.

The first thing to note is that we don't think Malthusian worries about exceeding K_h give us a good reason to let our own children starve. But if we don't let our children starve, then, as adults, they will probably procreate, thereby hastening the time when K_h is exceeded. If ecologically based, global human population concerns give us a reason to let distant children die, they give us an equally good reason to let our own children die. You wouldn't think of letting your own children die to help reduce human population. Thus you

must not find letting children starve to death to be a legitimate way to curb human population growth.

Second, there are other more effective ways of reducing human population growth: improving educational opportunities and employment opportunities *for women* (which drives up the opportunity cost of procreation), improving the economic security of the elderly, providing ready access to birth control, and providing abortion services.[11] Even more draconian policies, like mandatory sterilization after having one child, are preferable to letting children starve to death. Because there are numerous more effective means of curbing population growth than letting innocent children starve, anyone who accepts (B₁₉) must think it wrong to let innocent children starve as a means of population control.

Third, demographic studies repeatedly show that childhood morality rates and birthrates are positively correlated—as childhood mortality rates decline, so do birthrates—and so, supporting famine-relief organizations working to reduce the number of unnecessary childhood deaths is, paradoxically, a way of slowing population growth. But suppose you question the validity of these studies. Suppose you dig in your Malthusian heels and insist that feeding the world's starving children will increase the number of humans suffering from starvation down the road. Such insistence does not absolve you from obligation (O₁); it just means that you are obligated to fulfill it in a different way. Instead of being required to send money to a famine-relief organization, you will be obligated to send money to humanitarian organizations, like the IPPF, that are working to reduce the rate of population growth in underdeveloped countries through effective birth control measures.

Fourth, those who take Malthusian concerns seriously are even more obligated to refrain from consuming meat and other animal products, because intentionally breeding millions of cows and pigs and billions of chickens greatly reduces the world's K_h. Intentionally adding billions of farm animals to the world greatly increases the number of animal mouths that must be fed and, thus, greatly reduces the amount of food available for human consumption.

Appendix

Oxfam America
26 West St.
Boston, MA 02111
1-800-OXFAM US
    [1-800-693-2687].

International Planned
    Parenthood
    Federation (IPPF)
902 Broadway, 10th
    Floor
New York, NY 10010

United Nations
    Children's Fund
333 East 38th St.
New York, NY 10016
UNICEF: 1-800-
    FOR KIDS
    [1-800-367-5437]

CARE
151 Ellis St.
Atlanta, GA 30303
1-800-521-CARE
    [1-800-521-2273]

6. CONCLUSION

The implications of your beliefs are clear. Given your beliefs, it follows that we are morally obligated to (O_1)—to send a modest portion of our income to famine-relief organizations and/or other organizations working to reduce the amount of unnecessary pain, suffering, and death in the world—and to (O_2)—to refrain from squandering food that could be fed to the world's absolutely poor. (O_2), in turn, entails that we are obligated to adopt a quasi-vegan diet, rather than squander grain on a meat-based diet. These conclusions were not derived from some highly contentious ethical theory that you can easily reject, but from your own firmly held beliefs. Consequently, consistency demands that you embrace these obligations and modify your behavior accordingly.

NOTES

1. Following Peter Singer (who borrows the term from Robert McNamara), I use 'absolute poverty' to refer to "a condition of life so characterised by malnutrition, illiteracy, disease, squalid surroundings, high infant mortality and low life expectancy as to be beneath any reasonable definition of human decency" [Singer, *Practical Ethics,* Second Edition (Cambridge: Cambridge University Press, 1993), p. 219.]. Singer reports that, according to the World Watch Institute, as many as 1.2 billion people live in absolute poverty (pp. 219–20).

2. William Aiken, "The Right to Be Saved from Starvation" in *World Hunger and Moral Obligation,* eds. W. Aiken and H. LaFollette (Englewood Cliffs, NJ: Prentice-Hall, 1977), pp. 86 and 93. Aiken argues that one's right to be saved from starvation is claimable against all persons who satisfy three minimal conditions: (i) they must know that the person is starving, (ii) they must have the means necessary to save the person, and (iii) they must be able to save the person without placing themselves in an equally bad or worse situation than the person they are saving (pp. 91–93).

3. By "without sacrificing anything of comparable moral significance" Singer means "without causing anything else comparably bad to happen, or doing something that is wrong in itself, or failing to promote some moral good, comparable in significance to the bad thing that we prevent." ("Famine, Affluence, and Morality," *Philosophy and Public Affairs,* vol. 1, no. 3 [Spring 1972], p. 234).

4. Obviously, if you do not hold these beliefs (or enough of them), my argument will have no force for you, nor is it intended to. It is only aimed at those of you who do hold these widespread commonsense beliefs.

5. By "*unnecessary* suffering" I mean suffering which serves no greater, outweighing justifying good. If some instance of suffering is required to bring about a greater good (e.g., a painful root canal may be the only way to save a person's tooth), then that suffering is *not* unnecessary. Thus, in the case of (B_2), no *ceteris paribus* clause is needed, because if other things are *not* equal such that the suffering in question is justified by an overriding justifying

good that can only be achieved by allowing that suffering, then that suffering is *not* unnecessary.

6. By a "minimally decent person" I mean a person who does the very minimum required by morality and no more. I borrow this terminology from Judith Jarvis Thomson who distinguishes a *good* Samaritan from a *minimally decent* Samaritan. See her "A Defense of Abortion," *Philosophy and Public Affairs* 1 (1971): 62–65.

7. See my "The Immorality of Eating Meat" in *The Moral Life,* ed. Louis Pojman (New York and Oxford: Oxford University Press, 2000), pp. 856–889. There I documented that the routine unanaesthetized mutilations (castration, branding, dehorning, debeaking, dubbing, tail docking, and tooth pulling) and abysmal living conditions which farm animals are forced to endure in factory farms, along with inhumane transportation and slaughter processes, greatly increase the amount of unnecessary suffering in the world; and I argued that because you could easily take steps to help reduce such unnecessary suffering by eating something other than meat, consistency with your beliefs forces you to admit that eating meat is morally wrong.

8. Data on protein production and consumption and grain production and consumption taken from *Food, Energy, and Society*, Revised Edition, eds. David Pimentel and Marcia Pimentel (Niwot, CO: University of Colorado Press, 1996), pp. 77–78.

9. "Position of the American Dietetic Association: Vegetarian Diets," *Journal of the American Dietitic Association* 97 (November 1997): 1317. For those wishing to learn more about sound vegetarian nutrition, the ADA has published this article in its entirety at: www.eatright.org/adap1197.html.

10. (O_2) does not entail that it is wrong to eat meat *per se*, e.g. it does *not* entail that eating the flesh of wild animals is wrong. Hence, the use of 'quasi-vegan' in the text. However, (O_2) does entail that it is wrong to eat virtually all commercially produced meat and animal products because these products are obtained from grain-fed animals and their production necessarily squanders grain which could have been fed to starving humans.

11. Regardless of one's views on abortion, presumably it would be better to abort a fetus quickly and relatively painlessly than to let that fetus be born only to starve to death slowly and painfully.

STUDY QUESTIONS

1. Examine Engel's arguments for his two main principles. Discuss their premises. Do you see any problems with them?

2. Is Engel correct that virtually all major moral theories contain principles that require us to make some modest sacrifices for the welfare of the absolutely poor?

3. Examine the objections that Engel discusses against his position. Does he defeat them? Are there other objections you can think of?

4. How much should we give to the absolutely poor? Is Engel too lenient, too stringent, or about right?

5. Examine Engel's Day-Old Bread example and discuss its implications.

16

The World Food Supply: The Damage Done by Cattle-Raising

TRISTRAM COFFIN

Tristram Coffin was the editor of The Washington Spectator, *a public concerns newsletter.*

This article from The Washington Spectator *reports on the ecological costs of cattle-raising. For example, in California it takes 5214 gallons of water to produce one edible pound of beef, as compared to 23 gallons for the same amount of tomatoes. In addition, lowering one's meat diet is likely to result in greater health. Coffin calls on us to change our diet, for our own good and the good of humankind, from one heavy in meat to more grains, vegetables, and fruits.*

In this century, the number and impacts of livestock have swelled apace with human population and affluence. Since mid-century human numbers have doubled to [5.8] billion, while the number of four-legged livestock—cattle, pigs, sheep, goats, horses, buffalo and camels—has grown from 2.3 billion to 4 billion. At the same time, the fowl population multiplied from about 3 billion to nearly 11 billion. There are now three times as many domestic animals as people.[1]

"Currently, sufficient land, energy and water exist to feed well over twice the world's population" (*Earth Save Foundation*). But this is not the whole story. The Foundation adds, "Yet half of the world's grain harvest is fed to livestock, while millions of humans go hungry. In 1984 when thousands of Ethiopians were dying from famine, Ethiopia continued growing and shipping millions of dollars worth of livestock to the United States and other European countries."

Worldwatch Institute reports: "Rings of barren earth spread out from wells on the grasslands of Soviet Turkmenia. Heather and lilies wilt in the nature preserves of the southern Netherlands.

"Forests teeming with rare forms of plant and animal life explode in flame in Costa Rica. Water tables fall and fossil fuels are wasted in the U.S. Each of these cases of environmental decline issues from a single source: the global livestock industry."

The simple fact is that the livestock industry is a better paying customer than are hungry human beings. In turn, the industry is supported by the lusty appetite for meat of well-to-do individuals. Since 1985, North Americans have been eating 50% more beef, 280% more poultry and 33% more dairy products. In its tract "Our Food, Our World," the Foundation points out that this is a diet with one-third more fat, one-fifth less carbohydrate, and levels of protein consumption "far exceeding official recommendation."

Reprinted from *The Washington Spectator*, ed. Tristram Coffin, Vol. 19.2 (January 15, 1993).

"This increased demand for animal products has resulted in a vast reallocation of resources, has promoted the degradation of global systems, and has disrupted indigenous cultures. The impact on human health has been equally devastating."

Worldwatch advises: "Feeding the world's current population on an American-style diet would require two and a half times as much grain as the world's farmers produce for all purposes. A future world of 8 to 14 billion people eating the American ration of 220 grams a day can be nothing but a flight of fancy." Why? "In the U.S., over one-third of all raw materials—including fossil fuels—consumed for all purposes are devoted to the production of livestock" [*Earth Save*].

Example: it takes 16 pounds of grain and soy to produce one pound of beef. One half the Earth's land mass is grazed for livestock, as compared to the 2% used for fruits and vegetables.

Growing cattle crops is an "extremely energy-intensive process. Farmers must pump water, plow, cultivate and fertilize the fields, then harvest and transport the crops. The number of calories of fossil fuel expended to produce one calorie of protein from beef is 78, as compared to 2 calories to produce the same one calorie of soybeans." The energy used to produce one pound of grain-fed beef is equal to one gallon of gasoline, according to *Earth Save*.

What about water? "Our Food, Our World" estimates that livestock production accounts for more than half of all water consumed. In California it takes 5214 gallons of water to produce one edible pound of beef, as compared to 23 gallons for the same amount of tomatoes ... Water tables, like the Ogallala aquifer under the Great Plains states, are fast being depleted.

Marc Reisner writes in his book *California Desert,* "It offends me that we give three times more water to grow cows than we give to people in California."

The Growth of Deserts—"Our Food, Our World" contends that livestock grazing and overuse of land to grow food crops for cattle have played a major role in the growth of deserts. "Regions most affected by desertification are all cattle-producing areas, including the western half of the U.S., Central and South America, Australia and sub-Saharan Africa.

The main causes of desertification are overgrazing of livestock, overcultivation of land, improper irrigation techniques, deforestation [to clear land for cattle raising as is now occurring in the Brazilian Rain Forest]."

Why? "Under persistent grazing, the bare ground becomes impermeable to rainwater, which then courses off the surface, carrying away topsoil and scouring stream beds into deep gullies. Upstream, water tables fall for lack of replenishment; downstream, flooding occurs more frequently and sediment clogs waterways, dams and estuaries. In drier climates wind sweeps away the destabilized soil."

The U.N. Environment Program estimates that 73% of the world's 3.3 billion hectares of dry rangeland is at least moderately desertified, having lost more than 25% of its carrying capacity. "There is little debate that degradation is occurring in environments where rainfall is more plentiful and regular. The perennial plants that flourish in these zones are easily disrupted by cattle; clay soils are easily compacted and rendered impervious to water; and rains often arrive in strong, sudden downpours, sluicing away soils destabilized by cattle" (Worldwatch Institute).

Philip Fradkin, writing in *Audubon* magazine, says: "The impact of countless hooves and mouths over the years has done more to alter the type of vegetarian and land forms of the West than all the water projects, strip mines, power plants, freeways, and subdivision developments combined."

A few pertinent facts: Each year, an estimated 125,000 square miles of rainforest are destroyed, together with the loss of 1,000 plant and animal species. In Central America cattle ranching has destroyed more rainforests than has any other activity. A quarter of Central American rainforests have been cleared for pasture. This creates a profitable market for cattle sold to the U.S. market.

Livestock production creates other environmental problems—the pollution of the atmosphere by carbon dioxide and methane, of water by animal wastes and pesticides. Worldwatch Institute states: "The millions of tons of animal waste that accumulate at modern production facilities can pollute rivers and groundwater if precautions are not taken. If they get into rivers or open bodies of water, nitrogen and phosphorus in manure overfertilize algae, which grow rapidly, deplete oxygen supplies, and suffocate aquatic ecosystems. From the hundreds of algae-choked Italian lakes to the murky Chesapeake Bay, and from the oxygen-starved Baltic Sea to the polluted Adriatic, animal wastes add to the nutrient loads from fertilizer runoff, human sewage and urban and industrial pollution."

In the Netherlands, the 14 million animals in feeding houses in the southern part of the nation "excrete more nitrogen- and phosphorus-rich manure than the soil can absorb ... pushing fresh-water ecosystems into decline."

And, "manure nitrogen, mixed with nitrogen from artificial fertilizers, percolates through the soil into the underground water tables as nitrates.... In the U.S., roughly one-fifth of the wells in livestock states, such as Iowa, Kansas and Nebraska, have nitrate levels that exceed health standards. Manure nitrogen also escapes into the air as gaseous ammonia, a pollutant that causes acid rain."

The *Earth Save* study looks at three problems:

- "The metabolic processes of cattle result in the emission of large quantities of methane. Each cow produces 1 pound of methane for every 2 pounds of meat it yields. The amount of methane emitted by the world's cattle annually: 100 million tons." 20% of total world methane emissions comes from cattle.

- Wastes from factory farmers, feedlots and dairies create a buildup of toxins in the land and water. The E.P.A. estimates that almost half the wells and surface streams in the U.S. are "contaminated by agricultural pollutants."

- Chemical pesticides are used so widely and in such large quantities that they "poison the environment and the human food chain. The increase in overall pesticide use since 1945, when petro-chemical based agriculture became popular, is 3,300%."

Loss of Forests—Not only rangeland, but forests, too, suffer from heavy livestock production.

The Worldwatch study reports, "Forests suffer, as branches are cut for fodder or entire stands are leveled to make way for pastures. The roster of impacts from forest clearing includes the loss of watershed protection, loss of plant and animal species, and on a larger scale, substantial contributions of the greenhouse gas carbon dioxide to the atmosphere."

Examples: in Latin America, more than 20 million hectares of moist tropical forests have been cleared for cattle pasture. The U.N. Food and Agricultural Organization says that Central America has lost more than a third of its forest since the early 1960s. Nearly 70% of the deforested land in Panama and Costa Rica is now pasture.

"Eradicating tree cover sets the wheels of land degradation in motion. Shallow, acidic, and nutrient-poor, tropical soils lose critical phosphorus and other nutrients when the forest is converted to pasture.... Most pasture is abandoned within a decade for land newly carved from the forest ... Forest destruction for ranching also contributes to climate change. When living plants are cut down and burned, or when they decompose, they release carbon into the atmosphere as the greenhouse gas carbon dioxide. In the atmosphere, carbon dioxide traps the heat of the sun, warming the earth. The expansion of pastures into Latin American forests has released an estimated 1.4 billion tons of carbon into the atmosphere."

Worldwatch points out that methane, a byproduct of cattle-raising, is the second most important greenhouse gas.

Effect on Health—*Earth Save* warns, "Animal products contain large quantities of saturated fat, cholesterol and protein and no dietary fiber. The impact of this diet on human health has been devastating.... Fortunately, by observing a low-fat diet free of animal products, some diseases can be commonly prevented, consistently improved and sometimes cured." Some fats are associated with most of the diseases of affluence that are among the leading causes of death in industrialized countries: heart disease, stroke, breast and colon cancer. The study laments that physicians generally are taught to cure disease, but not how to prevent it. The majority "are taught little about nutrition as a preventative measure," but many are inquiring into this possibility.

"*Great Protein Fiasco*"—The Worldwatch study comments: "The adverse health impacts of excessive meat-eating stem in large part from what nutritionists call the *great protein fiasco*—a mistaken belief by many Westerners that they need to consume large quantities of protein. This myth, propagated as much as a century ago by health officials and governmental dietary guidelines, has resulted in Americans and other members of industrial societies ingesting twice as much protein as they need. Among the affluent, the protein myth is dangerous because of the saturated fats that accompany concentrated protein in meat and dairy products."

Low-fat diets are now recommended by the U.S. Surgeon General, the U.S. National Research Council, the American Heart Association, and the World Health Organization. They recommend lowering fat consumption to no more than 30% of calories, as compared to the U.S. norm of 37%. [Many health specialists recommend lowering the fat consumption to 10 to 15%—ed. note.]

Higher meat consumption among the well-to-do may also create a problem for the poor, "as the share of farmland devoted to feed cultivation expands, reducing production of food staples," says the Worldwatch study. It points out that in Egypt, for example, "over the past quarter-century, corn grown for animal feed has taken over cropland from wheat, rice, sorghum and millet—all staple grains fed to livestock rose from 10 to 36%."

Much the same is true in Mexico, where 30% of the grain is fed to livestock, "although 22% of the country's people suffer from malnutrition." The share of cropland growing animal food and fodder went up from 5% in 1960 to 23% in 1980. A study of agriculture in 23 third world countries showed that in 13 countries, farmers had shifted more than 10% of grain land from food crops to feed crops in the last 25 years. In nine countries, "the demand for meat among the rich was squeezing out staple production for the poor."

The picture in the U.S.: more than a million farms and ranches raise young beef, while four big companies slaughter nearly 60% of them. Since 1962, the number of huge American beef feedlots, capable of holding 16,000 head of cattle, has risen from 23 to 189. At the same time, small feedlots, holding no more than 1,000, have dropped by 117,000.

The big operations have no trouble getting government support, such as guaranteed minimum prices, government storage of surpluses, feed subsidies, import levies and product insurance. The Organization for Economic Cooperation and Development reports that in 1990 government programs in the industrial democracies gave subsidies to animal farmers and feed growers worth $120 billion.

What is the answer? The *Los Angeles Times* states: "The Seeds of Change [a group based in Santa Fe, NM] philosophy holds that adopting a plant-based diet is the best solution for improving individual health and lessening the toll of the human race on our Earth's limited resources." Seeds of Change founder Gabriel Howearth recommends:

> Bush acorn squash and bush buttercup squash, both high in vitamin A and free amino acids. Jerusalem artichokes, a native North American food plant with a varied vitamin balance and useful digestive enzymes. Hopi blue starch corn grown without irrigation in the Southwest and a traditional staple of the Hopi Indians … Okra, containing high amounts of vitamin C and amino acids, good in vegetable soup, stew and gumbo. Amaranth, a high-protein garden grain.

Howearth's goal "is to get all kinds of people, even those who work and have limited leisure time, to grow their own food—in their backyards, on their balconies, or on their rooftops."

This is not a goal everyone can follow. What many can do is change their diet from heavy meats to more vegetables and fruits. They will be less likely to become ill, and they will help save the planet Earth.

NOTE

1. From *The Worldwatch Institute*, quoted in "World Food Supply: The Damage Done by Cattle-Raising." *The Washington Spectator* (Jan. 15, 1993).

STUDY QUESTIONS

1. Go over the figures and damage caused by cattle-raising, mentioned in this essay. Are you convinced by the article that the situation is as bad as it is made out to be? Explain your answer.

2. If the raising of cattle and other livestock is so damaging to the environment and our health, what should we be doing about it?

17

Vegetarianism and Treading Lightly on the Earth

MICHAEL ALLEN FOX

Michael Allen Fox was educated at Cornell University and the University of Toronto, taught philosophy for thirty-nine years at Queen's University in Canada, and is now retired and living in Australia, where he is Adjunct Professor of Social Science at the University of New England. He has published work in such journals as Ethics, Environmental Ethics, Environmental Values, Ethics and the Environment, *and* International Journal of Applied Ethics, *and his most recent books are* Deep Vegetarianism *(also translated into Chinese) and* The Accessible Hegel.

The meat-based diet that is the prevailing choice in affluent, industrialized parts of the world is unhealthy and environmentally unsustainable in a number of ways. These claims are explained and documented in some detail in this essay. The negative effects of meat production on species diversity in particular are illustrated with special reference to rain forest destruction for cattle grazing. Also investigated here is the link between animal agriculture and the manipulative or dominating mindset that encourages viewing animals and ecosystems generally just as resources to be exploited at will. In contrast, it is argued, a vegetarian food system would enable us to take greater responsibility for our actions by minimizing our impact on the planet and help us regain a sense of being part of nature rather than existing apart from it.

Reprinted by permission of the author.

MOVING AWAY FROM MEAT

I begin with a basic assumption: Scientific evidence increasingly reveals that a vegetarian—even a vegan—diet is from a nutritional standpoint, at least as healthy as, and in all probability healthier than, one that features meat (Anonymous 1988a; Anonymous 1988b; U.S. National Research Council 1989; Barnard 1990; Chen 1990; Lappé 1992; White and Frank 1994; Melina and Davis 2003; Rice 2004; Saunders 2003). But beyond this important finding, many people are coming to understand that the amount of meat they consume individually and collectively has a profound effect on the way we use and manage natural resources—forests, land, water, and nonrenewable energy. To put it simply, the greater our dependence on meat and other animal products, the more we overexploit these resources to satisfy our food preferences. And if (as I argue here) the prevailing form of agroindustry significantly abuses and damages the environment, then it follows that the more meat we consume, the more the well-being of the planet, and consequently our own well-being, will suffer. This insight leads to an awareness that the dietary orientation of unhealthy, meat-dependent societies needs to change, not only for the good of each of their members, but also for the benefit of nature as a whole.

Many of us live in societies that encourage individuality, self-reliance, self-development, and the cultivation of personal taste. These are good things, to be sure. However, we are bombarded all the time by messages that encourage us to pursue the construction of selfhood by means of consumer choices—that is, by acting out self-centered desires and fantasies in our role as powerful purchasers within the global market system. We are all conditioned to view what we purchase as consumers simply as an expression of personal freedom, of consequence to ourselves alone. Numerous vested interests energetically promote this outlook: business leaders, industry spokespersons, the media, politicians, advertisers, and image-makers, to name a few. It therefore takes major effort to develop a contrasting form of awareness, namely, one that acknowledges that what we decide to buy has wider consequences.

Many of these consequences have an impact on the environment. When we begin to appreciate the connections between our purchases and the environment, we start to question our choices and the influences that helped bring them about. Being sensitized by ecological issues, as a growing number of citizens are today, opens our minds to the possibility of change through the formation of new values. The process of becoming a vegetarian is often part of this creative ferment.

THE ENVIRONMENTAL IMPACT
OF DIETARY CHOICE

The eco-destructive side of the meat industry's operations has been demonstrated with ample documentation from both government and non-government sources (Robbins 1987; Fiddes 1991; Durning & Brough 1995; Hill 1996; Fox 1999; Rice 2004; Gold 2004; Tudge 2004a, 2004b). These effects include:

- toxic chemical residues in the food chain
- pharmaceutical additives in animal feeds
- polluting chemicals and animal wastes from feedlot runoff in waterways and underground aquifers
- loss of topsoil caused by patterns of relentless grazing
- domestic and foreign deforestation and desertification resulting from the clearing of land for grazing and cultivating animal feed
- threatened habitats of wild species of plants and animals
- intensive exploitation of water and energy supplies
- ozone depletion caused by extensive use of fossil fuels and significant production of methane gas by cattle

A brief case study will help place these complex problems in context and help us comprehend their interconnections.

Canada is a typical Western industrialized country with a population only one-tenth that of the United States. Since the time of white settlement, expanding agriculture has been the major factor in an 85% reduction of wetlands (Government of Canada 1991: 9–9, 9–15). Agricultural acreage has increased fourfold since 1900, and the total area under irrigation more than doubled between 1970 and 1988 (Government of Canada 1991: 26–6, 9–14). We infer that the consumption of meat is a powerful force here, given that in North America some 95% of oats and 80% of corn crops end up as livestock feed (Animal Alliance of Canada 1991; Government of Canada 1991; Agriculture Canada 1994).

Farm animals in Canada produce 322 million liters (85 million U.S. gal) of manure *daily*, an overwhelming proportion of which comes from cattle. Each marketed kilogram (2.2 lb) of edible beef generates at least 40 kg (88 lb) of manure, and each marketed kilogram of pork 15 kg (33 lb). These wastes, plus the runoff of water used to clean farm buildings and equipment and pesticide residues and other agricultural chemicals, are often poorly handled, causing the contamination of waterways and soil, as well as air pollution (Government of Canada 1991: 9–26).

Now consider that to produce each quarter-pound hamburger costs the environment 11,000 L (2,904 gal) of water. This amounts to 96,800 L (25,555 gal) per kilogram. Meanwhile, a kilo of rice or cheese requires 5,000 L (1,320 gal) of water to produce, and a kilo of wheat only 1,000 L (264 gal) (Pearce 2006). Which is a better investment in the earth's future?

Finally, reflect on the accelerating demand for meat worldwide. As an example, whereas annual meat consumption in China averaged 4 kg (8.8 lb) in the 1960s, it is about 60 kg (132 lb) today (Porritt 2006).[1] This trend has prompted the prestigious World Watch Institute to focus attention on global problems of meat production in the latest edition of its *State of the World* report (Starke 2006).

Obviously not all of the environmentally negative effects of today's unsound agricultural practices can be blamed on livestock management. And

clearly some of the abuses already listed can be reduced or eliminated by a dedicated approach to recycling animal manure (and even human waste) into fertilizer, the use of natural means of pest control instead of harmful chemicals, and like measures. So it has been argued that the proper target of criticism is not meat production per se, but rather the intensive rearing methods used by contemporary agribusiness. There is some point to this rejoinder, and those who obtain meat from their own or others' free-range, organic, or biodynamic operations surely contribute less to the environmental toll on the planet. But, given the rate at which smaller-scale family farms are being forced out of competition (and out of existence) by larger and larger corporate conglomerates (Berry 1996), the opportunities for obtaining "environmentally friendly" meat are extremely rare. Taking current agricultural trends into account, then, only a tiny fraction of the population can conceivably exercise this option, and an even tinier group desires to do so in the first place. But the bottom line is that vegetarians are able to live more lightly on the land than do meat eaters of any description.

Is there evidence to back up this assertion? The short answer is yes. Consider the following observations.

Substituting a grass-feeding livestock system (using only ruminant animals) for the current grain and grass system was found to reduce the energy inputs about 60% and land resources about 8%.... [In addition, it] would free up about 300 million tons of grain for export each year. This amount of grain is sufficient to feed a human population of 400 million a vegetarian-type diet for an entire year (Pimentel 1990: 12).

All the grain fed to livestock could feed five times as many people. *(Proponents of intensive animal agriculture claim that we only put animals on land that could not support plant production. But we could grow more than enough plant food for human consumption if we used*

even a fraction of the land that is now used to grow plant food for livestock consumption.)
(Animal Alliance of Canada 1991)

Merely making animal agriculture more ecologically efficient would greatly reduce resource depletion and increase global food supplies. Imagine what a gradual and complete conversion of the meat economy to a vegetarian economy worldwide could achieve.

One of the accomplishments of environmental philosophy in its relatively short history is the establishment of ecologically informed ethical thinking. If this phrase stands for anything, it certainly must entail that an overarching goal of human life ought to minimize the harmful impact our existence—as individuals and as collectivities—has upon the biosphere. It follows that we also ought to make lifestyle choices that help secure this objective. Now a diet that relies heavily on meat appears affordable and environmentally sustainable only to those who (a) are unaware of the larger ecological costs of meat production; (b) assume that these costs do not have to be factored into our choices and a calculation of their consequences; or (c) believe that the costs can be passed on to others—people in developing nations, our children, and other future persons. We all have to eat and the earth inevitably has to absorb the impact of our pursuing this natural end, but we should aim to reduce and confine the ecological stresses that are under our species' control. Vegetarianism seems plainly to be the best way to manage the environmental harm and degradation caused by humans' quest for nourishment. Some of the eco-destructive effects of the meat industry listed earlier are not caused by plant-based agriculture, and with respect to other results, the effects are less severe. By enabling us to eat lower down on the food chain, a vegetarian regime makes more efficient use of solar and caloric energy inputs. (For example, by concentrating on plant sources of protein—such as soya, beans, and nuts—we get at it more directly than we do by eating animals that have processed cellulose into protein for us.) As an energy-saving diet, vegetarianism lightens the exploitative load we place upon the earth's ecosystems.

MEAT PRODUCTION AS A THREAT TO BIODIVERSITY

We have seen that the global environmental consequences of the meat production system are serious. They are also pervasive. To show this, I want to shift attention now to the effects of animal agriculture on planetary biodiversity and on our attitudes toward nature as a whole.

There are many causes of species extinction, both natural and human. In relation to human factors, no single activity accounts totally for the sort of ecocide that undermines species viability. We should not expect, therefore, that the process whereby the flesh of animals appears on our tables explains by itself why certain ecosystems and the life forms they support are either under threat or beyond recovery.

Let us begin by getting some idea of the scope of species eradication by humans. According to E. O. Wilson, who has conducted one of the most detailed studies of the problem, rain forest extinctions for which our species are responsible occur at between 1,000 and 10,000 times the natural rate (Wilson 1993). Wilson approximates that 27,000 species per year (74 per day, 3 per hour) are perishing at our hands. A more recently completed twenty-year study by the World Conservation Union shows that "at least one in eight plant species in the world—and nearly one in three in the United States—are under threat of extinction" (Stevens 1998). This appalling pace of destruction stems from several major dynamics, including the clearing of foreign and domestic forests for agricultural purposes and development, drainage and filling of wetlands, damming of rivers, use and abuse of coral reefs, and relentless high-tech ocean fishing. Among these, deforestation and overfishing are the most evident areas in which a relationship between human diet and species extinction is to be discovered. I shall focus here on the devastation of the irreplaceable rain forests of Latin America.

Most people who follow the news are conscious that global rain forests perform unique functions within the regulative cycles of the biosphere, helping to maintain global temperature, providing fresh supplies of oxygen and water to the atmosphere, and sheltering the most complex web of life imaginable. It is reported that 40% to 50% of the world's plant and animal species dwell in rain forests (McKisson & MacRae-Campbell 1990). This superabundance of life forms yields a wide range of raw materials used in the manufacture of all manner of consumer goods and pharmaceuticals, upon which the quality of human life crucially depends. Products of great value include hardwoods, rattan, natural rubber, waxes, essential oils, fruits, and nuts. One-quarter of all drug compounds obtained from pharmacies contain rain forest ingredients, whereas for most of the world's people, traditional medicines extracted from plants are used exclusively to treat ailments (Collins 1990; U.N. Food and Agricultural Organization 1995). Notwithstanding all this, a Smithsonian-sponsored research team found that an area of Amazon-basin rain forest equivalent to seven football fields is being cleared *per minute* for grazing land (Smithsonian Institution 2002). Sadly, "fewer than one percent of tropical rain forest plants have been chemically screened for useful medicinal properties" (Collins 1990: 32). Meanwhile, "studies in Peru, the Brazilian Amazon, the Philippines and Indonesia suggest that harvesting forest products sustainably is at least twice as profitable as clearing [the forests] for timber or to provide land for agriculture" (U.N. Food and Agricultural Organization 1995: 62).

That the rain forests are the earth's principal networks of species diversity seems unarguable. But why does this diversity matter so much? Thomas E. Lovejoy, a conservation biologist, places the matter in perspective:

> Assuming that the [earth's] biota contains ten million species, they then represent ten million successful sets of solutions to a series of biological problems, any one of which could be immensely valuable to us in a number of ways.... The point ... is not that the "worth" of an obscure species is that it may someday produce a cure for cancer. The point is that the biota as a whole is continually providing us with new ways to improve our biological lot, and that species that may be unimportant on our current assessment of what may be directly useful may be important tomorrow. (Lovejoy 1986:16–17)

Wilson has commented that "biodiversity is our most valuable but least appreciated resource" (Wilson 1993: 281), and Collins remarks that the rain forests comprise a unique "genetic library" of virtually untapped information (Collins 1990: 32).

Solid, human-centered reasons for preserving biological diversity are to be found in these reflections. But might there not be additional good grounds for promoting species diversity? We have no difficulty in valuing other species instrumentally—in terms of what they can do for us. Perhaps we can also value them for their own sake—that is, for having a marvellous way of being that is worthy of celebrating quite independently of any actual or potential use we might make of them, and no matter how remotely related to ourselves they may be.

We are now in a position to consider the role that animal agriculture plays in undermining species diversity on the planet. Former U.S. Vice President Al Gore has written that "at the current rate of deforestation, virtually all of the tropical rain forests will be gone partway through the next century" (Gore 1993: 119)—that is, the century we live in now.[2] It is difficult to establish a precise correlation between animal agriculture and rain forest decimation, but it should be noted that the World Watch Institute has observed that "the human appetite for animal flesh is a driving force behind virtually every major category of environmental damage now threatening the human future" (World Watch Institute 2004). Rain forests are cleared by humans seeking firewood, settlement space, farm plots, monocultural plantations, expanded land holdings, oil, minerals, pastureland for cattle, and, more recently, soybean cultivation.[3]

Hydroelectric projects, roads, and other development schemes also take their toll. Even though these pressures are numerous and diverse, grazing may be identified as a major threat (Greenpeace International 2006a).[4]

Conversion of tropical rain forests to pasture land for cattle has proceeded at a remarkable pace in Central America since the middle of the twentieth century. The inherent nature of rain forests is such that when they are cleared, only poor quality, unsustainable pastureland remains, and this contributes to the dynamics of expanding destruction as new grazing areas are sought to replace older, exhausted ones. Norman Myers contends that from Mexico to Brazil "the number one factor in elimination of Latin America's tropical forests is cattlegrazing" (Myers 1984: 127). Most of the beef produced in this region is exported to the American market, although an increasing portion goes to Western Europe and Japan (Myers 1984; Rifkin 1992). The United States contains only 5% of the world's population, yet it produces, imports, and consumes more beef than any other country (Myers 1984). The beef imported from Latin America ends up as fast food burgers, processed meats, and pet foods.[5] Myers notes that "convenience foods … constitute the fastest-growing part of the entire food industry in the United States"; 50% of all meals are now consumed in either fast food or institutional settings (Myers 1984: 130). These patterns demonstrate forcefully the connection between meat eating and rain forest destruction. We cannot save the forests just by saying no to fast-food hamburgers, but we can help turn things around if enough of us set an example by reducing the meat in our diets and if, in this way, we set an example for others.

MEAT PRODUCTION AND THE DOMINATION OF NATURE

The case of rain forest decimation for cattle grazing is a typical ecological horror story. But viewed through a slightly different prism, what we encounter here is one of the many forms of the human domination and manipulation of nature. I mean to point out here by that the range of our activities starkly display our species' tendency to treat nature and natural biological systems purely as instruments for achieving human and often very narrow, short-sighted objectives.

According to the manipulative mindset, nature or parts of nature (such as members of nonhuman species) merely constitute resources or materials for our use and disposal as we see fit. The slash-and-burn practice that seals the fate of rain forests as obstacles that are "in the way" of profit to be extracted from low-cost meat provides but one example of this mentality at work in the world. Whereas the rain forests are treated as dispensable, the animals subsequently bred on this land are themselves no more than commodities destined for some distant stockyard—just further contents of the organic cash till that is nature.

But the attitude evident here, which permits the ruthless exploitation of cattle from rain forest regions, is in reality no different from that which endorses the widespread practice of animal confinement on factory farms. Animals there have manifestly become machines or artefacts of production and reproduction (Mason & Singer 1990; Rice 2004; Gold 2004). New developments may yield even more ominous scenarios. Researchers have considered or are actively considering the application of genetic techniques to create freakish monster animals and to clone superproductive animals (U.S. Congress, Office of Technology Assessment 1985; British Medical Association 1992; Fox 1992; Spallone 1992). Other scientific fantasies include animals with modified physiologies that experience little or no stress (Mason & Singer 1990), animals with no pain receptors (Rollin 1995), and the manufacture of synthetic meat (Edelman et al. 2005; Reuters 2005). Greed is driving some of these developments; the thinking behind others must be that if the experiments are successful and lead to economical avenues of meat production, then it will be alright to treat the animal artifacts that result as mere things, and hence the major ethical objections to factory farming will simply melt away.[6]

What does all this add up to? The meat industry, itself feeding off human demand for certain types of food, is ushering in an era of activities that are totally lacking in compassion or a sense of connection with nature. Although we seem to be learning to connect to nature on one level—concern over ecological issues—on another level we have become out of touch with what matters most. The vast majority would not wish to visit a slaughterhouse for any reason,[7] and from what people know of modern livestock production processes, they would never want their pet or any animal they cared about to be treated the way food animals routinely are, let alone how they may be treated in the future. But at the same time, the consumers' selection of meat and meat products as foods of choice goes on with apparently little thought. In this manner, we accustom ourselves to accept the domination and manipulation of nature that as sensitive, caring people we ought to be aware of and reject. We thus find ourselves caught in a trap of our own making. We can, however, seek a way out by being reflective and deciding in favor of a lifestyle that does not rest upon the subjugation of the earth and the suffering of nonhuman forms of life. This is the vegetarian option, which is where I started.

CONCLUSION: A VEGETARIAN ETHIC

Vegetarianism encourages us to think of ourselves as *part of* nature rather than *apart from* nature. The vegetarian outlook recognizes the importance of ecologically sustainable human activity and affirms the requirement that we seek to minimize our impact on the planet, and this recognition includes the amount of harm we do in the course of looking after our essential needs. Mindfulness of both short- and long-term consequences of individual choice and collective behavior are hallmarks of a commitment to vegetarianism as a way of life. This choice also entails compassionate cohabitation with other species and respect for the earth to the greatest extent that these precepts can be followed, both in one's personal activities and in social policy and planning. The vegetarian way of life offers us a chance to re-establish contact with the land, eat locally grown foods, and recover connections with nature. Finally, vegetarianism is liberating in the sense that it frees us *from* the exploitation of animals and nature, while it frees us *to* discover who we are in more positive, life-affirming ways that are healthy for both humans and the planet that is our home.

NOTES

1. Also of interest here, it has been reported that nearly 15% of the Chinese population is now overweight, and childhood obesity in China has increased by 28 times over the past decade and a half, the causes of this being cited as greater meat consumption and lack of exercise (Guardian Weekly 2006).

2. See also his acclaimed environmental documentary film *An Inconvenient Truth* (2006).

3. Rain forest destruction for the purpose of creating soya plantations will cause concern among vegetarians, but this process is in fact geared toward supplying feed for livestock animals, not food for humans (Greenpeace International 2006b).

4. The radical transformation and degradation of *American* land by animal agriculture should not be underestimated and likewise presents a tragic story (Berry 1996; University of Washington Students n.d.).

5. Fast-food giants Burger King and McDonald's have pledged to stop using rain-forest-grown beef; others have made no such commitment. Greenpeace has recently charged that McDonald's beef and Kentucky Fried Chicken's chicken are fed on soya grown in cleared Amazon rain forests (Greenpeace International 2006c).

6. The case of synthetic or laboratory-grown meat is represented by smug journalists as a big "problem" for vegetarianism because its ethical position in

regard to meat eating would supposedly be undermined by the prospect of animal flesh being produced without pain, suffering, and killing. But first, this view shows little understanding of what vegetarianism is all about (see the final section of this article and Fox 1999). Second, synthetic meat is merely a possibility today; we are very far from seeing it drive conventional factory farms out of business. And if it did, this would cause as big an economic upheaval as a large-scale transition to vegetarianism. Third, if meat eaters so desperately want meat that they will queue up for fake, laboratory-cultured versions, let them do so and leave the fresh, healthy, naturally grown plants to the rest of us.

7. I have, and it is a profoundly disturbing experience. For readers with strong stomachs who might be willing to "visit" an abattoir through the pages of a book, I recommend Coe (1995) and Eisnetz (1997).

18

Can Frankenfood Save the Planet?

JONATHAN RAUCH

Jonathan Rauch is a writer for the Atlantic Monthly. *In this essay he presents evidence to the effect that genetically engineered food could provide enough nutrition to save future generations from starvation. He argues that environmentalists who oppose genetically modified food are actually working against the best interests of humankind and their pets.*

That genetic engineering may be the most environmentally beneficial technology to have emerged in decades, or possibly centuries, is not immediately obvious. Certainly, at least, it is not obvious to the many U.S. and foreign environmental groups that regard biotechnology as a bête noire. Nor is it necessarily obvious to people who grew up in cities, and who have only an inkling of what happens on a modern farm. Being agriculturally illiterate myself, I set out to look at what may be, if the planet is fortunate, the farming of the future.

It was baking hot that April day. I traveled with two Virginia state soil-and-water-conservation officers and an agricultural-extension agent to an area not far from Richmond. The farmers there are national (and therefore world) leaders in the application of what is known as continuous no-till farming. In plain English, they don't plough. For thousands of years, since the dawn of the agricultural revolution, farmers have ploughed, often several times a year; and with ploughing has come runoff that pollutes rivers and blights aquatic habitat, erosion that wears away the land, and the release into the atmosphere of greenhouse gases stored in the soil. Today, at last, farmers are working out methods that have begun to make ploughing obsolete.

Reprinted from the *Atlantic Monthly* (October 2003) by permission of the author.

At about one-thirty we arrived at a 200-acre patch of farmland known as the Good Luck Tract. No one seemed to know the provenance of the name, but the best guess was that somebody had said something like "You intend to farm this? Good luck!" The land was rolling, rather than flat, and its slopes came together to form natural troughs for rainwater. Ordinarily this highly erodible land would be suitable for cows, not crops. Yet it was dense with wheat—wheat yielding almost twice what could normally be expected, and in soil that had grown richer in organic matter, and thus more nourishing to crops, even as the land was farmed. Perhaps most striking was the almost complete absence of any chemical or soil runoff. Even the beating administered in 1999 by Hurricane Floyd, which lashed the ground with nineteen inches of rain in less than twenty-four hours, produced no significant runoff or erosion. The land simply absorbed the sheets of water before they could course downhill.

At another site, a few miles away, I saw why. On land planted in corn whose shoots had only just broken the surface, Paul Davis, the extension agent, wedged a shovel into the ground and dislodged about eight inches of topsoil. Then he reached down and picked up a clump. Ploughed soil, having been stirred up and turned over again and again, becomes lifeless and homogeneous, but the clump that Davis held out was alive. I immediately noticed three squirming earthworms, one grub, and quantities of tiny white insects that looked very busy. As if in greeting, a worm defecated. "Plant-available food!" a delighted Davis exclaimed.

This soil, like that of the Good Luck Tract, had not been ploughed for years, allowing the underground ecosystem to return. Insects and roots and microorganisms had given the soil an elaborate architecture, which held the earth in place and made it a sponge for water. That was why erosion and runoff had been reduced to practically nil. Crops thrived because worms were doing the ploughing. Crop residue that was left on the ground, rather than ploughed under as usual, provided nourishment for the soil's biota and, as it decayed, enriched the soil. The farmer saved the fuel he would have used driving back and forth with a heavy plough. That saved

money, and of course it also saved energy and reduced pollution. On top of all that, crop yields were better than with conventional methods.

The conservation people in Virginia were full of excitement over no-till farming. Their job was to clean up the James and York Rivers and the rest of the Chesapeake Bay watershed. Most of the sediment that clogs and clouds the rivers, and most of the fertilizer runoff that causes the algae blooms that kill fish, comes from farmland. By all but eliminating agricultural erosion and runoff—so Brian Noyes, the local conservation-district manager, told me—continuous no-till could "revolutionize" the area's water quality.

Even granting that Noyes is an enthusiast, from an environmental point of view no-till farming looks like a dramatic advance. The rub—if it is a rub—is that the widespread elimination of the plough depends on genetically modified crops.

It is only a modest exaggeration to say that as goes agriculture, so goes the planet. Of all the human activities that shape the environment, agriculture is the single most important, and it is well ahead of whatever comes second. Today about 38 percent of the earth's land area is crop land or pasture—a total that has crept upward over the past few decades as global population has grown. The increase has been gradual, only about 0.3 percent a year; but that still translates into an additional Greece or Nicaragua cultivated or grazed every year.

Farming does not go easy on the earth, and never has. To farm is to make war upon millions of plants (weeds, so-called) and animals (pests, so-called) that in the ordinary course of things would crowd out or eat or infest whatever it is a farmer is growing. Crop monocultures, as whole fields of only wheat or corn or any other single plant are called, make poor habitat and are vulnerable to disease and disaster. Although fertilizer runs off and pollutes water, farming without fertilizer will deplete and eventually exhaust the soil. Pesticides can harm the health of human beings and kill desirable or harmless bugs along with pests. Irrigation leaves behind trace elements that can accumulate and poison the soil. And on and on.

The trade-offs are fundamental. Organic farming, for example, uses no artificial fertilizer, but it does use a lot of manure, which can pollute water and contaminate food. Traditional farmers may use less herbicide, but they also do more ploughing, with all the ensuing environmental complications. Low-input agriculture uses fewer chemicals but more land. The point is not that farming is an environmental crime—it is not—but that there is no escaping the pressure it puts on the planet.

In the next half century the pressure will intensify. The United Nations, in its midrange projections, estimates that the earth's human population will grow by more than 40 percent, from 6.3 billion people today to 8.9 billion in 2050. Feeding all those people, and feeding their billion or so hungry pets (a dog or a cat is one of the first things people want once they move beyond a subsistence lifestyle), and providing the increasingly protein-rich diets that an increasingly wealthy world will expect—doing all of that will require food output to at least double, and possibly triple.

But then the story will change. According to the UN's midrange projections (which may, if anything, err somewhat on the high side), around 2050 the world's population will more or less level off. Even if the growth does not stop, it will slow. The crunch will be over. In fact, if in 2050 crop yields are still increasing, if most of the world is economically developed, and if population pressures are declining or even reversing—all of which seems reasonably likely—then the human species may at long last be able to feed itself, year in and year out, without putting any additional net stress on the environment. We might even be able to grow everything we need while *reducing* our agricultural footprint: returning cropland to wilderness, repairing damaged soils, restoring ecosystems, and so on. In other words, human agriculture might be placed on a sustainable footing forever: a breathtaking prospect.

The great problem, then, is to get through the next four or five decades with as little environmental damage as possible. That is where biotechnology comes in.

One day recently I drove down to southern Virginia to visit Dennis Avery and his son, Alex. The older Avery, a man in late middle age with a chinstrap beard, droopy eyes, and an intent, scholarly manner, lives on ninety-seven acres that he shares with horses, chickens, fish, cats, dogs, bluebirds, ducks, transient geese, and assorted other creatures. He is the director of global food issues at the Hudson Institute, a conservative think tank; Alex works with him, and is trained as a plant physiologist. We sat in a sun-room at the back of the house, our afternoon conversation punctuated every so often by dog snores and rooster crows. We talked for a little while about the Green Revolution, a dramatic advance in farm productivity that fed the world's burgeoning population over the past four decades, and then I asked if the challenge of the next four decades could be met.

"Well," Dennis replied, "we have tripled the world's farm output since 1960. And we're feeding twice as many people from the same land. That was a heroic achievement. But we have to do what some think is an even more difficult thing in this next forty years, because the Green Revolution had more land per person and more water per person—"

"—and more potential for increases," Alex added, "because the base that we were starting from was so much lower."

"By and large," Dennis went on, "the world's civilizations have been built around its best farmland. And we have used most of the world's good farmland. Most of the good land is already heavily fertilized. Most of the good land is already being planted with high-yield seeds. [Africa is the important exception.] Most of the good irrigation sites are used. We can't triple yields again with the technologies we're already using. And we might be lucky to get a fifty percent yield increase if we froze our technology short of biotech."

"Biotech" can refer to a number of things, but the relevant application here is genetic modification: the selective transfer of genes from one organism to another. Ordinary breeding can cross related varieties, but it cannot take a gene from a bacterium, for instance, and transfer it to a wheat plant. The organisms resulting from gene transfers are called "transgenic" by scientists—and "Frankenfood" by many greens.

Gene transfer poses risks, unquestionably. So, for that matter, does traditional crossbreeding. But many people worry that transgenic organisms might prove more unpredictable. One possibility is that transgenic crops would spread from fields into forests or other wild lands and there become environmental nuisances, or worse. A further risk is that transgenic plants might cross-pollinate with neighboring wild plants, producing "superweeds" or other invasive or destructive varieties in the wild. Those risks are real enough that even most biotech enthusiasts—including Dennis Avery, for example—favor some government regulation of transgenic crops.

What is much less widely appreciated is biotech's potential to do the environment good. Take as an example continuous no-till farming, which really works best with the help of transgenic crops. Human beings have been ploughing for so long that we tend to forget why we started doing it in the first place. The short answer: weed control. Turning over the soil between plantings smothers weeds and their seeds. If you don't plough, your land becomes a weed garden—unless you use herbicides to kill the weeds. Herbicides, however, are expensive, and can be complicated to apply. And they tend to kill the good with the bad.

In the mid-1990s the agricultural-products company Monsanto introduced a transgenic soybean variety called Roundup Ready. As the name implies, these soybeans tolerate Roundup, an herbicide (also made by Monsanto) that kills many kinds of weeds and then quickly breaks down into harmless ingredients. Equipped with Roundup Ready crops, farmers found that they could retire their ploughs and control weeds with just a few applications of a single, relatively benign herbicide—instead of many applications of a complex and expensive menu of chemicals. More than a third of all U.S. soybeans are now grown without ploughing, mostly owing to the introduction of Roundup Ready varieties. Ploughless cotton farming has likewise received a big boost from the advent of bioengineered varieties. No-till farming without biotech is possible, but it's more difficult and expensive, which is why no-till and biotech are advancing in tandem.

In 2001 a group of scientists announced that they had engineered a transgenic tomato plant able to thrive on salty water—water, in fact, almost half as salty as seawater, and fifty times as salty as tomatoes can ordinary abide. One of the researchers was quoted as saying, "I've already transformed tomato, tobacco, and canola. I believe I can transform any crop with this gene"—just the sort of Frankenstein hubris that makes environmentalists shudder. But consider the environmental implications. Irrigation has for millennia been a cornerstone of agriculture, but it comes at a price. As irrigation water evaporates, it leaves behind traces of salt, which accumulate in the soil and gradually render it infertile. (As any Roman legion knows, to destroy a nation's agricultural base you salt the soil.) Every year the world loses about 25 million acres—an area equivalent to a fifth of California—to salinity; 40 percent of the world's irrigated land, and 25 percent of America's, has been hurt to some degree. For decades traditional plant breeders tried to create salt-tolerant crop plants, and for decades they failed.

Salt-tolerant crops might bring millions of acres of wounded or crippled land back into production. "And it gets better," Alex Avery told me. The transgenic tomato plants take up and sequester in their leaves as much as six or seven percent of their weight in sodium. "Theoretically," Alex said, "you could reclaim a salt-contaminated field by growing enough of these crops to remove the salts from the soil."

His father chimed in: "We've worried about being able to keep these salt-contaminated fields going even for decades. We can now think about *centuries*."

One of the first biotech crops to reach the market, in the mid-1990s, was a cotton plant that makes its own pesticide. Scientists incorporated into the plant a toxin-producing gene from a soil bacterium known as *Bacillus thuringiensis*. With Bt cotton, as it is called, farmers can spray much less, and the poison contained in the plant is delivered only to bugs that actually eat the crop. As any environmentalist can tell you, insecticide is not very nice stuff—especially if you breathe it, which many Third World farmers do as they walk through their fields with backpack sprayers.

Transgenic cotton reduced pesticide use by more than two million pounds in the United States from 1996 to 2000, and it has reduced pesticide sprayings in parts of China by more than half. Earlier this year the Environmental Protection Agency approved a genetically modified corn that resists a beetle larva known as rootworm. Because rootworm is American corn's most voracious enemy, this new variety has the potential to reduce annual pesticide use in America by more than 14 million pounds. It could reduce or eliminate the spraying of pesticide on 23 million acres of U.S. land.

All of that is the beginning, not the end. Bio-engineers are also working, for instance, on crops that tolerate aluminum, another major contaminant of soil, especially in the tropics. Return an acre of farmland to productivity, or double yields on an already productive acre, and, other things being equal, you reduce by an acre the amount of virgin forest or savannah that will be stripped and cultivated. That may be the most important benefit of all.

Of the many people I have interviewed in my twenty years as a journalist, Norman Borlaug must be the one who has saved the most lives. Today he is an unprepossessing eighty-nine-year-old man of middling height, with crystal-bright blue eyes and thinning white hair. He still loves to talk about plant breeding, the discipline that won him the 1970 Nobel Peace Prize: Borlaug led efforts to breed the staples of the Green Revolution. (See "Forgotten Benefactor of Humanity," by Gregg Easterbrook, an article on Borlaug in the January 1997 *Atlantic*.) Yet the renowned plant breeder is quick to mention that he began his career, in the 1930s, in forestry, and that forest conservation has never been far from his thoughts. In the 1960s, while he was working to improve crop yields in India and Pakistan, he made a mental connection. He would create tables detailing acres under cultivation and average yields—and then, in another column, he would estimate how much land had been saved by higher farm productivity. Later, in the 1980s and 1990s, he and others began paying increased attention to what some agricultural economists now call the Borlaug hypothesis: that the Green Revolution has saved not only many human lives but, by improving the productivity of existing farmland, also millions of acres of tropical forest and other habitat—and so has saved countless animal lives.

From the 1960s through the 1980s, for example, Green Revolution advances saved more than 100 million acres of wild lands in India. More recently, higher yields in rice, coffee, vegetables, and other crops have reduced or in some cases stopped forest-clearing in Honduras, the Philippines, and elsewhere. Dennis Avery estimates that if farming techniques and yields had not improved since 1950, the world would have lost an additional 20 million or so square miles of wildlife habitat, most of it forest. About 16 million square miles of forest exists today. "What I'm saying," Avery said, in response to my puzzled expression, "is that we have saved every square mile of forest on the planet."

Habitat destruction remains a serious environmental problem; in some respects it is the most serious. The savannahs and tropical forests of Central and South America, Asia, and Africa by and large make poor farmland, but they are the earth's storehouses of biodiversity, and the forests are the earth's lungs. Since 1972 about 200,000 square miles of Amazon rain forest have been cleared for crops and pasture; from 1966 to 1994 all but three of the Central American countries cleared more forest than they left standing. Mexico is losing more than 4,000 square miles of forest a year to peasant farms; sub-Saharan Africa is losing more than 19,000.

That is why the great challenge of the next four or five decades is not to feed an additional three billion people (and their pets) but to do so without converting much of the world's prime habitat into second- or third-rate farmland. Now, most agronomists agree that some substantial yield improvements are still to be had from advances in conventional breeding, fertilizers, herbicides, and other Green Revolution standbys. But it seems pretty clear that biotechnology holds more promise—probably much more. Recall that world food output will need to at least double and possibly triple over the next several decades. Even if production could be increased that much using conventional technology, which is doubtful, the required amounts of pesticide and fertilizer and other polluting chemicals would be immense. If properly developed, disseminated, and used, genetically modified crops might well be the best hope the planet has got.

If properly developed, disseminated, and used, that tripartite qualification turns out to be important, and it brings the environmental community squarely, and at the moment rather jarringly, into the picture.

Not long ago I went to see David Sandalow in his office at the World Wildlife Fund, in Washington, D.C. Sandalow, the organization's executive vice-president in charge of conservation programs, is a tall, affable, polished, and slightly reticent man in his forties who holds degrees from Yale and the University of Michigan Law School.

Some weeks earlier, over lunch, I had mentioned Dennis Avery's claim that genetic modi-fication had great environmental potential. I was surprised when Sandalow told me he agreed. Later, in our interview in his office, I asked him to elaborate. "With biotechnology," he said, "there are no simple answers. Biotechnology has huge potential benefits and huge risks, and we need to address both as we move forward. The huge poten-tial benefits include increased productivity of arable land, which could relieve pressure on forests. They include decreased pesticide usage. But the huge risks include severe ecological disruptions—from gene flow and from enhanced invasiveness, which is a very antiseptic word for some very scary stuff."

I asked if he thought that, absent biotechnology, the world could feed everybody over the next forty or fifty years without ploughing down the rain forests. Instead of answering directly he said, "Biotechnology could be part of our arsenal if we can overcome some of the barriers. It will never be a panacea or a magic bullet. But nor should we remove it from our tool kit."

Sandalow is unusual. Very few credentialed greens talk the way he does about biotechnology, at least publicly. They would readily agree with him about the huge risks, but they wouldn't be caught dead speaking of huge potential benefits—a point I will come back to. From an ecological point of view, a very great deal depends on other

environmentalists' coming to think more the way Sandalow does.

Biotech companies are in business to make money. That is fitting and proper. But developing and testing new transgenic crops is expensive and commercially risky, to say nothing of politically controversial. When they decide how to invest their research-and-development money, biotech compa-nies will naturally seek products for which farmers and consumers will pay top dollar. Roundup Ready products, for instance, are well suited to U.S. farm-ing, with its high levels of capital spending on such things as herbicides and automated sprayers. Poor farmers in the developing world, or course, have much less buying power. Creating, say, salt-tolerant cassava suitable for growing on hardscrabble African farms might save habitat as well as lives—but commercial enterprises are not likely to fall over one another in a rush to do it.

If earth-friendly transgenics are developed, the next problem is disseminating them. As a number of the farmers and experts I talked to were quick to mention, switching to an unfamiliar new technol-ogy—something like no-till—is not easy. It requires capital investment in new seed and equipment, mastery of new skills and methods, a fragile transition period as farmer and ecology readjust, and an often considerable amount of trial and error to find out what works best on any given field. Such problems are only magnified in the Third World, where the learning curve is steeper and capital cushions are thin to nonexistent. Just handing a peasant farmer a bag of newfangled seed is not enough. In many cases peasant farmers will need one-on-one attention. Many will need help to pay for the seed, too.

Finally there is the matter of using biotech in a way that actually benefits the environment. Often the technological blade can cut either way, especially in the short run. A salt-tolerant or drought-resistant rice that allowed farmers to keep land in production might also induce them to plough up virgin land that previously was too salty or too dry to farm. If the effect of improved seed is to make farming more prof-itable, farmers may respond, at least temporarily, by bringing more land into production. If a farm becomes more productive, it may require fewer workers; and if local labor markets cannot provide jobs for them, displaced workers may move to a nearby patch of rain forest and burn it down to make way for subsistence farming. Such transition problems are solvable, but they need money and attention.

In short, realizing the great—probably unique—environmental potential of biotech will require stewardship. "It's a tool," Sara Scherr, an agricultural economist with the conservation group Forest Trends, told me, "but it's absolutely not going to happen automatically."

So now ask a question: Who is the natural constituency for earth-friendly biotechnology? Who cares enough to lobby governments to underwrite research—frequently unprofitable research—on transgenic crops that might restore soils or cut down on pesticides in poor countries? Who cares enough to teach Asian or African farmers, one by one, how to farm without ploughing? Who cares enough to help poor farmers afford high-tech, earth-friendly seed? Who cares enough to agitate for programs and reforms that might steer displaced peasants and profit-seeking farmers away from sensitive lands? Not politicians, for the most part. Not farmers. Not corporations. Not consumers.

At the World Resources Institute, an environmental think tank in Washington, the molecular biologist Don Doering envisions transgenic crops designed specifically to solve environmental problems: crops that might fertilize the soil, crops that could clean water, crops tailored to remedy the ecological problems of specific places. "Suddenly you might find yourself with a virtually chemical-free agriculture, where your cropland itself is filtering the water, it's protecting the watershed, it's providing habitat," Doering told me. "There is still so little investment in what I call design-for-environment." The natural constituency for such investment is, of course, environmentalists.

But environmentalists are not acting such a constituency today. They are doing the apposite. For example, Greenpeace declares on its Web site: "The introduction of genetically engineered (GE) organisms into the complex ecosystems of our environment is a dangerous global experiment with nature and evolution … GE organisms must not be released into the environment. They pose unacceptable risks to ecosystems, and have the potential to threaten biodiversity, wildlife and sustainable forms of agriculture."

Other groups argue for what they call the Precautionary Principle, under which no transgenic crop could be used until proven benign in virtually all respects. The Sierra Club says on its Web site,

> In accordance with this Precautionary Principle, we call for a moratorium on the planting of all genetically engineered crops and the release of all GEOs [genetically engineered organisms] into the environment, *including those now approved.* Releases should be delayed until extensive, rigorous research is done which determines the long-term environmental and health impacts of each GEO and there is public debate to ascertain the need for the use of each GEO intended for release into the environment. [italics added]

Under this policy the cleaner water and healthier soil that continuous no-till farming has already brought to the Chesapeake Bay watershed would be undone, and countless tons of polluted runoff and eroded topsoil would accumulate in Virginia rivers and streams while debaters debated and researchers researched. Recall David Sandalow: "Biotechnology has huge potential benefits and huge risks, and we need to address both as we move forward." A lot of environmentalists would say instead, "*before* we move forward." That is an important difference, particularly because the big population squeeze will happen not in the distant future but over the next several decades.

For reasons having more to do with policies than with logic, the modern environmental movement was to a large extent founded on suspicion of markets and artificial substances. Markets exploit the earth; chemicals poison it. Biotech touches both hot buttons. It is being pushed forward by greedy corporations, and it seems to be the very epitome of the unnatural.

Still, I hereby hazard a prediction. In ten years or less, most American environmentalists (European ones are more dogmatic) will regard genetic modification as one of their most powerful tools. In only the past ten years or so, after all, environmentalists have reversed field and embraced market mechanisms—tradable emissions permits and the like—as useful in the fight against pollution. The environmental logic of biotechnology is, if anything, even more compelling. The potential upside of genetic modification is simply too large to ignore—and therefore environmentalists will not ignore it. Biotechnology will transform agriculture, and in doing so will transform American environmentalism.

STUDY QUESTIONS

1. Discuss the promise of genetically modified food. What environmental problems can it solve? How can it help alleviate world hunger?

2. Discuss the risks involved in producing genetically modified food. Why are so many environmentalists against it?

3. How do you think we should proceed with regard to genetically modified food?

19

The Unholy Alliance

MAE-WAN HO

Mae-Wan Ho, trained as a geneticist, is a leading social and environmental activist. She is the author of numerous books and articles, including most recently Genetic Engineering, Dream or Nightmare? *She proposes an immediate moratorium on genetically modified foods until their safety, in all phases, can be properly tested.*

Genetic engineering biotechnology is inherently hazardous. It could lead to disasters far worse than those caused by accidents to nuclear installations. In the words of the author, "genes can replicate indefinitely, spread and recombine." For this reason the release of a genetically engineered micro-organism that is lethal to humans could well spell the end of humanity. Unfortunately the proponents of this terrifying technology share a genetic determinist mindset that leads them to reject the inherently dangerous nature of their work. What is particularly worrying at first sight is the irresistible power of the large corporations which are pushing this technology.

From *The Ecologist*, Vol. 27, No. 4 (July/August 1997). Reprinted by permission of *The Ecologist*, www.theecologist.org.

Suddenly, the brave new world dawns.

Suddenly, as 1997 begins and the millennium is drawing to a close, men and women in the street are waking up to the realization that genetic engineering biotechnology is taking over every aspect of their daily lives. They are caught unprepared for the avalanche of products arriving, or soon to arrive, in their supermarkets: rapeseed oil, soybean, maize, sugar beet, squash, cucumber.... It started as a mere trickle less than three years ago—the BST-milk from cows fed genetically engineered bovine growth hormone to boost milk yield, and the tomato genetically engineered to prolong shelf-life. They had provoked so much debate and opposition, as did indeed the genetic screening tests for an increasing number of diseases. Surely, we wouldn't, and shouldn't, be rushed headlong into the brave new world.

Back then, in order to quell our anxiety, a series of highly publicized "consensus conferences" and "public consultations" were carried out. Committees were set up by many European governments to consider the risks and the ethics, and the debates continued. The public were, however, only dimly aware of critics who deplored "tampering with nature" and "scrambling the genetic code of species" by introducing human genes into animals, and animal genes into vegetables. Warnings of unexpected effects on agriculture and biodiversity, of the dangers of irreversible "genetic pollution," warnings of genetic discrimination and the return of eugenics, as genetic screening and prenatal diagnosis became widely available, were marginalized. So too were condemnations of the immorality of the "patents on life"—transgenic animals, plants and seeds, taken freely by geneticists of developed countries from the Third World, as well as human genes and human cell lines from indigenous peoples.

By and large, the public were lulled into a false sense of security, in the belief that the best scientists and the new breed of "bioethicists" in the country were busy considering the risks associated with the new biotechnology and the ethical issues raised. Simultaneously, glossy information pamphlets and reports, which aimed at promoting "public understanding" of genetic "modification," were widely distributed by the biotech industries and their friends, and endorsed by government scientists. "Genetic modification," we are told, is simply the latest in a "seamless" continuum of biotechnologies practised by human beings since the dawn of civilization, from bread and wine-making, to selective breeding. The significant advantage of genetic modification is that it is much more "precise," as genes can be individually isolated and transferred as desired.

Thus, the possible benefits promised to humankind are limitless. There is something to satisfy everyone. For those morally concerned about inequality and human suffering, it promises to feed the hungry with genetically modified crops able to resist pests and diseases and to increase yields. For those who despair of the present global environmental deterioration, it promises to modify strains of bacteria and higher plants that can degrade toxic wastes or mop up heavy metals (contaminants). For those hankering after sustainable agriculture, it promises to develop Greener, more environmentally friendly transgenic crops that will reduce the use of pesticides, herbicides and fertilizers.

That is not all. It is in the realm of human genetics that the real revolution will be wrought. Plans to uncover the entire genetic blueprint of the human being would, we are told, eventually enable geneticists to diagnose, in advance, all the diseases that an individual will suffer in his or her lifetime, even before the individual is born, or even as the egg is fertilized *in vitro*. A whole gamut of specific drugs tailored to individual genetic needs can be designed to cure all diseases. The possibility of immortality is dangling from the horizons as the "longevity gene" is isolated.

There are problems, of course, as there would be in any technology. The ethical issues have to be decided by the public. (By implication, the science is separate and not open to question.) The risks will be minimized. (Again, by implication, the risks have nothing to do with the science.) After all, nothing in life is without risk. Crossing roads is a risk. The new biotechnology (i.e. genetic engineering biotechnology) is under very strict government regulation, and the government's scientists and other experts will see to it that neither the consumer nor the environment will be unduly harmed.

Then came the relaxation of regulation on genetically modified products, on grounds that over-regulation is compromising the "competitiveness" of the industry, and that hundreds of field trials have demonstrated the new biotechnology to be safe. And, in any case, there is no essential difference between transgenic plants produced by the new biotechnology and those produced by conventional breeding methods. (One prominent spokesperson for the industry even went as far as to refer to the varieties produced by conventional breeding methods, *retrospectively,* as "transgenics.")[1] This was followed, a year later, by the avalanche of products approved, or seeking, approval marketing, for which neither segregation from non-genetically engineered produce nor labelling is required. One is left to wonder why, if the products are as safe and wonderful as claimed, they could not be segregated, as organic produce has been for years, so that consumers are given the choice of buying what they want.

A few days later, as though acting on cue, the Association of British Insurers announced that, in future, people applying for life policies will have to divulge the results of any genetic tests they have taken. This is seen, by many, as a definite move towards open genetic discrimination. A few days later, a scientist of the Roslin Institute near Edinburgh announced that they had successfully "cloned" a sheep from a cell taken from the mammary gland of an adult animal. "Dolly," the cloned lamb, is now seven months old. Of course it took nearly 300 trials to get one success, but no mention is made of the vast majority of the embryos that failed. Is that ethical? If it can be done on sheep, does it mean it can be done for human beings? Are we nearer to cloning human beings? The popular media went wild with heroic enthusiasm at one extreme to the horror of Frankenstein at the other. Why is this work only coming to public attention now, when the research has actually been going on for at least 10 years?[2]

I should, right away, dispel the myth that genetic engineering is just like conventional breeding techniques. It is not. Genetic engineering bypasses conventional breeding by using the artificially constructed vectors to multiply copies of genes, and in many cases, to carry and smuggle genes into cells. Once inside cells, these vectors slot themselves into the host genome. In this way, *transgenic* organisms are made carrying the desired *transgenes.* The insertion of foreign genes into the host genome has long been known to have many harmful and fatal effects including cancer; and this is born out by the low success rate of creating desired transgenic organisms. Typically, a large number of eggs or embryos have to be injected or infected with the vector to obtain a few organisms that successfully express the transgene.

The most common vectors used in genetic engineering biotechnology are a chimaeric recombination of natural genetic parasites from different sources, including viruses causing cancers and other diseases in animals and plants, with their pathogenic functions 'crippled,' and tagged with one or more antibiotic resistance 'marker' genes, so that cells transformed with the vector can be selected. For example, the vector most widely used in plant genetic engineering is derived from a tumour-inducing plasmid carried by the soil bacterium *Agrobacterium tumefaciens.* In animals, vectors are constructed from *retroviruses* causing cancers and other diseases. A vector currently used in fish has a framework from the Moloney marine leukaemic virus, which causes leukaemia in mice, but can infect all mammalian cells. It has bits from the Rous Sarcoma virus, causing sarcomas in chickens, and from the vesicular stomatitis virus, causing oral lesions in cattle, horses, pigs and humans. Such mosaic vectors are particularly hazardous. Unlike natural parasitic genetic elements which have various degrees of host specificity, vectors used in genetic engineering, partly by design and partly on account of their mosaic character, have the ability to overcome species barriers and to infect a wide range of species. Another obstacle to genetic engineering is that all organisms and cells have natural defence mechanisms that enable them to destroy or inactivate foreign genes, and transgene instability is a big problem for the industry. Vectors are now increasingly constructed to overcome those mechanisms that maintain the integrity of species. The result is that the artificially constructed vectors are especially good at carrying out horizontal gene transfer.

Let me summarize why rDNA technology differs radically from conventional breeding techniques.

1. Genetic engineering recombines genetic material in the laboratory between species that do not interbreed in nature.

2. While conventional breeding methods shuffle different forms (alletes) of the same genes, genetic engineering enables completely new (exotic) genes to be introduced with unpredictable effects on the physiology and biochemistry of the resultant transgenic organism.

3. Gene multiplications and a high proportion of gene transfers are mediated by vectors which have the following undesirable characteristics:

   a. Many are derived from disease-causing viruses, plasmids and mobile genetic elements—parasitic DNA that have the ability to invade cells and insert themselves into the cell's genome causing genetic damages.

   b. They are designed to break down species barriers so that they can shuttle genes between a wide range of species. Their wide host range means that they can infect many animals and plants, and in the process pick up genes from viruses of all these species to create new pathogens.

   c. They routinely carry genes for antibiotic resistance, which is already a big health problem.

   d. They are increasingly constructed to overcome the recipient species' defence mechanisms that break down or inactivate foreign DNA.

The public are totally unprepared. They are being plunged headlong, against their will, into the brave new genetically engineered world, in which giant, faceless multinational corporations will control every aspect of their lives, from the food they can eat to the baby they can conceive and give birth to.

Isn't it a bit late in the day to tell us that? you ask. Yes and no. Yes, because I, who should, perhaps, have known better, was caught unprepared like the rest. And no, because there have been so many people warning us of that eventuality, who have campaigned tirelessly on our behalf, some of them going back to the earliest days of genetic engineering in the 1970s—although we have paid them little heed. No, it is not too late, if only because that is precisely what we tend to believe, and are encouraged to believe. A certain climate is created—that of being rapidly overtaken by events—reinforcing the feeling that the tidal wave of progress brought on by the new biotechnology is impossible to stem, so that we may be paralysed into accepting the inevitable. No, because we shall not give up, for the consequence of giving up is the brave new world, and soon after that, there may be no world at all. The gene genie is fast getting out of control. The practitioners of genetic engineering biotechnology, the regulators and the critics alike, have *all* underestimated the risks involved, which are *inherent* to genetic engineering biotechnology, particularly as misguided by an outmoded and erroneous worldview that comes from bad science. The dreams may already be turning into nightmares.

That is why people like myself are calling for an immediate moratorium on further releases and marketing of genetically engineered products, and for an independent public enquiry to be set up to look into the risks and hazards involved, taking into account the most comprehensive, scientific knowledge in addition to the social, moral implications. This would be most timely, as public opposition to genetic engineering biotechnology has been gaining momentum throughout Europe and the USA.

In Austria, a record 1.2 million citizens, representing 20 percent of the electorate, have signed a people's petition to ban genetically engineered foods, as well as deliberate releases of genetically modified organisms and patenting of life. Genetically modified foods were also rejected earlier by a lay people consultation in Norway, and by 95 percent of consumers in Germany, as revealed by a recent survey. The European Parliament has voted by an overwhelming 407 to 2 majority to censure the

Commission's authorization, in December 1996, for imports of Ciba-Geigy's transgenic maize into Europe, and is calling for imports to be suspended while the authorization is re-examined. The European Commission has decided that in the future genetically engineered seeds will be labelled, and is also considering proposals for retroactive labelling. Commissioner Emma Bonino is to set up a new scientific committee to deal with genetically engineered foods, members of which are to be completely independent of the food industry. Meanwhile, Franz Fischler, the European Commissioner on Agriculture, supports a complete segregation and labelling of production lines of genetically modified and non-genetically modified foods.

In June this year, President Clinton imposed a five-year ban on human cloning in the USA, while the UK House of Commons Science and Technology Committee (STC) wants British law to be amended to ensure that human cloning is illegal. The STC, President Chirac of France and German Research Minister Juergen Ruettgers are also calling for an international ban on human cloning.

Like other excellent critics before me,[3] I do not think there is a grand conspiracy afoot, though there are many forces converging to a single terrible end. Susan George comments, "They don't have to conspire if they have the same world-view, aspire to similar goals and take concerted steps to attain them."[4]

I am one of those scientists who have long been highly critical of the reductionist mainstream scientific world-view, and have begun to work towards a radically different approach for understanding nature.[5] But I was unable, for a long time, to see how much science really matters n the affairs of the real world, not just in terms of practical inventions like genetic engineering, but in how that scientific world-view takes hold of people's unconscious, so that they take action, involuntarily, unquestioningly, to shape the world to the detriment of human beings. I was so little aware of how that science is used, without conscious intent, to intimidate and control, to obfuscate, to exploit and oppress; how

that dominant world-view generates a selective blindness to make scientists themselves ignore or misread scientific evidence.

The point, however, is not that *science* is bad—but that there can be *bad science* that ill-serves humanity. Science can often be wrong. The history of science can just as well be written in terms of the mistakes made than as the series of triumphs it is usually made out to be. Science is nothing more, and nothing less, than a system of concepts for understanding nature and for obtaining reliable knowledge that enables us to live sustainably with nature. In that sense, one can ill-afford to give up science, for it is through our proper understanding and knowledge of nature that we can live a satisfying life, that we can ultimately distinguish the good science, which serves humanity, from the bad science that does not. In this view, science is imbued with moral values from the start, and cannot be disentangled from them. Therefore it is bad science that purports to be "neutral" and divorced from moral values, as much as it is bad science that ignores scientific evidence.

It is clear that I part company with perhaps a majority of my scientist colleagues in the mainstream, who believe that science can never be wrong, although it can be misused. Or else they carefully distinguish science, as neutral and value-free, from its application, technology, which can do harm or good.[6] This distinction between science and technology is spurious, especially in the case of an experimental science like genetics, and almost all of biology, where the techniques determine what sorts of question are asked and hence the range of answers that are important, significant and relevant to the science. Where would molecular genetics be without the tools that enable practitioners to recombine and manipulate our destiny? It is an irresistibly heroic view, except that it is totally wrong and misguided.

It is also meaningless, therefore, to set up Ethical Committees which do not question the basic scientific assumptions behind the practice of genetic engineering biotechnology. Their brief is severely limited, often verging on the trivial and banal—such as whether a pork gene transferred to food plants might be counter to certain religious beliefs—in comparison with the much more fundamental questions of eugenics, genetic discrimination and, indeed, whether gene transfers should be carried out at all. They can do nothing more than make the unacceptable acceptable to the public.

The debate on genetic engineering biotechnology is dogged by the artificial separation imposed between "pure" science and the issues it gives rise to. "Ethics" is deemed to be socially determined, and therefore negotiable, while the science is seen to be beyond reproach, as it is the "laws" of nature. The same goes for the distinction between "technology"—the application of science—from the science. Risk assessments are to do with the technology, leaving the science equally untouched. The technology can be bad for your health, but not the science. In this article, I shall show why science cannot be separated from moral values nor from the technology that shapes our society. In other words, bad science is unquestionably bad for one's health and well-being, and should be avoided at all costs. Science is, above all, fallible and negotiable, because we have the choice, to do or not to do. It should be negotiated for the public good. That is the only ethical position one can take with regard to science. Otherwise, we are in danger of turning science into the most fundamentalist of religions that, working hand in hand with corporate interests, will surely usher in the brave new world.

BAD SCIENCE AND BIG BUSINESS

What makes genetic engineering biotechnology dangerous, in the first instance, is that it is an unprecedented, close alliance between two great powers that can make or break the world: science and commerce. Practically all established molecular geneticists have some direct or indirect connection with industry, which will set limits on what the scientists can and will do research on, not to mention the possibility of compromising their integrity as independent scientists.[7]

The worst aspect of the alliance is that it is between the most reductionist science and multinational monopolistic industry at its most aggressive and exploitative. If the truth be told, it is bad science working together with big business for quick profit, aided and abetted by our governments for the banal reason that governments wish to be re-elected to remain in 'power.'[8]

Speaking as a scientist who loves and believes in science, I have to say it is bad science that has let the world down and caused the major problems we now face, not the least among which is by promoting and legitimizing a particular world-view. It is a reductionist, manipulative and exploitative world-view. Reductionist because it sees the world as bits and pieces, and denies there are organic wholes such as organisms, ecosystems, societies and community of nations. Manipulative and exploitative because it regards nature and fellow human beings as objects to be manipulated and exploited for gain, life being a Darwinian struggle for survival of the fittest.

It is by no means coincidental that the economic theory currently dominating the world is rooted in the same *laissez-faire* capitalist ideology that gave rise to Darwinism. It acknowledges no values other than self-interest, competitiveness and the accumulation of wealth, at which the developed nations have been very successful. Already, according to the 1992 United Nations Development Programme Report, the richest fifth of the world's population has amassed 82.7 per cent of the wealth, while the poorest fifth gets a piddling 1.4 per cent. Or, put in another way, there are now 477 billionaires in the world whose combined assets are roughly equal to the combined annual incomes of the poorer half of humanity—2.8 billion people.[9] Do we need to be more "competitive" still to take from the poorest their remaining pittance? That is, in fact, what we are doing.

The governmental representatives of the superpowers are pushing for a "globalized economy" under trade agreements which erase all economic borders. "Together, the processes of deregulation and globalization are undermining the power of both unions and governments and placing the power of global corporations and finance beyond the reach of public accountability."[10] The largest corporations continue to consolidate that power through mergers, acquisitions and strategic alliances. Multinational corporations now comprise 51 of the world's 100 largest economies: only 49 of the latter are nations. By 1993, agricultural biotechnology was being controlled by just 11 giant corporations, and these are now undergoing further mergers. The OECD (Organization for Economic Co-operation and Development) member countries are at this moment working in secret in Paris on the Multilateral Agreements on Investment (MAI), which is written by and for corporations to prohibit any government from establishing performance or accountability standards for foreign investors. European Commissioner, Sir Leon Brittan, is negotiating in the World Trade Organization, on behalf of the European Community, to ensure that no barriers of any kind should remain in the South to dampen exploitation by the North and, at the same time, to protect the deeply unethical "patents of life" through Trade Related Intellectual Property Rights (TRIPS) agreements.[11] So, in addition to gaining complete control of the food supply of the South through exclusive rights to genetically engineered seeds, the big food giants of the North can asset-strip the South's genetic and intellectual resources with impunity, up to and including genes and cell lines of indigenous peoples.

There is no question that the mindset that leads to and validates genetic engineering is *genetic determinism*—the idea that organisms are determined by their genetic makeup, or the totality of their genes. Genetic determinism derives from the marriage of Darwinism and Mendelian genetics. For those imbued with the mindset of genetic determinism, the major problems of the world can be solved simply by identifying and manipulating genes, for genes determine the characters of organisms; so by identifying a gene we can predict a desirable or undesirable trait, by changing a gene we change the trait, by transferring a gene we transfer the corresponding trait.

The Human Genome Project was inspired by the same genetic determinism that locates the "blueprint" for constructing the human being in the human genome. It may have been a brilliant political move to capture research funds and, at the same time, to revive a flagging pharmaceutical industry, but its scientific content was suspect from the first.

Genetic engineering technology promises to work for the benefit of mankind; the reality is something else.

- It displaces and marginalizes all alternative approaches that address the social and environmental causes of malnutrition and ill-health, such as poverty and unemployment, and the need for a sustainable agriculture that could regenerate the environment, guarantee long-term food security and, at the same time, conserve indigenous biodiversity.

- Its purpose is to accommodate problems that reductionist science and industry have created in the first place—widespread environmental deterioration from the intensive, high-input agriculture of the Green Revolution, and accumulation of toxic wastes from chemical industries. What's on offer now is more of the same, except with new problems attached.

- It leads to discriminatory and other unethical practices that are against the moral values of societies and community of nations.

- Worst of all, it is pushing a technology that is untried, and, according to existing knowledge, is inherently hazardous to health and biodiversity.

Let me enlarge on that last point here, as I believe it has been underestimated, if not entirely overlooked by the practitioners, regulators and many critics of genetic engineering biotechnology alike, on account of a certain blindness to concrete scientific evidence, largely as a result of their conscious or unconscious commitment to an old, discredited paradigm. The most immediate hazards are likely to be in public health—which has already reached a global crisis, attesting to the failure of decades of reductionist medical practices —although the hazards to biodiversity will not be far behind.

GENETIC ENGINEERING BIOTECHNOLOGY IS INHERENTLY HAZARDOUS

According to the 1996 World Health Organization Report, at least 30 new diseases, including AIDS, Ebola and Hepatitis C, have emerged over the past 20 years, while old infectious diseases such as tuberculosis, cholera, malaria and diphtheria are coming back worldwide. Almost every month now in the UK we hear reports on fresh outbreaks: *Streptococcus,* meningitis, *E. coli.* Practically all the pathogens are resistant to antibiotics, many to multiple antibiotics. Two strains of *E. coli* isolated in a transplant ward outside Cambridge in 1993 were found to be resistant to 21 out of 22 common antibiotics.[12] A strain of *Staphylococcus* isolated in Australia in 1990 was found to be resistant to 31 different drugs.[13] Infections with these and other strains will very soon become totally invulnerable to treatment. In fact, scientists in Japan have already isolated a strain of *Staphylococcus aureus* that is resistant even to the last resort antibiotic, vancomycin.[14]

Geneticists have now linked the emergence of pathogenic bacteria and of antibiotic resistance to *horizontal gene transfer*—the transfer of genes to unrelated species, by infection through viruses, though pieces of genetic material, DNA, taken up into cells from the environment, or by unusual mating taking place between unrelated species. For example, horizontal gene transfer and subsequent genetic recombination have generated the bacterial strains responsible for the cholera outbreak in India in 1992,[15] and the Streptococcus epidemic in Tayside in 1993.[16] The *E. coli* 157 strain involved in the recent outbreaks in Scotland is believed to have originated from horizontal gene transfer from the pathogen, *Shigella.*[17] Many unrelated bacterial pathogens, causing diseases from bubonic plague to tree blight,

are found to share an entire set of genes for invading cells, which have almost certainly spread by horizontal gene transfer.[18] Similarly, genes for antibiotic resistance have spread horizontally and recombined with one another to generate multiple antibiotic resistance throughout the bacterial populations.[19] Antibiotic resistance genes spread readily by contact between human beings, and from bacteria inhabiting the gut of farm animals to those in human beings.[20] Multiple antibiotic-resistant strains of pathogens have been endemic in many hospitals for years.[21]

What is the connection between horizontal gene transfer and genetic engineering? Genetic engineering is a technology designed specifically to transfer genes horizontally between species that do not interbreed. It is designed to break down species barriers and, increasingly, to overcome the species' defence mechanisms which normally degrade or inactivate foreign genes.[22]

For the purpose of manipulating, replicating and transferring genes, genetic engineers make use of recombined versions of precisely those genetic parasites causing diseases including cancers, and others that carry and spread virulence genes and antibiotic resistance genes. Thus the technology will contribute to an increase in the frequency of horizontal gene transfer of those genes that are responsible for virulence and antibiotic resistance, and allow them to recombine to generate new pathogens.

What is even more disturbing is that geneticists have now found evidence that the presence of antibiotics typically increases the frequency of horizontal gene transfer 100-fold or more, possibly because the antibiotic acts like a sex hormone for the bacteria, enhancing mating and exchange of genes between unrelated species.[23] Thus, antibiotic resistance and multiple antibiotic resistance cannot be overcome simply by making new antibiotics, *for antibiotics create the very conditions to facilitate the spread of resistance.* The continuing profligate use of antibiotics in intensive farming and in medicine, in combination with the commercial-scale practice of genetic engineering, may already be major contributing factors for the accelerated spread of multiple antibiotic resistance among new and old pathogens that the WHO

1996 Report has identified within the past 10 years. For example, there has been a dramatic rise both in terms of incidence and severity of cases of infections by *Salmonella*,[24] with some countries in Europe witnessing a staggering 20-fold increase in incidence since 1980.

That is not all. One by one, those assumptions on which geneticists and regulatory committees have based their assessment of genetically engineered products to be "safe" have fallen by the wayside, especially in the light of evidence emerging within the past three to four years. However, there is still little indication that the new findings are being taken on board. On the contrary, regulatory bodies have succumbed to pressure from the industry to relax already inadequate regulations. Let me list a few more of the relevant findings in genetics.

We have been told that horizontal gene transfer is confined to bacteria. That is not so. It is now known to involve practically all species of animal, plant and fungus. It is possible for any gene in any species to spread to any other species, especially if the gene is carried on genetically engineered gene-transfer vectors. Transgenes and antibiotic resistance marker genes from transgenic plants have been shown to end up in soil fungi and bacteria.[25] The microbial populations in the environment serve as the gene-transfer highway and reservoir, supporting the replication of the genes and allowing them to spread and recombine with other genes to generate new pathogens.[26]

We have been assured that "crippled" laboratory strains of bacteria and viruses do not survive when released into the environment. That is not true. There is now abundant evidence that they can either survive quite well and multiply, or they can go dormant and reappear after having acquired genes from other bacteria to enable them to multiply.[27] Bacteria co-operate much more than they compete. They share their most valuable assets for survival.

We have been told that DNA is easily broken down in the environment. Not so. DNA can remain in the environment where they can be picked up by bacteria and incorporated into their genome.[28]

DNA is, in fact, one of the toughest molecules. Biochemists jumped with joy when they didn't have to work with proteins anymore, which lose their activity very readily. By contrast, DNA survives rigorous boiling, so when they approve processed food on grounds that there can be no DNA left, ask exactly how the processing is done, and whether the appropriate tests for the presence of DNA have been carried out.

The survival of "crippled" laboratory strains of bacteria and viruses and the persistence of DNA in the environment are of particular relevance to the so-called contained users producing transgenic pharmaceuticals, enzymes and food additives. "Tolerated" releases and transgenic wastes from such users may already have released large amounts of transgenic bacteria and viruses as well as DNA into the environment since the early 1980s when commercial genetic engineering biotechnology began.

We are told that DNA is easily digested by enzymes in our gut. Not true. The DNA of a virus has been found to survive passage through the gut of mice. Furthermore, the DNA readily finds its way into the bloodstream, and into all kinds of cell[s] in the body.[29] Once inside the cell, the DNA can insert itself into the cell's genome, and create all manner of genetic disturbances, including cancer.[30]

There are yet further findings pointing to the potential hazards of generating new disease-causing viruses by recombination between artificial viral vectors and vaccines and other viruses in the environment. The viruses generated in this way will have increased host ranges, infecting and causing diseases in more than one species, and hence very difficult to eradicate. *We are already seeing such viruses emerging.*

- Monkeypox, a previously rare and potentially fatal virus caught from rodents, is spreading through central Zaire.[31] Between 1981 and 1986 only 37 cases were known, but there have been at least 163 cases in one eastern province of Zaire alone since July 1995. For the first time, humans are transmitting the disease directly from one to the other.

- An outbreak of hantavirus infection hit southern Argentina in December 1996, the first time the virus was transmitted from person to person.[32] Previously, the virus was spread by breathing in the aerosols from rodent excrement or urine.

- New highly virulent strains of infectious bursal disease virus (IBDV) spread rapidly throughout most of the poultry industry in the Northern Hemisphere, and are now infecting Antarctic penguins, and are suspected of causing mass mortality.[33]

- New strains of distemper and rabies viruses are spilling out from towns and villages to plague some of the world's rarest wild animals in Africa[34]: lions, panthers, wild dogs, giant otter.

None of the plethora of new findings has been taken on board by the regulatory bodies. On the contrary, safety regulations have been relaxed. The public is being used, against its will, as guinea pigs for genetically engineered products, while new viruses and bacterial pathogens may be created by the technology every passing day.

The present situation is reminiscent of the development of nuclear energy which gave us the atom bomb, and the nuclear power stations that we now know to be hazardous to health and also to be environmentally unsustainable on account of the long-lasting radioactive wastes they produce. Joseph Rotblat, the British physicist who won the 1995 Nobel Prize after years of battling against nuclear weapons, has this to say. "My worry is that other advances in science may result in other means of mass destruction, maybe more readily available even than nuclear weapons. Genetic engineering is quite a possible area, because of these dreadful developments that are taking place there."[35]

The large-scale release of transgenic organisms is much worse than nuclear weapons or radioactive nuclear wastes, as genes can replicate indefinitely, spread and recombine. There may yet be time enough to stop the industry's dreams turning into nightmares if we act now, before the critical genetic "melt-down" is reached.

NOTES

1. The first time I heard the word "transgenic" being used on cultivars resulting from conventional breeding methods was from Henry Miller, a prominent advocate for genetic engineering biotechnology, in a public debate with myself, organized by the Oxford Centre for Environment, Ethics and Society, in Oxford University on February 20, 1997.

2. "Scientists scorn sci-fi fears over sheep clone," *The Guardian*, February 24, 1997, p. 7. Lewis Wolpert, development biologist at University College London was reported as saying, "It's a pretty risky technique with lots of abnormalities." Also report and interview in the Eight O'Clock News, BBC Radio 4, February 24, 1997.

3. As for instance, Spallone, 1992.

4. George, 1988, p. 5.

5. My colleague Peter Saunders and I began working on an alternative approach to neo-Darwinian evolutionary theory in the 1970s. Major collections of multi-author essays appeared in Ho and Saunders, 1984: Pollard, 1981: Ho and Fox, 1988.

6. Lewis Wolpert, who currently heads the Committee for the Public Understanding of Science, argues strenuously for this 'fundamentalist' view of science. See Wolpert, 1996.

7. See Hubbard and Wald, 1993.

8. This was pointed out to me by Martin Khor, during a Course on Globalization and Economics that he gave at Schumacher College, February 3–10, 1997.

9. See Korten, 1997.

10. Korten, 1997, p. 2.

11. See Perlas, 1994; also WTO: New setback for the South, *Third World Resurgence* issue 77/78, 1997, which contains many articles reporting on the WTO meeting held in December 1996 in Singapore.

12. Brown *et al.,* 1993.

13. Udo and Grubb, 1990.

14. "Superbug spectre haunts Japan," Michael Day, *New Scientist* 3 May, 1997, p. 5.

15. See Bik *et al.,* 1995; Prager *et al.,* 1995; Reidl and Makalanos, 1995.

16. Whatmore *et al.,* 1994; Kapur *et al.,* 1995; Schnitzler *et al.,* 1995; Upton *et al.,* 1996.

17. Professor Hugh Pennington, on BBC Radio 4 News, February 1997.

18. Barinaga, 1996.

19. Reviewed by Davies, 1994.

20. Tschape, 1994.

21. See World Health Report, 1996; also Garret, 1995, chapter 13, for an excellent account of the history of antibiotic resistance in pathogens.

22. See Ho and Tappeser, 1997.

23. See Davies, 1994.

24. WHO Fact Sheet No. 139, January 1997.

25. Hoffman *et al.,* 1994; Schluter *et al.,* 1995.

26. See Ho, 1996a.

27. Jager and Tappeser, 1996, have extensively reviewed the literature on the survival of bacteria and DNA released into different environments.

28. See Lorenz and Wackernagel, 1994.

29. See Schubert *et al.,* 1994; also *New Scientist* January 24, p. 24, featured a short report on recent findings of the group that were presented at the International Congress on Cell Biology in San Francisco, December 1996.

30. Wahl *et al.,* 1984; see also relevant entries in Kendrew, 1995, especially "slow transforming retroviruses" and "Transgenic technologies."

31. "Killer virus piles on the misery in Zaire" Debora MacKenzie, *New Scientist* April 19, 1997, p. 12.

32. "Virus gets personal," *New Scientist* April 26, 1997, p. 13.

33. "Poultry virus infection in Antarctic penguins," Heather Gardner, Knowles Kerry and Martin Riddle, *Nature* 387, May 15, 1997, p. 245.

34. See Pain, 1997.

35. Quoted in "The spectre of a human clone" *The Independent,* February 26, 1997, p. 1.

STUDY QUESTIONS

1. What is a 'vector,' and how are vectors used in modifying organisms?

2. What is horizontal gene transfer, and what are the concerns about it?

3. It is often claimed that genetic modification of food is not substantively different from conventional food breeding. Discuss three of Ho's reasons for disputing this claim.

4. We are typically taught that the aim of science is 'knowledge.' Although Ho does not disagree that this is *an* aim of science, she believes that science now more often aims to serve the ends of business. Discuss some of her examples.

20

The ETC Report: The Poor Can Feed Themselves

By 2050, or much sooner, we will be growing food under climatic conditions we've never seen before and learning that "normal" weather is an illusive fiction. Yet, we are told that global land grabs and plantations of agrofuels are a "win-win." The truth is that policymakers don't know enough about our food supply. We don't know where our food comes from and we don't know who is feeding the hungry today. We have absolutely no idea who will feed us in 2050. This report raises more questions than answers. It begins with a comparison of the likelihood of the industrial food chain and the peasant food web getting us through climate chaos.

THE INDUSTRIAL FOOD CHAIN

Ninety-six percent of all recorded food and agricultural research takes place in industrialized countries, and 80% of that research is on food processing and retailing. Over the last half-century, the industrial food chain has consolidated so that each link in the chain—from seed to soup—is dominated by a handful of multinationals working with an ever-narrower commodity list that has left half of humanity either dangerously malnourished or overweight.

The industrial food chain focuses on far fewer than 100 breeds of five livestock species. Corporate plant breeders work with 150 crops but focus on barely a dozen. Of the 80,000 commercial plant varieties in the market today, well over half are ornamentals. What remains of our declining fish stocks comes from 336 species accounting for almost two-thirds of the aquatic species we consume. Along with the loss of diversity has come a loss of quality. The nutritional content of

many of our grains and vegetables has dropped between 5 and 40% so that we have to eat more calories to get the same nutrition.

In the face of climate chaos, the industrial chain is imposing a patent regime that prizes uniformity over diversity and enforces a technological model that costs more and takes more time to breed one genetically engineered variety than it does to breed hundreds of conventional varieties. The industrial food chain doesn't know who the hungry are, where they are, or what they need.

THE PEASANT FOOD WEB

Eighty-five percent of the world's food is grown and consumed if not within the "100 mile diet" within national borders and/or the same ecoregional zone. Most of this food is grown from peasant-bred seed without the industrial chain's synthetic fertilizers. Peasants breed and nurture 40

Reprinted with permission of ETC Group-Action Group on Erosion, Technology and Concentration, 431 Gilmour St, Second Floor Ottawa, ON Canada. As found at www.etcgroup.org.

livestock species and almost 8000 breeds. Peasants also breed 5000 domesticated crops and have donated more than 1.9 million plant varieties to the world's gene banks. Peasant fishers harvest and protect more than 15,000 freshwater species. The work of peasants and pastoralists maintaining soil fertility is 18 times more valuable than the synthetic fertilizers provided by the seven largest corporations.

Peasants have not consolidated but they have organized. There are 1.5 billion on 380 million farms; 800 million more growing urban gardens; 410 million gathering the hidden harvest of our forests and savannas; 190 million pastoralists and well over 100 million peasant fishers. At least 370 million of these are also indigenous peoples. Together these peasants make up almost half the world's peoples and they grow at least 70% of the world's food. Better than anyone else, they feed the hungry. If we are to eat in 2050 we will need all of them and all of their diversity.

Food Chain or Food Web?   The industrial agricultural model talks about a food "chain" with Monsanto at one end and Wal-Mart at the other—a linked chain of agricultural input companies (seed, fertilizer, pesticides, machinery) at the start that is attached to traders, processors and retailers. In fact, most of the world's food doesn't follow a chain; food moves within a web: peasants are also consumers who exchange with one another; urban consumers are also peasant producers growing and exchanging food; farmers are often fishers and foragers and their lands exist within an ecosystem with multiple functions. Eighty-five percent of the food that is grown is consumed within the same eco-region or (at least) within national borders and most of it is grown beyond the reach of the multi-national chain.

> The dominant food system—for most of history and much of humanity still today— is a web, not a chain—of relationships.

The World Bank and many bilateral development agencies have bought into the urban legend that agricultural development can pick and choose the links in the food chain they like. This is naïve. The reason Monsanto, DuPont and Syngenta (which control half the proprietary commercial seed supply and about the same share of global pesticides) are focused on breeding crops like maize, soybeans, wheat and (now) rice is because the big processors like Nestlé, Unilever, Kraft and ConAgra can manipulate these cheap carbohydrate fillers (the four crops account for two-thirds of U.S. consumer calories) into thousands of food (and non-food) products that can "bulk up" more expensive goods. The processors, in turn, are scrambling to meet the exigencies of consumer-attuned retailers like Wal-Mart, Tesco, Carrefour, and Metro that demand cheap, uniform and predictable products on their shelves and show no hesitation to reach back down the food chain to dictate how farmers (and which farmers) will produce food.

> *"Small scale food producers are those men and women who produce and harvest field and tree crops as well as livestock, fish and other aquatic organisms. They include smallholder peasant/ family crop and livestock farmers, herders/ pastoralists, artisanal fisherfolk, landless farmers/workers, gardeners, forest dwellers, indigenous peoples, hunters and gatherers, and any other small scale users of natural resources for food production."*—Michel Pimbert

Through a shared corporate culture and shared markets, different parts of the food chain have developed strong informal bonds: there are close links between Syngenta and Archer Daniels Midland, for example, and between Monsanto and Cargill and between DuPont and Bunge. *The industrial model comes with chains attached. Buying into any part of it means buying into all of it.*

But, Who Will Feed Us?   Answering this question first requires an understanding of who "we" are now and how we might change en route to 2050. Then we need to understand the conditions under which food will be provided in the decades ahead. Once we have this sorted out, we can evaluate the likelihood of different production models meeting our future needs. We must not assume that any of the existing models will be adequate. One of the most important findings in this report is that neither the chain nor the web is prepared to confront climate change.

Who Are the Hungry and How Are They Changing? At the height of the media surge around the 2008 food crisis, for the first time in history, half of the world's population became "urban." The predictions being written into policy are that, in 2050, two-thirds of the planet's projected 9.2 billion people will be living in cities and that all of this increase (2.6 billion) will be not only in the global South but also in the South's urban areas. Between now and 2050 at least 1.3 billion people will (policymakers are told) migrate —be migrated—from country to city in the largest land grab (or enclosure) ever. Left behind will only be those too old to move and the indigenous peoples determined to stay. The best that can be done for the world's 1.5 billion peasant farmers (again, policymakers are being told) is to buy them one-way bus tickets to the city so that the land can be cleared for a "carbohydrate economy" that churns out "biomass" food, fodder or fuel and, especially, carbon credits where and as needed.

The food crisis has increased the ranks of the "hungry" (i.e., those taking in insufficient calories for daily living) from 840 million around 2003 to just over 1 billion today—a jump of 160 million in less than six years. Another billion people may have enough calories but are malnourished in chronic ill-health due to micronutrient shortfalls. Of the world's 6.6 billion in 2009 then, close to one-third are suffering from hunger and malnutrition. But there are another 1.3 billion people overweight or obese who are also "malnourished." Although this last 1.3 billion elicits less sympathy, many of them are the victims of predatory commercial practices that condemn them to cheap, calorie-rich, nutrition-poor processed foods. *By any measure,* *almost half the world's population is badly served by today's food production systems.*

There are at least 370 million indigenous peasants on at least 92 million farms.

Where Are the Hungry, and Who Is Feeding the Hungry and Malnourished Now?

Despite a plethora of official statistics, there is considerable ambiguity about where the hungry can be found and who is feeding them. Nine hundred and fifty million (95%) of the "hungry," it is assumed, live in the global South. Three-quarters (712 million) are said to be "rural," meaning that 238 million live in towns and cities. This rural/urban imbalance among the hungry (three quarters rural, one quarter urban) needs further study. There is no doubt, however, that government policies are forcing a rapid exodus from the countryside into the cities. The very scale and speed of the transition works against food security and leads to a substantial under-estimation of the urban food problem. The 712 million rural hungry are significantly less cash-dependent than their urban counterparts and have greater access to land and livestock and to the fish and forest products that can be crucial to adequate calories and reasonable nutrition. Meanwhile, the 238 million urban hungry are spending between 60 and 80% of their income on food—about one-third more than people in rural areas—and getting fewer calories to boot. But a surprising proportion of the urban hungry also manage rooftop/back gardens and livestock pens, where they grow a critical share of their own food and sell to local markets. The UNDP conservatively estimates that some 800 million people are actively engaged in urban food production. Nevertheless, when food prices start to climb, urban peasants often begin trekking back to the countryside.

Peasants?

"The language around us is changing all the time. Historically, we were peasants. Then when that term came to mean 'backward' we became 'farmers.' In these days 'farmer' has the connotation of inefficiency and we are strongly encouraged to be more modern, to see ourselves as managers, business people or entrepreneurs capable of handling increasingly larger pieces of territory. Well, I am a farmer and I am a peasant. I learned that I had much more in common with peasants than I did with some of my agribusiness neighbours. I am reclaiming the term peasant because I believe that small is more efficient, it is socially intelligent, it is community oriented. Being a peasant stands for the kind of agriculture and rural communities we are striving to build."

—Karen Pedersen, past-president, National Farmers Union (Canada)

"This debate in the literature...is a fabrication at a higher level, by those who know more. In the countryside, out there, there is no such debate. We continue being peasants. That's the way it is."

—Emiliano Cerros Nava, an executive commission member of UNORCA in Mexico

---

Peasants currently manage over half of the world's arable land. (See Annex.) From regional data, it is fair to estimate: 17 million peasant farms in Latin America grow between a half to two-thirds of staple foods; Africa's 33 million peasant farms (mostly female-led) account for 80% of farms and most of the domestic food consumption; Asia's 200 million peasant rice farms produce most of its harvest. Although their well-being fluctuates sometimes tragically, and they survive under harsh conditions with little external support, the 1,520 million peasant farm family members mostly feed themselves. The 712 million rural hungry (who can't afford to buy much of their food in the industrial food chain's markets) likely depend on peasants for whatever food they have. There are another 1.1 billion in the rural South who may not be hungry but also have limited access to the industrial chain and who are also likely to rely heavily on peasant surpluses as well as their own hunting, gathering and gardening.

Peasants are also the ones who feed the hungry. Rural peasant production is closest to the 712 million rural people who make up three-quarters of the world's hungry. These people are not only rural but also remote and impoverished or, in other words, of little interest to the industrial chain that prefers middle-class urban markets. Meanwhile, urban peasants grow at least a quarter of the food in the South's cities—the food that is most accessible to the 238 million hungry people who can't afford high food prices. By these estimates, at least 70% of the world's population is fed by peasants.

Policymakers must re-examine the common fallacy that, even when properly supported, the world's peasant food network lacks the bounty, efficiency and resilience to confront the food and climate crises. At the same time, policymakers must deconstruct the mythology surrounding the effectiveness of the industrial food system. The reality is that the world's 3 billion or so indigenous and peasant producers rural and urban, fishers and pastoralists not only feed a majority of the world's people and most of the world's malnourished, they create and conserve most of the world's biodiversity and are humanity's best defense against climate change.

As we prepare for 2050, then, logic suggests the need for policies that will make it possible for rural people to remain rural and for urbanites to grow as much of their own food as possible.

The bottom line for both Rome and Copenhagen is that in the middle of a crisis—do no harm! Do nothing to disrupt the existing sources of food security. This means safeguarding peasant farms, respecting their resource rights, guaranteeing access to uncultivated lands, and protecting/ promoting urban gardens.

What do we need to do to ensure food security?

If we can't be sure what will grow well where, and if we are sure that extreme weather events will disrupt the food supply much more than in the past, then the central policy questions for shaping a sound food system become clear:

1. How can we ensure that food production for human consumption is given priority over other consumption demands?
2. How can we increase the species diversity of plants, livestock and aquatic species in order to adjust to changing climatic conditions?
3. How can we protect and improve the genetic diversity within plants, aquatic species and livestock to withstand extreme weather events, new pests and diseases, and changing climates?

4. How can we encourage breeders to reset goals to develop diverse and reliable plants and animals?
5. How can we protect and improve biological controls and soil nutrients to safeguard food and reduce reliance on synthetic chemicals?
6. How can we strengthen local community food production to reduce energy dependence and increase food quality?
7. How can we minimize loss and waste throughout the food system?
8. How do we ensure that food is nutritious, adequate, appropriate, and accessible to all?
9. How do we guarantee that peasant producers have stable and equitable production and marketing arrangements?

QUESTION 1

How Can We Ensure That Food Production for Human Consumption Is Given Priority Over Other Consumption Demands?

Because climate change means that we can't be sure what will grow where or with what consistency, common sense dictates that if we don't know otherwise we have to assume that land and natural resources already support endangered livelihoods and that changes in use should not be permitted in the absence of study and consultation (i.e., if we don't know—don't change it). We must operate on the assumption that marginalized rural populations have a high dependence on non-cultivated biomass (roadsides, forests, savannas, marine and freshwater species, etc.) and that marginalized urban and peri-urban populations have a high food production dependence on all accessible urban soils and water. And, despite our focus on food, we must recognize that both rural and urban peasants also produce other survival essentials such as community fuels, fibres, shelters and medicines.

Climate-Ready Failures. In October 2008, GRAIN first exposed the new "land grab" in the global South, a rush to control overseas farmland, led by corporate investors and governments. Nowhere is this development more foolhardy than in sub-Saharan Africa. A recent report coordinated by Bioversity International warns that climate-induced crop losses in this region could be as high as 50% just 10 years from now. By 2050, the report says, the majority of African countries will be experiencing "novel" growing conditions on most of their crop land. "Novel" doesn't mean good. Overwhelmingly, Africa will be hotter, drier and more exposed to extreme weather events than any time in the past century. The hotter Sahelian countries, the study says, will have climates with few analogs for any crop (meaning that they have no place to look today for the breeding material they will need tomorrow). Nevertheless, some of these countries like Sudan, Cameroon, and Nigeria—major land grab targets—actually have crop areas that are analogs to many future climates. Not only are they unlikely to be able to help themselves but, also, their potentially valuable germplasm is poorly represented in major gene banks. If large areas are sown to uniform export crops, this unique genetic diversity may become extinct before it can be collected. Such land grabs not only threaten national food security but they endanger the future food security of many other (including OECD) countries.

Lamb Grab. Another growing (but reversible) threat to our land-use is from grain-fed livestock production. Forty percent of our global grain supply feeds animals. Forty-seven million hectares are sown annually to fodder grasses and legumes. The protein and calorie loss in feeding crops to cattle, rather than food to people, is massive. UNEP (United Nations Environment Programme) calculates that the loss of calories by feeding cereals to animals instead of using the cereals as human food represents the annual calorie need for more than 3.5 billion people. Despite this, policy-makers are told they must anticipate a 3% per annum rise in meat and dairy consumption. Such a dietary shift is unhealthy and unsustainable as well as unacceptable given the climate changes ahead. The logical policy response is to invest in educational and regulatory initiatives that encourage consumption of more grains, vegetables and fruits.

This is not to suggest that peasant livestock production doesn't have a role. The UN Framework Convention on Climate Change (UNFCCC) sees livestock as a prominent source of greenhouse gas (GHG) emissions while the negotiators addressing the food crisis often look upon peasant livestock keepers and pastoralists as either a disease threat or a barrier to agrofuel production. In reality, peasant livestock systems (mobile or sedentary) can be extremely efficient at enriching biodiversity and in sequestering greenhouse gases. While industrial livestock operations are the leading emitter of nitrous oxide, most extensive livestock systems (i.e., smallholder) are climate friendly. Peasant herds logically occupy the slopes and soils not suitable for crops. These grazing lands cover over 45% of the earth's surface—1.5 times more than forest. While forests may add only about 10% to their biomass each year, savannas can reproduce 150% and tropical savannas have a greater potential to store carbon below ground than any other terrestrial ecosystem.

Manure, generated by peasant livestock holds, when deposited on fields and pastures, doesn't produce significant amounts of methane. By contrast, factory farms produce manure in liquid form releasing 18 million tones of methane annually. The peasant web is agro-ecologically sound—the industrial chain is not. The obvious solution to curtail nitrous oxide and methane emissions generated by industrial livestock is to shut down factory farm production.

Agrofuels. Policymakers are frequently told that there is plenty of unused, marginal land to grow biomass crops (for agrofuels, bio-electricity and bio-chemicals) in the global South. This self-serving argument is nonsense—especially when no one knows how our crops and livestock will withstand climate change. Many of the plants now being established for bio-energy production on plantations in Africa, Asia, and Latin America have been sparsely studied and their performance and environmental impact is unknown. *Jatropha curcas*, a small tree native to Latin America, is being planted over large areas of Ethiopia, Mozambique and Tanzania, and each country expects to produce 60,000 tons of agrofuel by 2017. Some of the most commonly introduced fuel/biomass crops, *Jatropha curcas* among them, are believed to have a very narrow genetic base as well as production problems. No matter what plant species is employed, agrofuels/biomass plants compete with food crops for land, water and nutrients. Governments and corporations do not have the right to take this risk. By encouraging biofuel production, governments are failing to meet their obligations on the progressive realization of the right to adequate food.

The absurdity of growing biomass for export (not for local community use) in Africa is overwhelming. Maize is one of Africa's most important and preferred food crops. It is also a major first-generation agrofuel. In parts of East Africa, however, peasants are abandoning maize for crops that are more suited to drier conditions such as sorghum and millet even though stover production—used for either feed or fuel—is substantially lower. Yet European governments in pursuit of climate carbon credits are pressing for greater agrofuel/biomass production in Africa.

Hidden Harvest. So-called underutilized lands are the "commons" from which rural and peri-urban peasants collect and manage medicinal plants, fuel, as well as fish, game, uncultivated vegetables, nuts, fruit, and fungi. The "hidden harvest" not only provides irreplaceable nutrients in their diet, it is also essential for food security. Collection of "wild" and uncultivated materials takes place throughout the year but can become critical for survival in the weeks or months leading up to harvest when family food stocks are lowest. In some areas of Africa, wild resources cover up to 80% of household food needs during staple crop shortages. Even when the annual proportion of the hidden harvest seems low, its availability can mean the difference between life and death. Turning the commons into a global link in the industrial food or fuel chain could massively increase food insecurity.

For example, peasant communities in Borneo routinely gather nourishment from 800 different plants and more than 100 species of ground fauna along with hundreds of bird species. Only a third of their diet comes from cultivated crops. During the rainy season in one region of Kenya, women draw 35% of their plant material (for food, fibre and medicines) from so-called "marginal" lands. Other peasants in Kenya draw a quarter of their annual food supply from the "wild" but their dependence rises to almost half during the dry months. Peasant women in Uttar Pradesh, India, derive almost half their income from forest species. Even middle-class women in the same region obtain a third of their income from the same source. In one semi-arid region in India where common lands have declined between a third and a half since the 1960s, peasants still derive 14–23% of their nourishment from "wild" plants and animals. In drought years, this vital harvest can rise to half of their food intake. The Mende of Sierra Leone take more than half their food from forests, streams and fallow fields. In sum, it is safe to estimate that no less than 15% of the annual food supply of rural peasants in the

global South comes from lands and life that the peasants nurture—but don't cultivate and that economists don't calculate. *But the most important reality for rural peoples and policymakers is that the absence of this 15% of the food supply in the weeks before crop harvests could mean mass starvation.*

Urban Harvest. Urban peasant food production may be even more substantial. According to one estimate cited by Canada's International Development Research Centre (IDRC), 25% of the entire global food output is grown in cities. Undertaken before the recent food crisis, it is likely that this figure significantly underestimates the current level of urban food production. History shows that urban agriculture production rises with food prices. Some years ago, UNDP estimated that at least 800 million urbanites produce some of their own food, including at least 200 million urban families that sell some of their produce in local markets. Again, these figures are probably much higher today. Almost 18% of the land in downtown Hanoi is used to grow food. In Quito, about 35% of urban land is used for agriculture and in the Argentinian city of Rosario, 80% of the land grows some food. In Abomey and Bohicon, two cities in Benin, half of the population in the peri-urban area is growing food as their primary activity.

Urban food production is a second "hidden harvest" that is usually overlooked or opposed by city and national administrations but is vital to local food security. As multinational hypermarket chains spread throughout the cities and towns of Latin America, Asia, and now Africa, urban production is seen as competition and the city water and sanitation regulations are sometimes employed to destroy the competitors. Yet, in the middle of a food crisis and with climate change all around, every effort must be made to strengthen city farming. Urban gardening and livestock keeping would benefit from policies that promote sound farming practices and safeguard water and soil quality.

The industrial food chain seems to be unaware that not less than 15% of the food critical to the rural hungry and perhaps 25% of the food critical to the urban hungry lie outside the conventional agricultural system. This being the case, how can they protect food security? How is it that the industrial chain can deny the importance of these unconventional food webs? And, most importantly, how can policy-makers at a time of food and climate crisis safeguard and strengthen this web?

POLICYMAKERS SHOULD CONSIDER:

1. Discouraging industrial-scale meat and dairy production and encouraging diets high in grains, vegetables and fruit. This could liberate 40% of the world's grain production, reduce energy consumption through transportation savings and reduce GHG emissions while improving human nutrition and lowering health costs.

2. Rejecting agrofuels/biomass crops except for locally produced, community-based consumption.

3. Prohibiting land speculation and "land grabs."

4. Strengthening customary use of land and resource rights, while taking special measures to protect women's rights to productive assets.

5. Encouraging urban and peri-urban food production and distribution, again taking into account and supporting the important contribution of women producers.

QUESTION 2

How Can We Increase the Species Diversity of Plants, Aquatic Species and Livestock in Order to Adjust to Changing Climatic Conditions?

The history of the industrial food chain is a history of biological reductionism. Over the latter half of the 20th century, the chain has persistently narrowed our capacity to ensure food security. Can the chain reverse its trendline? Can the chain change?

Field. Global crop production concentrates on 12 plant species (including maize, rice, wheat, soybeans, potatoes, sweet potatoes, bananas and plantains, sorghum, cassava, millets, sunflowers and canola). Only about 150 plant species are grown commercially around the world. Peasants have domesticated at least 5,000 plant species, but the industrial food chain uses only 3% of them.

An estimated 640 million peasant farmers and an additional 190 million pastoralists raise livestock for their own consumption and local markets.

Thanks to the ingenuity of farmers, literally hundreds of local plant species have been shown to have remarkable plasticity (e.g., adaptability, resilience) when confronted with extraordinarily different growing conditions including temperature, altitude, photosensitivity, soil conditions and pests and diseases. In harmony with the reductionist trendline (perhaps, understandably, given limited resources), national and international gene banks have also focused on the major global commercial species and have poor collections of the marginalized species that might feed humanity through the climate crisis. Of the 628,000 documented accessions within the Consultative Group on International Agricultural Research (CGIAR)—the largest international gene bank network—for example, nine crops account for more than half of the total collection and two crops—rice and wheat—account for almost one quarter. This means that public breeders don't have access to the ex situ species diversity they need now to prepare for tomorrow. It also means that only the peasant web maintains this species diversity (*in situ*). But, the important message for everybody is that the species that are absent in the ex situ gene bank collections are exposed to genetic erosion in the *in situ* ("on farm") environment.

Fowl. Although peasants have domesticated 40 livestock species, the industrial food chain has concentrated livestock production on just five species (bovines, chickens, pigs, sheep and goats). This shortsighted industrial approach must be reversed if we are to utilize the best species for different slope and soil conditions and new climatic challenges. Our focus must be on the exploration of the 35 livestock species that are largely outside commerce today.

We must also protect, develop and expand beyond the 60 fodder species important to livestock ruminants. Ninety percent of the world's forage grasses originate in sub-Saharan Africa, for example. Forage legumes such as alfalfa, vetch and clover are nearly universal. We need new pasture species for new conditions. Dependence on a few species increases the risk of food losses in a world of climate chaos.

Fish. Currently, 336 species from 115 families of fish and invertebrates are commercially farmed with 47% of all fish production coming from aquaculture. However, the potential number of edible aquatic species vastly exceeds current use. There are more than 15,200 freshwater species and at least 20,000 marine species. Almost two-thirds of global species consumption (industrial catch) comes from five groups: finfish families (Salmonidae, Cyprinidae and Cichlidae), marine crustaceans and the bivalve mollusks (mussels, clams, scallops, and oysters), which are over-exploited and endangered. Tragically, ocean trawlers discard at least 40% of their annual catch. By contrast, coastal and inland fishers use a vastly greater (although uncounted) range of species and discard very little. Freshwater species play an important role in feeding people but the ecosystems in which they live also provide invaluable ecosystem services important to survive climate change. In terms of goods and services, FAO reports, inland waters contribute more to global economies than all terrestrial ecosystems combined, including forests, grasslands and rangelands. The only group that has demonstrated the capacity to monitor and manage either the food stocks and the ecology of inland waters is the artisanal fishers themselves.

The importance of inland peasant fishponds to food security can't be exaggerated. Asian aquaculture, for example, is mostly on peasant farms of less than 2 hectares (ha). Thai freshwater fish ponds are usually less than 0.3 ha but they produce an average of 2,300 kg/ha. Over 90% of Indian shrimp farms are less than 2 ha. Vietnam's tiny catfish ponds still produce 400,000 kg/ha, and backyard water holes in Bangladesh, amazingly, yield substantial quantities of catfish for household diets and local markets. Not only must the small-scale production be protected, it must also be recognized as the basis for strengthening rural and urban aquaculture.

POLICYMAKERS SHOULD CONSIDER:

1. Supporting farmers, livestock keepers and fishers, especially the role of women, in *in situ* conservation and use of diverse local species.

2. Promoting priority market access for underutilized species (aquatic, crop and livestock) that show climate resilience and disease resistance.

3. Encouraging but only with the approval and oversight of peasants gene banks, sperm banks, etc., to collect and characterize underutilized species as an urgent national and global priority.

QUESTION 3

How Can We Protect and Improve Genetic Diversity within Plants, Aquatic Species and Livestock to Withstand Extreme Weather Events, New Pests and Diseases, and Changing Climates?

The genetic diversity within a species can be as extraordinary as the diversity between species. Faced with uncertain and inconsistent conditions on land and at sea, governments must not only explore underutilized species but also encourage genetic diversity within species. Understandably, prior to the recognition of climate change, government conservation efforts focused on the most important plant, livestock and aquatic species (through gene banks for orthodox seed, *in situ* collections for vegetatively propagated plants; cryogenically preserved eggs and sperm, etc.). Collection efforts within the species also concentrated upon yield and uniformity characteristics to maximize profit and meet industrial processing requirements. The food crisis and climate change require a paradigm shift.

Now, the key words must be *diversity* and *plasticity*.

Field. Thanks to the ingenuity of farmers, the world's major food crops have been encouraged to grow at a remarkable range of altitudes and latitudes in a variety of ecosystems. From early in the 20th century and especially since the 1960s, public and private commercial breeding has narrowed the genetic base of the world's top food crops and massively eroded their genetic diversity. Beginning in the 1960s, the Green Revolution's emphasis on wheat, rice and maize and the focus of commercial breeders on soybeans, alfalfa, cotton and canola (oilseed rape) pushed so-called "poor people's crops" to the margins causing genetic erosion even in low-priority species. By the early 1990s it was roughly estimated that genetic diversity in the world's leading crops was declining by about 2% per annum and that perhaps three-quarters of the germplasm pool for these crops was already extinct. This loss of diversity severely limits the resilience of crops to respond to climate change.

More than the hunger crisis, the climate crisis points to the need to conserve and utilize genetic diversity in both the major food crops and in other crops that show a great potential to be productive while withstanding new pests, diseases and conditions. Who is best able to do this?

Fowl. The world's dominant five livestock species—along with the handful of commercial breeds that dominate industrial production—can be found on every continent except Antarctica. Reports commissioned by FAO warn that climate change may require the mass movement of livestock breeds and express concern that globalization—especially vertical integration along the food chain and standardization trends among the major food retailers—could further narrow the genetic base of commercial species at a time when diversity is needed most. The report specifically warns that new developments in biotechnology will combine with retail standardization to adversely affect small livestock keepers and their ability to conserve livestock genetic diversity.

The lack of genetic diversity within the five commercial livestock species is astonishing—and the loss is accelerating. While 21% of all livestock breeds are thought to be endangered, not enough is known about another 36% to determine their condition. Ten breeds are becoming extinct every year. Among the five livestock species an average of just five breeds dominate commercial production around the world. Leading the cattle herd is the Holstein-Friesian dairy breed (128 countries). The White Leghorn chicken is found almost everywhere. The Large White pig is farmed in 117 countries. Marino sheep, with derivatives, is probably in more than 60 countries, and the Saanen dairy goat can be found in 81 countries. Artificial insemination in the 1960s, embryo transfer in the 1980s and embryo sexing in the mid-1990s encouraged the overuse of a handful of superior animals for millions of progeny. Although the result has been a major increase in productivity, the consequent genetic uniformity, combined with genetic erosion, could spell disaster down the road.

Who can help us conserve and utilize livestock genetic diversity to meet new climatic challenges? To date, the industrial food model has encouraged uniformity, destroyed diversity and increased vulnerability. Is there any evidence that it can change? Avian influenza and Mexican swine flu (H1N1) are just two recent examples of global pandemics largely provoked by extreme genetic uniformity in commercial breeds raised in confined and crowded conditions. Genetically uniform and intensively raised livestock are much more vulnerable to disease and climate change. Peasant-bred breeds are more diverse and more resilient but because they tolerate diseases that kill their more fragile cousins in the industrial food chain, industry and governments cull (i.e., exterminate) these hardy breeds at the first sign of problems rather than building upon the sturdier stock to withstand new threats.

> To protect those livestock breeds that have been bred weak, we are culling those that have been bred hardy—rendering the genetic traits of the hardy extinct.

A handful of companies control livestock genomics and production. Out front is Tyson Foods (USA), which operates in 90 countries and is the world's largest processor and marketer of chicken, beef and pork. The company—with annual sales of $27 billion—is also one of the four global corporations that control broiler genetics. Among others, EW Gruppe in Germany is the world's top breeder in broilers, chickens and turkeys and provides the genetics for 68% of white egg layers and 17% of brown egg layers. Hendrix Genetics (Netherlands) ranks first in the worldwide supply of brown egg layers, second in turkey genetics, fourth in broilers and number two in pig genetics. The company sells layer hen breeding stock in over 100 countries.

> This level of corporate concentration represents a direct threat to our long-term food security.

What can we hope for from the peasant web? Livestock keepers and pastoralists are breeding all 40 domesticated species and, according to FAO, are currently protecting 7,616 breeds. If we are going to have the kind of livestock we need for the soils and slopes best suited for livestock-keeping, it would be better to work with those who have practical incentive, animal germplasm, ecosystem knowledge, and breeding experience to do the job.

Fish. The world's marine fish stocks are already in rapid decline. Freshwater species are equally suffering from industrial and agricultural pollution and the barriers erected by the world's 45,000 dams. Strains of salmon, shrimp, oyster, carp and tilapia are found almost everywhere. From its possible origins in the Danube River, carp is now harvested in 96 countries. Nile tilapia is native to West Africa and the Nile River but is grown in 61 countries on all continents today. Tiger shrimp are farmed in 23 countries in the Indian and Pacific oceans. Pacific oysters originated in Japan and are now harvested in 31 countries. Atlantic salmon were originally native to both sides of the North Atlantic. Today's Atlantic salmon are grown in at least 19 countries and Chile is one of the world's most important exporters.

Despite their geographic diversity, many commercial species have an extraordinarily narrow and narrowing genetic base. Most experts agree that so-called "wild" carp no longer exist but there is some genetic variability in escapees derived from domesticated varieties. The salmon farmed in 19 countries is based upon a single Norwegian breeding program that has been privatized into a company called Nofima.

So, who will best steward our fisheries through climate change? The industrial food chain that jettisons all but a handful of species and whose breeding programs have increased uniformity and vulnerability? Or, the tens of millions of inshore and freshwater fishers who welcome species diversity and know how to protect fragile ecosystems?

POLICYMAKERS SHOULD CONSIDER:

1. Eliminating industrial farming/fishing subsidies and adopting regulatory systems that encourage genetic diversity among plant, animal and aquatic food species.

2. Supporting the conservation of endangered genetic diversity first through *in situ* collections and, secondarily, *ex situ* collections, with the permission and guidance of peasants.

3. Prioritizing the conservation and enhancement strategies of peasant producers and orienting conservation programs in gene banks etc., to meet their breeding requirements.

QUESTION 4

How Can We Encourage Breeders to Reset Goals to Develop Diverse and Reliable Plants and Animals?

Perhaps it's hard for the industrial food system to be innovative when it is caught up in chains. For all its vaunted research investment, the industrial model has yet to develop and introduce a single new crop or livestock species (although there are at least 80,000 higher-order plants and many hundreds of mammals, birds and aquatic species potentially available). The uncertainties of climate change demand a complete rethink of our research (and especially breeding) priorities. Plant breeders need to nurture species and genetic diversity in the field during the same growing season.

Rights Make a Wrong

The major legacy of the industrial agricultural research chain will be the creation of intellectual property rights over crops, livestock and fish (including their genetic parts and components). Attempts to monopolize plant varieties began in the 1930s but grew into a global force in the 1960s with the formation of an International Convention for the Protection of New Varieties of Plants (UPOV). In order to assert legal ownership over living material, breeders abandoned diversity and marginalized agronomic priorities in order to develop varieties that were "distinct, uniform and stable." These are the mirror opposites of what we need today and tomorrow. Physical distinctiveness may help defend ownership in court,

but it is not necessarily beneficial in the field. If it doesn't serve an economic purpose, breeders' efforts to achieve distinctiveness simply means a waste of time and money. The industrial food chain prizes uniformity and stability. But these attributes fight against climate readiness and food security. Today, our crops and livestock desperately need genetic diversity, not uniformity. While we don't want "unstable" varieties and breeds, we do want "plasticity" the genetic capacity of plants and animals to respond rapidly to changing conditions. Replanted seed adapts over generations to local agronomic conditions and offers higher and more reliable yields. Both patents and related regulations are forcing farmers to buy new and, therefore, unadapted seed every season, denying agriculture one of its most important tools. Any restrictions on the right to conduct research using patented breeding material must be struck down since it blocks peasants from their customary breeding activities.

> We need as many breeders and as much diversity as possible. *Intellectual property regulations are a direct attack on global food security.*

Can the industrial chain breed for diverse conditions? In fact, the research food chain isn't even very good at breeding with readily available genetic diversity. In 2007 there were over 72,500 proprietary plant varieties (including ornamentals) ostensibly available in the marketplace. And, over the last 40 years, Green Revolution plant breeders have released 8,000 new crop varieties.

By contrast, since the 1960s peasants have bred far more than 1.9 million plant varieties. We know this because peasants have donated that number of unique farm-bred varieties to the world's gene banks. But, since the gene banks have mostly been looking for the major crop species, some of the most important peasant plant breeding has been ignored. As already discussed, peasants grow thousands of plant species annually and at least 103 of these species each contributes 5% or more of the human calories available in one or more countries. If policymakers are informed by the track record, it is clearly peasant farming systems that are the proven leaders in using genetic diversity to help crops withstand climate change.

Lab Lobotomy?   Even if we revoke monopolistic intellectual property regimes, can we reorganize conventional agricultural research to address these new breeding goals? The second legacy of the agricultural genetic-engineering industry will be its fragmentation and privatization of the crop improvement system established one hundred years ago. University training is now oriented to molecular biology and combinatorial technologies designed to identify and transfer genes between species. Graduates have no real understanding of plant breeding or agriculture. Today's institutional plant breeders and taxonomists are yesterday's news—themselves a dying breed. For example, FAO's 2006 assessment of plant breeding capacity in Africa shows less support for plant breeders today than in 1985, noting that "local plant breeding programs are generally poorly funded, including funds for field trials, staff travel, data analysis and infrastructure." In the USA, the number of public sector breeders working on fruit and vegetable crops declined by 43% from 1994 to 2001. At the moment when taxonomy, conventional plant breeding, and a holistic sense of ecosystem adaptation are vital to withstand climate change, the biosciences have given themselves a frontal "labotany."

Since the 1960s peasants have bred far more than 1.9 million plant varieties.

Cash Crunch.   Can we afford to make the shift from the industrial breeding strategy toward a more diversified approach? The third legacy of the agbiotech industry is the entrenchment of an extraordinarily slow and expensive research model. Corporate wastefulness at the breeding end of the food chain is already damaging to food security. According to Monsanto, it takes at least 10 years and between $100 and $150 million to introduce a new genetically modified trait into plant varieties. One public researcher reports that it took 16 years to introduce the well-known and well-characterized *Bt* trait into GM crops. This is in contrast to conventional, commercial breeders who rarely spend more than $1 million to breed a plant variety. (DNA marker-assisted breeding technologies can speed the pace of conventional breeding.) In short, for every new biotech variety, conventional breeders can introduce between 100 and 150 standard varieties in less time. Despite this, the world's largest seed companies are working almost exclusively on GM seeds.

Let Them Eat Chrysanthemums?   If data from the European Plant Variety Protection Office accurately reflects the orientation of the world's industrial food chain, then the chain is having trouble getting its priorities sorted. Fully 59% of all the plant variety "rights" granted between 1995 and 2009 went to ornamental species (notably roses and chrysanthemums), while only 27% went to agricultural varieties that feed people or livestock and just 14% went to vegetables and fruits over a time period in which the ranks of the hungry swelled by more than 160 million. The UPOV registry of protected plant varieties includes more than 29,000 roses and chrysanthemums—almost exactly the count for wheat, rice and maize combined.

The bottom line critique of industrial plant and livestock breeding is that it focuses on too few species, the wrong species and the wrong breeding goals. It is also too slow, too expensive, and its dependence on intellectual property forces the development of varieties that exacerbate climate vulnerability.

The peasant breeding system creates vastly more varieties of many more species that has as its primary goal ecosystem adaptability and yield reliability. However, this in no way means that the peasant web will manage climate change without consequences. Peasants, too, will experience growing conditions they have never seen before and they will need to work with novel species and breeding material in order to survive.

There is a desperate need to encourage germplasm exchanges between and among peasant organizations around the world, and to insure that they have priority access to whatever gene bank materials they need.

See-Through Systems? Some public (institutional) breeders while acknowledging their situation and limitations can't see how they can get "there" from "here." How is it possible to work with so many species for so many environments? How is it possible to work with peasants? To do so will require a social re-organization of scientific research. However, peasant organizations have never been better prepared to meet these challenges. Communications technologies make it vastly easier to maintain a constant exchange of research information between all the concerned parties. Conventional public researchers and peasant breeders could and should be able to work together.

*In the early 1980s, the seed industry trade group, ASSINSEL, lobbied strenuously for worldwide adoption of plant breeder's rights (patent-like protection for corporate plant breeders). ASSINSEL's booklet, **Feeding the 500 Million,** argued that breeders' rights would be essential to stimulate plant breeding and feed the world's hungry. Thirty years later, corporate breeders have patented more ornamentals than food crops. And the 500 million hungry have more than doubled in number. Let them eat roses and chrysanthemums!*

Today's climate change emergency should also encourage policymakers to consider a "tried-and-true" participatory breeding strategy that brought tremendous plant diversity to a range of new ecosystems in one country. Between the 1860s and 1920s, the U.S. Department of Agriculture annually mailed millions of small packets of experimental seeds to farmers throughout the United States. Farmers in much of the country were breaking sod for the first time and there were few certainties about growing conditions. The initiative was highly successful. Tens of thousands of farmers/plant breeders produced their own varieties, exchanged seed with their neighbors, and turned their country into a breadbasket. *Today, national and international gene banks should follow USDA's example, multiply appropriate seed stocks, and—working with peasant organizations—send small packets of experimental seed to producers around the world.*

POLICYMAKERS SHOULD CONSIDER:

1. Reorienting breeding programs to ensure both seasonal and long-term species and genetic diversity.

2. Promoting "bulk population" breeding strategies for developing materials that can withstand extreme weather events.

3. Eliminating intellectual property regimes or unnecessary phytosanitary regulations that privilege genetic uniformity.

4. Prohibiting any measures—public or private—that constrain the right of peasants to save or exchange food genetic resources.

5. Introducing a seed multiplication program through gene banks to distribute experimental seed packets to peasant organizations for distribution to interested members.

QUESTION 5

How Can We Protect and Improve Biological Controls and Soil Nutrients to Safeguard Food and Reduce Reliance on Synthetic Chemicals?

Peak Oil Meets Peak Soil.   As we struggle to feed the world in the decades ahead, we either will not have—or will not be able to afford—fossil carbon to drive farm machinery or to provide synthetic fertilizers and pesticides. Studies suggest, however, that pests and diseases will migrate around the world putting new pressures on productivity. Even in the regions expected to benefit from climate change (northern USA, Canada and much of Western Europe) increased temperatures and CO_2 levels portend a boom in rusts, blight and insects and, most worryingly, a speedup in the pace of disease and insect mutation. Microbes play a crucial role in climate mitigation. Soil organic matter, as FAO points out, is the major global storage reservoir for carbon (not forests). Microbe diversity turns this material into soil nutrients beneficial to crops and contributes to climate regulation and stabilization. An estimated 140–170 million tons of nitrogen, for example, are fixed by microbes worldwide annually—equivalent to US $90 billion worth of nitrogen fertilizers. (By comparison, the big seven fertilizer companies have total annual sales of less than $5 billion.) The use of synthetic fertilizer is a major contributor to emissions of nitrous oxide in agriculture.

Global fertilizer production has risen more than 31% since the World Food Summit of 1996 and is expected to climb further with the expansion of the industrial food chain's promotion of agrofuels and the removal of cellulose fiber from fields. Already, fertilizers account for 1.2% of total GHG emissions equivalent to the total emissions from countries like Indonesia or Brazil.

Monocultures of genetically uniform crops deplete microbial diversity while increasing crop vulnerability. The best way to ensure that beneficial microbe diversity maintains soil nutrients is to promote the species and genetic diversity already discussed.

POLICYMAKERS SHOULD CONSIDER:

1. Expanding public research on the beneficial use of microbes for soil fertility and as biocontrol agents.

2. Working with peasants to monitor beneficial microbe environments as well as the advance of new pests and diseases.

3. Through regulation and education, encourage moves away from dependence on fossil carbons.

QUESTION 6

How Can We Strengthen Local Food Production to Reduce Energy Dependence and Increase Food Quality?

Can the industrial food chain be made more efficient and effective? The total energy in the food system in OECD states is approximately 4 kcal invested to supply 1 kcal of food, while in the global South, the ratio is approximately 1 kcal invested to supply 1 kcal of food.

If you live in an OECD country, there is an almost automatic assumption that the whole world is part of a globalized food chain. This is entirely wrong. It bears repeating that 85% of the world's cultivated food is grown and consumed domestically (i.e., if not within sight of the farm, at least within the same country or eco-region). The percentage of world food sold through the industrial food chain is uncertain but likely includes almost all of the 15% that is exported across national borders and the vast majority of food marketed in OECD countries.

It is equally likely that the majority of the world's food does not depend upon industry-based agricultural inputs. In 1996, for example, FAO estimated that 1.4 billion people depend upon farm-saved seed. That figure roughly equaled the total number of peasant farmers at that time. While peasants may occasionally purchase seed or fertilizer or pesticides, the majority (either by choice or by necessity) produce their food without external inputs. In other words, "conventional" food production is not industrialized while "unconventional" production is dependent upon a globalized industrial system. *The web is much bigger than the chain.*

Setting aside small farm production, at least 15% of the global South's consumed food in rural areas isn't cultivated and at least 25% of its urban food is grown by urban-dwelling peasants who are not associated with the industrial food chain. Conservatively, then, at least 20% of the global South's food supply comes from the uncalculated "hidden harvest" of rural and urban production. This figure must, at the very least, be added to the productivity of peasant farmers and pastoralists. In other words, not less than 70% of the South's food supply is the work of peasants.

POLICYMAKERS SHOULD CONSIDER:

1. Making urban and peri-urban food production a national priority.

2. Developing special breeding initiatives intended to support urban agriculture.

3. Supporting peasant-based food production and facilitating direct peasant-consumer marketing arrangements, with special attention to the role of women.

4. Encouraging organic production.

QUESTION 7

How Can We Minimize Loss and Waste Throughout the Food System?

Waste to Waist. The industrial chain is enormously wasteful. Food spoilage in the industrial food system's markets is higher (+/−30%) because of distance, time, storage, and other wasteful (including consumer) practices. One study estimates that U.S. households throw out 1.28 lbs. of food a day in their trash (14% of all meats, grains, fruits and vegetables coming into the home), the equivalent of $43 billion worth of food. On top of that, commercial retail food establishments (convenience stores, fast-food, groceries) throw away 27 million tons of food annually.

Even recognizing that the majority of the world's hungry live in tropical or sub-tropical areas where food losses—from field to fork—are often devastating, the industrial food chain—mostly in temperate climes with better storage—is unconscionably wasteful. A 2009 industry survey of the most efficient UK food supply chains concluded that on average, 20% of costs in the chain add no value.

> Of the 3,900 calories available to the average U.S. consumer daily, 1,100 calories are wasted.

During the World Food Summit in November 2009, the U.S. National Institute of Diabetes and Digestive and Kidney Diseases reported that, since the previous food crisis of 1974, U.S. food wastage had risen from 28% to 40% of the country's total food supply—an average per capita waste of 1,400 kilocalories a day (nationally, 150 trillion kilocalories a year). This figure does not take into account the calorie loss from turning grain into meat and dairy products or from wasting good food on fat waists. The environmental damage is also substantial: the unnecessary consumption of more than 300 million barrels of oil a year and a quarter of the U.S. freshwater supply to make food that goes uneaten.

As a result of breeding for high yields and factory farming practices, U.S. and UK data show that essential nutrients in the food supply have declined in recent decades, with double-digit percentage declines of iron, zinc, calcium, selenium, etc. A 2009 study reports declines of 5% to 40% or more in some minerals in vegetables and fruits. Fewer nutrients per serving translate into less nutrition per calorie served. Fast-growing plants tend to dilute nutrient concentrations. In addition, high levels of nitrogen fertilizers reduce nutrient density and flavour. Similarly, Green Revolution wheat varieties bred for higher yields contain diminished protein content.

When the industrial food chain moves south, the waste and the expense come along with it. On average, the South's urban consumers spend at least 30% more on food than rural consumers and, still, their average calorie intake is lower. Studies show that poor urbanites spend as much as 60–80% of family income on food—and that their lack of cash translates more directly into food shortages and malnutrition than for their country cousins. It is hard to see how the industrial food chain can shake off its wasteful habits. Eighty percent of all research on food and agriculture concentrates not on farm-based food production but on food processing and retailing. And 96% of this research takes place in OECD countries. Despite industry's attempts to make the chain more efficient and profitable, the losses and abuses are staggering.

POLICYMAKERS SHOULD CONSIDER:

1. Reducing post-harvest losses (including consumer waste) as an important strategy for food security.

2. Recognizing and reversing industrial breeding strategies that diminish essential nutrients of food crops.

QUESTION 8

How Can We Ensure That Food Is Nutritious, Adequate, Appropriate, and Accessible to All?

After decades of consolidation, the world's largest grocery retailers occupy the most powerful position on the agroindustrial food chain. The top 100 global food retailers—with sales of US $1.8 trillion in 2007—account for 35% of all grocery sales worldwide. The top 3 mega-grocery retailers—Wal-Mart, Carrefour and Tesco—account for 50% of the revenues earned by the top 10 companies. In a single decade, Latin American markets saw the same level of supermarket penetration that took five decades in USA and

Europe. The pace of market penetration continues in Asia, and now Africa.

In South Africa, four supermarket chains control 94.5% of the retail food market. The country's 1,700 supermarkets (most of which have been established since 1994) have displaced an estimated 350,000 "spazas" (Mom 'n Pop food shops). Giant grocery retailers also have major impacts on the other end of the food chain—buying or contracting with farmers. Wal-Mart says it will buy from more than one million Chinese farmers by 2011. Retail giants (including Tesco, Metro, Car-refour, Wal-Mart) advise governments on WTO compliance and *codex alimentarius* regulations. The impact of food retailers on diet and obesity is undeniable. In Guatemala, for example, a proudly indigenous country and homeland to global crops like maize and beans, the expansion of supermarket chains has been especially damaging to the nutrition of poor consumers who are pressed to buy cheap, highly processed pastries, cookies and crackers instead of their native staples. A 2007 study found that a 1% increase in supermarket purchases translates into a 41% decline in maize calorie consumption and a 6.5% falloff in bean consumption.

POLICYMAKERS SHOULD CONSIDER:

1. Regulatory incentives to protect and enhance local markets, local production and consumption.

2. Before allowing the entry of global retail food giants: examine the social and economic impacts of oligopolistic retail food markets, including potential impacts on peasant food producers (both rural and urban), the survival of small businesses in the formal and informal sectors, and the nutrition and diets of poor consumers.

3. Insuring that food retailers do not exploit agricultural workers in the global South through labor contracts or procurement standards.

4. Rejecting industry-driven food safety and phytosanitary standards and so-called "sustainable" procurement standards that discriminate against peasant farmers and small-scale businesses.

5. Incorporating the Right to Food in binding law, nationally and internationally.

QUESTION 9

How Can We Be Sure That Peasant Producers Have Equitable and Stable Production and Marketing Arrangements?

Chain Reaction? There is growing recognition and support for peasant farmers and their role in confronting the food and climate crisis. The first-ever independent global assessment of agricultural science and technology, the International Assessment of Agricultural Knowledge, Science & Technology (IAASTD), sponsored by the World Bank, the Food & Agriculture Organization and other U.N. agencies, warns that the world can't rely on technological fixes—such as transgenic crops—to solve systemic problems of persistent hunger, poverty and environmental crises, and affirms the crucial role of small-scale farmers and low-impact farming.

UNEP's February 2009 report, *The Environmental Food Crisis*, calls for a global micro-financing fund to boost small-scale farmer productivity and the development of diversified and resilient eco-agriculture systems that provide critical ecosystem services, as well as adequate food to meet local needs. The *Córdoba Call for Coherence and Action on Food Security and Climate Change* asserts that the interests of peasant producers must be at the center of the food and climate debate and that "excessive reliance on market-based approaches is a mistake." The authors of the Call are food and agriculture specialists and include the first and current UN Special Rapporteurs on the Right to Food.

Peasants must take the lead in developing strategies—including technological strategies—to meet the food and climate crises. This doesn't mean abandoning the potential for conventional science. The Western model of science and technology has developed micro-techniques that can have macro-applications—high-tech advances that are often widely deployed. By contrast, peasant research often develops macro-technologies for micro-environments—that is, wide-tech and complex, integrated strategies that are location specific. Over the last hundred years since the rediscovery of Mendel's law, these two scientific solitudes have rarely been integrated. These strategies can only be brought together appropriately when leadership comes from the peasant organizations that are both closest to the land and closest to the hungry. Food sovereignty—the right of nations and peoples to democratically determine their own food systems—is paramount.

POLICYMAKERS SHOULD CONSIDER:

1. Most international agricultural policies dictated by free trade agreements and international financial institutions work against peasant farming systems. These policies have aggravated hunger and contributed to unsustainable farming practices. The seriousness of today's crises demands that policymakers revoke failed agricultural trade policies.

2. Supporting farmers and small producers to remain on the land and maintain their livelihoods through access to land, water, credit and markets. Respect and uphold resource rights, including the right to save and exchange seed and genetic resources. This includes Farmers' Rights, Livestock Keepers' Rights, and "aquatic rights."

3. Supporting proposals for food sovereignty put forth by the world's largest peasant organizations, fishers, pastoralists and other important small producers, environmentalists and consumer networks, in the Nyeleni World Forum for Food Sovereignty, organized in Mali 2007 (see box, on next page).

CONCLUSION

In the final analysis, there is no reason to be sanguine. We are deeply in trouble and there is no guarantee that humanity will rise to the challenges ahead. Neither the industrial food chain nor the peasant web has all that is necessary to get us through our compounding crises. The industrial food chain—rigid, reductionist and centrally regulated—doesn't have the resilience to respond to the current food crisis or the coming climate chaos. The peasant system—diverse, decentralized, and dynamic—has the natural resources, research capacity and resilience to better meet the challenges ahead. It is not the capacity or competence of the peasant system that we need to worry about, it is the lack of capacity and incompetence of government and science to "scale up" their systems to meet the potential of peasant provisioning.

Annex: Peasants—Counting Up

While statisticians think in terms of 1.5 billion (or so) smallholder farmers, the more realistic figure is probably double that number when full account is taken of the urban gardeners and livestock keepers, nomadic pastoralists, fishers and forest-keepers around the world. Urban gardeners often move back and forth between town and country and fishers often farm as well. Here is a different calculation...

Farmers.   Of the 450 million farms, 382 million (85%) have 2 hectares or less and statisticians customarily refer to them as smallholders or peasants. Close to 380 million peasant farms are in the global South, meaning that at least 1.5 billion people per farm) live there. Very significantly, 370 million are indigenous peasants on at least 92 million farms. In total, peasants probably have significantly more than half of the world's cropland. Of the global 1.56 billion hectares in arable and permanent crops (many countries classify "peasants" as holding 5 hectares or less), 764 million hectares could be held by peasants and not less than 225 million are held by big farmers. Mid-size farmers would then hold 571 million hectares (or an average of 36.8 ha). In some definitions, some researchers

---

Six Pillars of Food Sovereignty from Nyeleni 2007

Focuses on Food for People, putting the right to food at the centre of food, agriculture, livestock and fisheries policies; *and rejects* the proposition that food is just another commodity or component for international agri-business.

Values Food Providers and respects their rights; and rejects those policies, actions and programmes that undervalue them, threaten their livelihoods and eliminate them.

Localises Food Systems, bringing food providers and consumers closer together; *and rejects* governance structures, agreements and practices that depend on and promote unsustainable and inequitable international trade and give power to remote and unaccountable corporations.

Puts Control Locally over territory, land, grazing, water, seeds, livestock and fish populations; *and rejects*

the privatisation of natural resources through laws, commercial contracts and intellectual property rights regimes.

Builds Knowledge and Skills that conserve, develop and manage localised food production and harvesting systems; *and rejects* technologies that undermine, threaten or contaminate these, e.g. genetic engineering.

Works with Nature in diverse, agroecological production and harvesting methods that maximise ecosystem functions and improve resilience and adaptation, especially in the face of climate change; *and rejects* energy-intensive industrialised methods which damage the environment and contribute to global warming.

---

tend to incorporate peasant "farms" that have much less than one-tenth of a hectare per person. The inclusion of these almost-landless peasants into productivity calculations grossly distorts the productivity of most peasant farms.

Pastoralists. An estimated 640 million peasant farmers and an additional 190 million pastoralists raise livestock for their own consumption and local markets. Since pastoralists move about and routinely cross national boundaries, they are seldom included in food security calculations.

Fishers. There are about 30-35 million peasant fishers but probably more than 100 million peasants are involved in fishing, processing and distributing what amounts to half the world's fish caught for direct human consumption (or 30 million metric tons). These figures, however, only speak to peasant production for the market and not the fishing and—aquaculture activities of indigenous—peoples or rural and urban peasants outside the market. In total, 2.9 billion people get 15% or more of their protein from ocean or freshwater fish. In the poorest countries, 18.5% of protein

comes from artisanal (small scale and/or subsistence) fishers. Unlike most commercial fisheries and ocean-going fish factories, peasant fishers focus almost exclusively on fish for human consumption as opposed to fishmeal for livestock feed.

Urban Gardeners. Before the current food crisis, an estimated 800 million peasants were involved in urban farming. Of these, 200 million produce food primarily for urban markets and manage to provide full-time employment for about 150 million family members. On average, the world's cities produce about one-third of their own food consumption. In times of high food prices, the amount of urban and peri-urban gardening and livestock-keeping increases significantly.

Hunters and Gatherers. It is not possible to quantify the proportion of the food supply that comes from forests, roadsides, and other "marginal" land. We do know that at least 410 million people live in—or adjacent to—forests and derive much of their food and livelihood from forests. In total, 1.6 billion people get some portion of their food and livelihood from forests around the world.

REFERENCES

Agriculture Canada, Market Information Service. 1994. *Livestock Market Report, 1993*. Ottawa: Agriculture Canada.

Animal Alliance of Canada. 1991. "Enviro Facts about Livestock Production (compiled from World Watch Paper No. 103). Toronto: Animal Alliance of Canada.

Anonymous. 1988a. "Position of the American Dietetic Association: Vegetarian Diets." *Journal of the American Dietetic Association* 3: 351–355.

Anonymous. 1988b. "The Vegetarian Advantage." *Health* 20 (October): 18.

Barnard, Neal D. 1990. *The Power of Your Plate*. Summertown, TN: Book Publishing.

Berry, Wendell. 1996. *The Unsettling of American Culture and Agriculture*. Berkeley: University of California Press.

British Medical Association. 1992. *Our Genetic Future: The Science and Ethics of Genetic Technology*. Oxford: Oxford University Press.

Chen, Junshi. 1990. *Diet, Lifestyle and Mortality in China: A Study of 65 Chinese Counties*. Ithaca, NY: Cornell University Press.

Coe, Sue. 1995. *Dead Meat*. New York: Four Walls Eight Windows.

Collins, Mark, ed. 1990. *The Last Rain Forests: A World Conservation Atlas*. New York: Oxford University Press.

Durning, Alan T. and Brough, Holly B. 1995. "Animal Farming and the Environment." In *Just Environments: Intergenerational, International and Interspecies Issues*. Ed. David E. Cooper and Joy A. Palmer. London: Routledge.

Edelman, P. D. et al. 2005. "*In Vitro*-Cultured Meat Production." *Tissue Engineering* 11, No. 5/6: 659–662.

Eisnetz, Gail. 1997. *Slaughterhouse*. Buffalo: Prometheus Books.

Fiddes, Nick. 1991. *Meat: A Natural Symbol*. London: Routledge.

Fox, Michael Allen. 1999. *Deep Vegetarianism*. Philadelphia: Temple University Press.

Fox, Michael W. 1992. *Superpigs and Wondercorn: The Brave New World of Biotechnology and Where It All May Lead*. New York: Lyons & Burford.

Gold, Mark. 2004. "The Global Benefits of Eating Less Meat" (a 76-page report). Compassion in World Farming Trust. www.cifw.org.uk/education/eat.html

Gore, Albert. 1993. *Earth in the Balance: Ecology and the Human Spirit*. New York: Plume.

Government of Canada. 1991. *The State of Canada's Environment*. Ottawa: Supply and Services Canada.

Greenpeace International. 2006a. *Eating Up the Amazon* (a 64-page report). 6 April.

Greenpeace International. 2006b. "Greenpeace closes Amazon soya facilities in Brazil and Europe." 22 May press release. www.greenpeace.org.uk/forests

Greenpeace International. 2006c. "Greenpeace prevents soya from Amazon rain forest destruction entering Europe." 7 April press release. www.greenpeace.org/international/press/releases/greenpeace-prevents-soya-from-2

Guardian Weekly. 2006. "China's Expanding Girth." 25–31 August: 2.

Hill, John Lawrence. 1996. *The Case for Vegetarianism: Philosophy for a Small Planet*. Lanham, MD: Rowman & Littlefield.

Lappé, Frances Moore. 1992. *Diet for a Small Planet* (20th ed.). New York: Ballantine.

Lovejoy, Thomas E. 1986. "Species Leave the Ark One by One." In *The Preservation of Species: The Value of Biological Diversity*. Ed. Brian G. Norton. Princeton: Princeton University Press.

Mason, Jim and Singer, Peter. 1990. *Animal Factories* (rev. ed.). New York: Harmony Books.

McKisson, Nicki and MacRae-Campbell, Linda. 1990. *The Future of Our Tropical Rainforests*. Tucson: Zephyr Press.

Melina, Vesanto and Davis, Brenda. 2003. *The New Becoming Vegetarian: The Essential Guide to a Healthy Vegetarian Diet* (2nd rev. ed.). Summer-town, TN: Healthy Living Publications.

Myers, Norman. 1984. *The Primary Source: Tropical Forests and Our Future*. New York: Norton.

Pearce, Fred. 2006. "The Parched Planet." *New Scientist*, 26 February: 32–36.

Pimentel, David. 1990. "Environmental and Social Implications of Waste in U.S. Agriculture and

Food Sectors." *Journal of Agricultural Ethics* 3: 5–20.

Porritt, Jonathon. 2006. "Hard facts to swallow." *Guardian Weekly*, 13–19 January: 18.

Reuters. 2005. "Scientists propose growing artificial meat." 7 July dispatch. www.msnbc.msn.com/id/8498629/

Rice, Pamela. 2004. *101 Reasons Why I'm a Vegetarian*. New York: Lantern Books.

Rifkin, Jeremy. 1992. *Beyond Beef: The Rise and Fall of the Cattle Culture*. New York: Dutton.

Robbins, John. 1987. *Diet for a New America*. Walpole, NH: Stillpoint.

Rollin, Bernard E. 1995. *The Frankenstein Syndrome: Ethical and Social Issues in The Genetic Engineering of Animals*. New York: Cambridge University Press.

Saunders, Kerrie K. 2003. *The Vegan Diet as Chronic Disease Prevention: Evidence Supporting the New Four Food Groups*. New York: Lantern Books.

Smithsonian Institution. 2002. "Smithsonian researchers show Amazonian deforestation accelerating." *Science Daily Online*, 15 January. www.science-daily.com/releases/2002/01/020115075118.htm

Spallone, Pat. 1992. *Generation Games: Genetic Engineering and the Future for Our Lives*. Philadelphia: Temple University Press.

Starke, Linda, ed. 2006. *State of the World 2006*. Washington, DC: World Watch Institute.

Stevens, William K. 1998. "Plant Species Threats Cited." *The Globe and Mail* (Toronto), 9 April: A15.

Tudge, Colin. 2004a. "It's a Meat Market." *New Scientist*, 13 March: 19.

———, 2004b. *So Shall We Reap: What's Gone Wrong with the World's Food—and How to Fix It*. Harmondsworth, Middlesex: Penguin.

U.N. Food and Agricultural Organization. 1995. *Dimensions of Need: An Atlas of Food and Agriculture*. Santa Barbara: ABC-CLIO.

University of Washington Students. n.d. "Rape of Mother Earth." www.students.washington.edu/careuw/rapeofmotherearth.pdf

U.S. Congress, Office of Technology Assessment. 1985. *Technology, Public Policy, and the Changing Structure of American Agriculture: A Special Report for the 1985 Farm Bill*. Washington, DC: US Government Printing Office.

U.S. National Research Council. 1989. *Diet and Health: Implications for Reducing Chronic Disease Risk*. Washington, DC: National Academy Press.

White, Randall and Frank, Erica. 1994. "Health Effects and Prevalence of Vegetarianism." *Western Journal of Medicine* 160: 465–471.

Wilson, Edward O. 1993. *The Diversity of Life*. New York: Norton.

World Watch. 2004. "Is Meat Sustainable?" (editorial). *World Watch Magazine* 17(4), July/August.

STUDY QUESTIONS

1. Fox argues that our food choices have consequences that extend beyond our personal lives and that we should take responsibility for them. What do you think of his argument?

2. If you were convinced that eating meat is morally wrong, would you give it up? Why, or why not?

3. Toward the end of this reading, Fox alleges that humans have a "manipulative mindset" in relation to the natural world. Is animal agriculture part of this mindset? Discuss.

4. What sort of diet, in your opinion, would be consistent with the principle that humans ought to minimize their impact on the biosphere? Explain your answer.

5. If synthetic meat (meat made in laboratories) were widely available, would there remain any moral objection to eating meat? Defend your answer.

FOR FURTHER READING

Aiken, William, and Hugh LaFollette, eds., *World Hunger and Moral Obligation,* 2nd ed., Englewood Cliffs, N. J.: Prentice Hall, 1996. The best collection of readings available, containing four of the readings in this chapter, plus others of great importance.

Ehrlich, Paul. *The Population Bomb.* New York: Ballantine Books, 1971. An important work, warning of the dangers of the population explosion.

Lappé, Francis, and Joseph Collins. *Food First: Beyond the Myth of Scarcity.* New York: Ballantine Books, 1978. An attack on Neo-Malthusians like Hardin in which the authors argue that we have abundant resources to solve the world's hunger problems.

O'Neill, Onora. *Faces of Hunger.* London: Allen & Unwin, 1986. A penetrating Kantian discussion of the principles and problems surrounding world hunger.

Rifkin, Jeremy. *Beyond Beef.* New York: Plume, 1993.

Simon, Arthur. *Bread for the World.* New York: Paulist Press, 1975. A poignant discussion of the problem of world hunger from a Christian perspective with some thoughtful solutions.